BOURNE: WHY CIVILIZATIONS FALL AND CA

WHY CIVILIZATIONS FALL
And Cannot Rise Again

THE NATURAL EVOLUTION OF CAPITAL ECONOMIES
AND THE DESTRUCTIVE FORCES
OF CULTURAL ENTROPY

Copyright 2019 Ralph Bourne
ralphbourne@sbcglobal.net

"We are outside (not inside) God's Garden. No benign presence commands human civilizations here. To return to the Garden, we must use the tools God has given us, reason and love."
   Dr. B. Franklin, 1779

INTRODUCTION – (~X+-)

CH. 1 – (~3+-)
Capital Development in Nature (and cultural entropy) long before human beings.

CH 2 – (~33)
WHAT IS CULTURAL ENTROPY?
Cultural Entropy opposes Capitalism and Capital Sharing Cultures in Animal and Human Cultures
Entropy in physics

CH 3 – (~51)
CULTURAL ENTROPY: FORCES UNIQUE TO *HUMAN* CULTURES:

CH. 4 – (~77)
**THE ECONOMIC EVOLUTION OF HUMAN CULTURES
WONDERFUL HUMAN ECONOMIC INNOVATIONS THAT GREATLY ASSIST THE FLOW OF CAPITAL:**
Human economic changes emphasize cooperative capitalism over competitive (predatory) capitalism

CH. 5 -- (~97)

HUMAN ECONOMIC DISTORTIONS THAT GREATLY *IMPAIR*
CAPITAL CIRCULATION OVER TIME,
AND THUS ASSIST THE CORROSIVE AND DIVISIVE EFFECTS OF
CULTURAL ENTROPY.

CH 6 -- (~123)
*CULTURAL ENTROPY DECAYS HUMAN FAMILIES -- HOW ENTROPY
WORKS IN HUMAN ECONOMIES TO STIFLE CAPITAL CIRCULATION,
POLARIZE POPULATIONS, AND ASSIST THE FORCES OF DIVISION AND
CONFLICT: CAPITAL IS LIFE.*

CH. 7 – (~143)
POPULATION WARS
CULTURAL ENTROPY CREATES COMPETITIVE CAPITALISM AND (OVER)
POPULATION WARS.
*(POPULATION WARS AND COMPETITIVE CAPITALISM STRESS RESOURCES
AND DEVALUE LIFE.)*

CAP CH 8-- (~157)
HOW CULTURAL ENTROPY DESTROYS CIVILIZATIONS
Rome and Greece
The Anasazi
Stonehenge
The Maya
The Ottoman Empire
The Chinese
The Khmer
The African Continent
The Norse in Greenland
The Americas

CH. 9 -- (~177)
THE ECONOMY (CULTURE) OF SELF
The Malleable Human Self

CH. 10 – (~195)
CONCLUSIONS AND THE LITERATURE Cultural Entropy
Cultural Entropy impacts Democratic Concepts
What is Capitalism?
Population Wars in Philosophy
In Religion
In Literature
Theatre of the Absurd

Catch-22
Human Monsters from Chaos

CH. 11 – GLOSSARY OF TERMS

THE CREATION OF CAPITAL ECONOMIES
AND THE DESTRUCTIVE FORCES
OF CULTURAL ENTROPY

INTRODUCTION:
Most human difficulties—from intolerance and homelessness to world wars--also occurred in nature billions of years ago, long before humans. Human life inherited problems they did not uniquely create.

More to the point, the random forces (colliding numbers), that created these problems long ago, still command the table today. Human reason does not.

Why should we care? These invisible numerical forces contain no *qualitative* concept. Numbers are *quantities* only. If we allow unthinking, random, *quantitative* forces to control the future as they have controlled the past, the **quality** of human life will not be in the equation—life will continue to be violent and unreasonable. The **numbers** *(quantities)* don't care.

Humans probably *do* care. And human understandings can change the equation; we can choose to seek value and *quality* (over quantity) in our individual human lives.

So, what are these malignant natural forces? How do they invisibly control us? How can we fight back? And what are the real rules of the game?

THE CAPITAL FLOW
In police investigations, following the capital flow often leads investigators to important facts—such as, why crimes are committed and who the criminals are. Most crimes are disputes over capital.

Following the capital flow, seeking the facts, is the design of this book. We hope to encounter the true criminals of natural history.

And to be thorough, we need to start at the beginning, the true beginning of capital exchanges--this capital economy, the economy of **life,** *started long before humans arrived, billions of years ago.*

CHAPTER 1 –
WHY CIVILIZATIONS FALL
And Cannot Rise Again

Capital Development in Nature
(Before Humans Arrived)

A civilization collapses when its capital economy falls apart.
This civilization may, incidentally, be immoral or pious. The civilization may be warlike or peaceful. The civilization may be a few groups in the jungle or contain vast populous cities. Great leaders or clowns may govern the civilization. The civilization's soldiers may be heroic or not. Terrible calamites may intermittently plague the civilization. As long as the civilization's economy works, the civilization will continue to stumble on.

Leaders may be deposed; religions may change; incidental wars may slaughter many, many young men; but, if the civilization's economy works, the population will still increase. Males in every species possess ample fertility to make up for a few battle casualties.

On the contrary, if a civilization's economy collapses, if capital stops circulating, women and children starve and the population disappears. No economy; no women and children; no future civilization.

This book investigates why **economies** fall apart. But before economies fall apart, they must be created initially. To understand the entire process (what is an economy?), we must start at the beginning of capital economics, not the *human* beginning, but the beginnings of *life* billions of years ago.

The economy of all life (that today **includes** humans) truly started billions of years ago, long before humans. To start a business requires **capital** or *original-energy*. **Life is a business.**

What is Capital? How does a business start?
Economists often refer to capital as an inert, human-centered concept—token dollar bills in a wallet, stocks in a portfolio, bonds in a bank vault, assets in land or labor.

But capital, or tradable *value*, or stuff able to energize or feed life, actually began growing and accumulating billions of years ago. Biological infrastructures and fossil fuels are examples of essential capital energies created long, long before humans; these capital items may still be in circulation today.

In nature, the most **valuable, tradable** commodity is actually life, itself. Life is the primary food-energy for all other life. Thus life is capital, and capital is life. And humans were not the ones who invented it.

Life-capital began constructing itself billions of years ago using energy—mostly from the sun--and resources borrowed from the earth. When life so constructed is de-constructed—or is digested by another life form—the energy and materials of construction are exchanged; they are not lost. This exchange is capitalism.

To repeat: Plants use sun-energy and resources to create capital items, or life. This life-capital flows progressively through a succession of other organisms. Each organism utilizes some of the life energy until the energy is exhausted. Eventually, only original resources are left; these recirculate again and again. Capital resources that once flowed through dinosaurs still flow through humans today. **This capital circulation, again, is called capitalism.**

A. CAPITAL CREATION IN NATURE: CALL IT VALUE OR LIFE-ENERGY, CAPITAL, FOOD, PROFIT, BLOOD, OR FISH OIL!! THE MIRACLE SOLUTION!! WILL CURE ALL ILLS!

CAPITAL:

Humans may *feel* they **invented** capital. Humans also reluctantly take credit for inventing world wars, depressions, environmental catastrophes, homelessness, overpopulation, criminal gangs, greedy aristocrats, slavery, cultural genocides—and many other *human* problems.

Actually, **all** this stuff was invented long, long, long before humans arrived at the party. And more important, the invisible forces that created such stuff billions of years ago are still **in control** today. We'll consider such forces throughout this book.

But now, we're still on capital--humans did not invent it.

For *absolute* proof, here are some early news clippings:

A. CAPITAL CREATION:

WHY CIVILIZATIONS FALL: CAPITAL DEVELOPMENT AND ENTROPY IN NATURE

> **The Single-Cell Sentinel** -4.1 BILLION yrs ago
> First edition exclusive! This reporter has noticed for some time, we organic molecules are grabbing energy from the sun or even volcanic vents. We use this energy to invest in *ourselves*; we are creating life! We value us, so we are creating VALUE OR CAPITAL!
> Wow! We should pat each other on the backs! Oops! But we don't appear to have backs. In fact, we don't appear to have hands either. Hm.
> Well, anyway, we would like to announce the beginning of life. Thank you Lord! We feel life is sort of important. We *may* have a future. Or not.

SOME FORCES **OPPOSE** CAPITAL (LIFE) DEVELOPMENT:
We might note here: Life capital does not exist unopposed. Numerous random forces (of entropy) oppose the order life requires. These many forces—moving water molecules, ultra violet rays, random chemical reactions, radiation, for example--will dissolve the atomic structures of life back to elemental particles.

To continue living, life must continue **working** to maintain its integrity against many, chaotic, random forces pushing against it that would cause divisions and errors. To continue working against chaos to establish stability, life requires a source of **energy**; this energy is generally provided by sunlight, but other sources may also be tapped, including the random forces themselves, volcanic vents, or chemical reactions.

B. CAPITAL PROFITS IN NATURE: $$
Life started about 4.1 billion years ago. Since life valued itself it could also call itself **capital**. Life was a *valuable* trade item. **But without capital *profits*, life could not go very far.** Why?

> **THE BACTERIA BUGLE – 4.1 BILLION years ago**
> Today we would like to proudly announce!
> LIFE HAS BEGUN HERE TOO!! YEAH! THANK YOU GOD! However, this reporter has just noticed a problem: When the sun doesn't shine, our life processes apparently stop completely. This reminds me, it is getting dark and--- uumph!

> **The NEXTDAY FISHYOIL FORUM**
> News Alert: FISHY OIL FAT PROFIT!!
> MIRACLE SERUM WILL CURE ALL ILLS!!
> *We are proud to report today the newest high-tech product, Fish Oil, fat, also called profit! Dr. Diatom's miracle elixir, profit, now allows us to continue our life processes even in the dark! We have learned to produce this profit-energy product after years of difficult struggles!*
> *Pick up a bottle from any fish fat vendor!*
> *The nightlife begins! !*
> *The paaarty is on!*
> *Great celebrations!*
> *FAT CITY! Profit POWER!*
> Capitalism has officially begun!!
> We now have valuable capital profits to invest and trade in our future! Our CAPITAL lives are valuable!!!!

C. CAPITAL CIRCULATION OR CAPITALISM:

AGAIN, WHAT IS CAPITAL?

Capital is packaged life-energy, food, usually taken from the sun, valuable *stuff* life values and trades. Capital *is* life because life values and trades itself. Capital is food since life values, and also **is**, food. Capital is valuable **energy and resources** life needs to continue and grow. Fat or profit, is **extra** energy-capital life can use later.

By this rather broad definition, capital includes capital **resources**, a non-living set of items, such as land locations, minerals, and tech innovations—*valuable stuff* life absolutely needs to create more capital (life), and prosper. Most important: Capital is **us**—all living organisms are collections of valuable, energy capital, food. Wow! We are valuable! It's nice to be valuable!

WHY CIVILIZATIONS FALL: CAPITAL DEVELOPMENT AND ENTROPY IN NATURE

Unfortunately the capital process makes us edible to others. Oops! Watch out! We *are* food! We are fish oil! We *are* capital. We are energy. We <u>are</u> valuable <u>trade</u> items.

AND WHAT IS CAPITAL PROFIT?
Profit is simply *extra* fish oil, fat, **extra us**, something we don't need right now, but we can use later, trade for value, or give to others in the future. Without capital **profit**, we cannot grow, we have nothing to give to our children, we have no choices, and we have nothing to circulate within ourselves so we can become more complex creatures.

So capital **profit,** fat, is **absolutely** necessary for growth and progress.

AND MOST IMPORTANT: WHAT IS CAPITAL CIRCULATION? OR CAPITALISM?
The most important talent of capital profit—or fish oil--is that, <u>like our blood</u>, it can circulate. By circulating from life form to life form, from parent to child, from prey to predator, from death to decay, from decayed resources to new life, by re-circulating again and again, capital-energy allows the life cycle to continue in a circle.

Everyone has heard of the circle of life. ***Capital is what is circling!***

When capital circles or is exchanged, life can prosper; this is capitalism. But when capital stops circling, or gets hoarded, misplaced, or impacted (as in digestion), bad, bad things happen, awful things like recessions or depressions or the devaluation or **end of all life**. *We don't really like these things—that's why they are bad.*

Incidentally, some good-intentioned people, in the past, decided capitalism and all its processes were evil. By opposing capital processes, however, they created some bad results—namely, death and stagnation. Without circulation, an organism cannot survive.

Capital circulation is **capitalism**. Capital is life. Life energy must circulate to allow life to continue living.

TWO KINDS OF CAPITALISM
We might stop here just a moment and recognize all capitalism is not the same.

In **COMPETITIVE CAPITALISM** all capital exchanges between unrelated organisms are violent. Ouch! One organism wins, the other loses violently.

In **COOPERATIVE CAPITALISM**, exchanges of ***profits*** take place—profits are *extra*, not life or death—and all participants in the exchange can benefit.

Cooperative capitalism occurs within a single organism or culture when capital is *shared* for mutual benefit. When we eat, food energy is **shared** by millions of separate cells, from our toes to our ears. **Cooperative capitalism** also takes place between **unrelated** individuals in the *flower-fruit exchange*, when plants trade fruits or nectar to animals for **work**.

We will discuss the ***flower-fruit cooperative*** later in this chapter. Bare in mind, however, **cooperative exchanges** are *rare* in nature. For the most part, all capital exchanges between unrelated organisms in nature are **violent**!!! Ouch! Death! Pain! We are food! Watch out!

Capital is life. Life requires energy capital. Life must grab energy from some source, either sunlight or another organism. Without capital circulation, or capitalism, animal life cannot exist. But the normal system to grab capital, **competitive capitalism**, can be nasty, create population wars, stress resources, and make destructive toxicities.

And incidentally, cancer cells also create toxicities when they **stop cooperation:** *C*haotic divisions (entropy) may create over-reproducing cancers *within* cooperating cultures or organisms. Selfish or ignorant cancerous cells in cooperating cultures **stop *cooperating***; cancerous cells over-reproduce to the degree they kill both their parent organism and themselves.

Cancers are not smart; they have no brains. Cancerous divisions change **cooperative capitalism** *within* a single organism into **competitive capitalism**. Ouch!

Cancers are dangerous to all *cooperating* cultures. We will meet more ignorant and selfish cultural cancers later.

D. FOSSIL FUELS – Forgotten Capital left behind

And finally, important for later: **Fossil fuels**--if valuable fish oil food-energy is buried, sometimes for millions and millions and millions of years, some of it can *still* be useful as gasoline, or plastic, or asphalt in some **weird** future civilization—if that foolish civilization doesn't mind breathing a few toxic byproducts.

Misplaced fish oil, profits, or fossil fuels, have been described as, *"God's bread basket for humanity."* Fossil fuels can be turned into energy or even directly back into food in the future. Thank you fish oil! Thank you petroleum! Thank you, old, old capital profit, created by our forefathers and foremothers long ago!

Wow! What is not to *love* about fish oil capital? What more can be said?

WHY CIVILIZATIONS FALL: CAPITAL DEVELOPMENT AND ENTROPY IN NATURE

Well, um, there is that **one** small thing to **repeat:** Remember? Some neighbors will gladly <u>eat</u> *us* because we are food! Oops! We are fish oil. Others value us as food or slave-energy. Seeking capital creates violent, mean, population warfare, also known as, competitive capitalism. You or me--only one can survive; this makes friendships difficult.

In nature, all capital exchanges between unrelated individuals are violent!!!

E. POPULATION or CULTURAL WARS ALSO STRESS RESOURCES!!!!

Population wars stress resources.
Population wars create extremes.
Extremes create toxicities
Toxicities destroy and divide populations
When populations recover, the wars continue and continue and continue until...FOREVER.

Billions of years ago, **competitive capitalism** began—us verses them! My bacterial/biological culture against your biological culture... And why are we playing? Well, to keep living first, but even as important—**we, life, are playing to claim the future for our progeny!**

Single organisms have limited life expectancies, but *cultures* of organisms can continue with some certainty into the future. Cultures, or big **numbers** of organisms, have **unlimited** lifespans. If we view a culture of organisms as a single animal, this animal can live forever. Cultures or species are fighting for *immortality.*

Immortality is great—only eternal spirits and cultures possess immortality.

To continue to continue, however, each culture (bacterial or human) must battle other cultures to control resources and the **future**. A culture/species can succeed into the immortal future only if its **numbers** continue to grow into the future. A culture that fails to grow in numbers into the future faster than death and competing species simply disappears; it is overwhelmed by other cultures that grow faster in numbers. In **culture wars**, big **numbers** battle against other big **numbers**. So numbers growth is everything in cultural survival.

Bare in mind for later: **Human cultures must abide by the same rules. Humans are also food-capital!**

<u>**NUMBERS WARS**</u> **HAVE TERRIBLE CONSEQUENCES:**
  Resource Depletion
  Toxicities
  Population destruction
AND THEN THE PROCESS REPEATS, AGAIN, AND AGAIN, AND AGAIN, AND.... (Over billions of years the AGAINS can mount up.) Numbers don't care.

SIZE AND NUMBERS MATTER
And all else being equal, between complex animals, the animals with the largest size and the most vicious dispositions overwhelm animals of smaller size and more docile dispositions in numbers competitions.

Our children are our soldiers: We (early organisms) make war against other cultures by churning out vast numbers of our own children. These children serve to overwhelm other cultures with their raw **numbers**. We need to battle in such fashion, since other cultures are trying to destroy us using *their* children. We recognize children from all cultures will be massive casualties of this mutual warfare, but we have no choice. Children are expendable. Children are bullets in our guns. If we don't fight, we will disappear. This is competitive capitalism.

Whether we are talking protozoans or dinosaurs, the game is to claim the future with growing **numbers or size**.

To repeat the repeat: The future is crowded; every culture is in violent competition for resources. So more of us than you, numbers or size, and we'll kick *you* out of the sunlight. On the contrary, more of *you* than *us*, and *we* are out. Ouch! It's lonely in the dark. This is competitive capitalism!

Competitive capitalism, the violent war of numbers against numbers, the race of us against them, is on!! Hurray!!! **The economy (violent though it may be) is booming! Booming!** Children are weapons of mass destruction. And we are **all** food! We are all *in circulation*. Whoopee!!

But we don't like being eaten. That is rather impolite.
Capital is life. Capital circulation is capitalism. Competitive capitalism is violent.

Recall: This is still 3.7 billion years ago. Humans have not arrived to take the blame.

WHY CIVILIZATIONS FALL: CAPITAL DEVELOPMENT AND ENTROPY IN NATURE

BACK TO CAPITAL HISTORY: THE MORNING EDITIONS
    F. Capital Hoarding
    G. Gang violence,
    H. Toxic byproducts,
    I. World wars,
    J. Predation, Parasites, Prejudice, and Intolerance
    K. Homelessness,
    L. Sex,
    M. Intolerance, Polarization.
    N. The flower-fruit cooperative exchange.
    O. LIVE EVOLVES NEW TECHNOLOGIES TO SOLVE ITS PROBLEMS, but the problems—violence, wars, and toxicities—strangely, continue.
    P. Dinosaur Demise: Death of a climax population

F. CLIMAX POPULATIONS AND CAPITAL HOARDING—NECESSARY RESOURCES HOARDED BY A FEW!!

The Bacteria Bugle – Late Edition 3.7 BILLION years ago

CLIMAX POPULATIONS HOARDING CAPITAL: Rich film stars and celebrities are hoarding capital and the sun. Life gathers in layers of film. This film now occupies much of the earth. The aristocrats at the top hoard much of the useable capital and resources.

    Others are left in the dark out of the cycle. "They have far more resources than they need. We have nothing. This is inequity!" the homeless are crying. "Let us in!" But the lucky film stars just smile securely and sign autographs. "We have it made!" they sigh.

News report: THIEVERY BECOMES EXTREMELY POPULAR!!
Some innovators are finding great success by stealing their neighbor's capital. No one seems to know whether this is right or wrong. *Morality has yet to be invented.*
But robbery is becoming common.
"Beware! Beware! Evil is among us!" the moral majority cry.

WHY CIVILIZATIONS FALL: CAPITAL DEVELOPMENT AND ENTROPY IN NATURE

> "Whoopee! Go get 'em!" cry the thieves.

G. YOUTH GANG VIOLENCE! (A semi-result of hoarding): Some young predatory organisms find it easier to *steal* a neighbor's capital than to create their own. At the same time, some lucky organisms—aristocrats and film stars--hoard capital resources, stifle change, and block the sun, so thievery is understandable. **Does this sound familiar to today?? It should. But remember, this is billions of years ago.**

By the way: These guys didn't have brains. Stuff like this could never happen to smart guys like us! Right?

Or, maybe we aren't that smart.

The next Sentinel issue should seem very familiar:

H. TOXIC BYPRODUCTS threaten Earth!!!

> **The Single-Cell Sentinel –**
> Late Edition 2.7 Billion yrs ago
> PHOTOSYNTHESIS – THE NEW RAGE!
>
> Everybody's doing it! Doing it! Doing it! Using sun energy and grabbing some carbon from CO_2, we are all having a great time. What fun! We only expel a little oxygen to have a great party! Some say oxygen is toxic, but who cares?
> Time to party! Tanning solons are open for business everywhere. Fun in the sun! Grim statistics about oxygen are simply fake news. FAKE NEWS! Warnings are propaganda! Pay no attention. Party on! Ignore fake news!

> **The Single-Cell Sentinel** – LAST EDITION!! circa -2.3 Billion yrs ago
> IF YOU HAVEN'T NOTICED YET – WE ARE ALL APPARENTLY DEAD!!
> Foul toxic byproduct, oxygen, has killed everyone!

WHY CIVILIZATIONS FALL: CAPITAL DEVELOPMENT AND ENTROPY IN NATURE

> "The doomsayers were right! We did it to ourselves!" scientists cry. We were all madly chasing capital and destroying our world, and gosh, we succeeded!
>
> Incidentally, there is no hope! The end is nigh!! Foul oxygen breathing aliens are arriving. They are taking over. The old ways are being disrespected! Oh, the inhumanity!

H. **TOXIC BYPRODUCTS:** This might sound familiar: 2.3 BILLION years ago, life's toxic byproduct, *oxygen*, destroyed almost *all* species on earth. Oxygen producers killed themselves off. A few alien aerobic organisms survived to take over. Is this a reminder for today? It might be.

Later, oxygen toxicity changed the world's climate drastically; oxygen toxicity helped create the Huronian Ice age, the longest ice age ever, over 100 million years, an ice age that covered much of the earth. Brrr!

NOTE: Population or numbers wars stress resources and create toxicities. Is this still true today?

*The reader should verify everything online or in a geology textbook: THE HURONIAN ICE AGE.

I. More late news: ***WORLD WARS*** BETWEEN CULTURES!

> **THE BACTERIA REVOLUTION circa -2.2 Billion yrs ago**
> **OOPS!**
>
> Don't look now, but apparently we are all dead again! All life down the tubes. Gosh! Déjà vu all over again! We have written this same story over and over. Terrible dying is reported from all areas.
>
> WORLD WARS: Some selfish species were over-reproducing, stressing resources, and causing red tides that kill everything, including themselves. That's dumb. (But understand, we don't have brains.)
>
> Additional report: If this wasn't bad enough, apparently volcanic eruptions have vented massive amounts of sulfur. This sulfur is combining with the by-product oxygen and hydrogen in the air to created sulfuric acid, which is deadly to *everything*.
>
> And did we mention? This is also creating a new Huronian ice age covering the *entire* earth? "Nice knowing everyone. Bye!"

DIPLOMACY ENDS!!!: WORLD POPULATION WARS ERUPT and CONTINUE FOREVER!!!
RED TIDES: TERRIBLE LOSSES
Bacteria cultures wage cultural/species wars against each other.

A united organic species shares resources and breeding. Cultures that no longer **share** are in competition or population wars. These wars changes cooperative capitalism to competitive capitalism.

Population wars over millions of years place stresses on resources. Population wars stress all populations. And more, when numbers and toxicity get out of control, everything dies. Oops! We did not see that coming! But then again, we don't have brains. Wars **can** be hell!

Constant warfare diminishes the *quality* of life (for every type of life). World wars tend to do that. (And still, apparently, do.)

Numbers are only quantities, with an (n). ***Quality* with an(l) has no meaning to naked numbers.**

Over and over again, life repeatedly tries to destroy itself and make itself miserable—just like humans!
"If it is smaller or weaker than you, eat it!' is the motto. "Eat everything," cry the parasites.

NOTE: *The population wars that began billions of years ago <u>continue today</u> unabated between all cultures!*
    Note: Population wars stress resources
        Population wars create toxicities
        Toxicities destroy populations

WHY CIVILIZATIONS FALL: CAPITAL DEVELOPMENT AND ENTROPY IN NATURE

In ignorance, when populations recover, the wars repeat and repeat

By the way...billions of years ago:
Nature created PREJUDICE AND INTOLERANCE!!

J. PARASITES ARE EVERYWHERE!!! SO <u>PREJUDICE AND INTOLERANCE</u> ARE THE RAGE!!!

Lazy parasites on welfare infect every nook and cranny and every hard-working organism. Parasites take other's assets without work; this places a great strain on life's development. Anything that works must work even harder to accommodate parasites and predators, muggers, and con artists. Sound like today?

Only the species that reproduce the fastest can survive the onslaught.

Intolerance, prejudice, and overpopulation <u>are necessary</u> to avoid parasites and predation. We must be intolerant of everything that doesn't look just like us—and the world is filled with imposters! Cultures, that fail to reproduce quickly, simply disappear. Cultural wars between all species are ongoing and involve the entire world, and no one can win them. **Children are expendable, edible soldiers.** These world wars continue eternally nonstop.

Everyone agrees on one thing: "*Individual* lives have little <u>value</u>. Only big *numbers* are important: Q*uantity, with an 'n'*, is everything. Q*uality, with an 'l',* means nothing." Is that true today?
Note: Population wars create INTOLERANCE.

THE BIVALVE BUGLE – 1.4 BILLION YEARS AGO.
INTOLERANCE AND PREJUDICE ARE ABSOLUTELY NECESSARY FOR SURVIVAL!!!
VICIOUS PARASITES ARE TAKING OVER. PROTECT YOURSELVES AT ALL COSTS! PRACTICE INTOLERANCE!!
Vicious gangs of parasites and predators are everywhere. These thugs will try to steal your capital—in other words, they will try to eat you—maybe from inside! You don't want that! Grow intolerant!!! Avoid everything that is not you or your immediate family.
The arms war is on! Prejudice is power!! Buy guns! Lock your doors! We must out reproduce our enemies!! The more we reproduce, the more we survive parasites and predation!

WHY CIVILIZATIONS FALL: CAPITAL DEVELOPMENT AND ENTROPY IN NATURE

> "DON'T EAT ME!" the children cry, but we all know children are not important. We *all* eat children. Don't we? Yum! Love children.
>
> MEANWHILE: **HIGH TECH VIRUSES ARE ATTACKING FROM INNER SPACE!!!** Watch out everyone!! These alien viruses are hacking people's genetic codes!! Keep your passwords safe. Avoid everything that doesn't speak your DNA language! Suspect all strangers!
>
> **PRACTICE INTOLERANCE!!** Resist all immigrants! Stay with your home tribe. **PREJUDICE IS POWER!!** Trust no one. Strange aliens are taking over! Build fences! Install security! Aaargh! They got me!

Sound familiar?

TO SURVIVE WE MUST PRACTICE INTOLERANCE AND PREJUDICE. Wars are costly and eat up everyone's profits. Parasitic viruses hijack genetic secrets. Parasites parasitize everything; and some parasites even parasitize other parasites.

Everyone eats everyone else, so family dinnertime can be tense!

Millions of children have to be born for a few to survive. **Children are capital** or food. **Children are capital soldiers in population wars.** Prime real estate becomes ever more important. The numbers race constantly reduces the *value* of *individual* lives. The competition for capital grows violent. **We must all practice intolerance**!!! Help!

And recall: Humans haven't even arrived at the party! **Don't blame us! Not yet!**

K. **AND THE HOMELESS PROBLEM REMAINS EVER PERSISTENT:**

WHY CIVILIZATIONS FALL: CAPITAL DEVELOPMENT AND ENTROPY IN NATURE

> ### THE BIVALVE BUGLE
> **REAL ESTATE VALUES ARE SKYROCKETING!** VALUES ARE GOING OUT OF SIGHT! HOMELESS PROBLEM INTOLERABLE! Yes, your reporter has witnessed the price of property growing beyond the reach of normal organisms. Only the luckiest can inherit prime properties now. The poor homeless circulate the seas in poverty, quickly eaten, doomed to substandard life styles. Success is one in a million. The population is obsessed by the rampant pursuit of capital and a proper home in a good neighborhood!
> TERRIBLE WASTE OF RESOUCES Scientists also report a terrible flow of resources moving to the bottom of the sea out of reach of all life forms. Climax populations of film stars and the wealthy hoard capital in layers of floating algae. These selfish few own the best sites; they block others from the sun and hoard resources! What can we do about this inequity?
> How about sex? SEX??

WHY CIVILIZATIONS FALL: CAPITAL DEVELOPMENT AND ENTROPY IN NATURE

L. SEX!! OKAY!! HOORAY!!! WONDERFUL!!! 1.3 BILLION YEARS AGO!

> **THE MULTICELLED PLAYMATE MAGAZINE** circa -1.3 billion yrs ago
> **SEXUAL REPRODUCTION IS THE RAGE!!**
> If you haven't tried it, it's time to swing! Improve your genes with sex. Get rid of your parasites by having heterosexual unions. Let only the uninfected males win. Party time for all!
>
> Classified ads: "This is Lola. I am sweet and available, but only to a large male with no parasites. See me at…"

EDITOR'S NOTE. "We are still talking about microorganisms here."

SEX AND CAPITAL: About 1.3 billion years ago, sex becomes popular. Exchanging and mixing genetic material allows organisms to quickly change to adapt to new survival challenges.

HETEROSEXUAL SEX allows males with defects or parasites to be deleted from the flow. Males are ***expendable***. Ladies can accept only the healthiest males. Sex helps animals reduce parasitism, and stay healthy, so they can pursue more capital and have more sex.

Unfortunately, the capital everyone is consuming is each other. Oops! The numbers would grow even larger except for this mutual consumption. Mass predation keeps things somewhat in line, but family gatherings can be very awkward.

> "Where is uncle Bert?
> "We ate him for breakfast."
> "Oh? Well then-- Where is aunt Ruth? Yum."

NEW INVENTIONS: SEX
Sexual reproduction 1.3 billion years ago increases the varieties of species. Heterosexual reproduction decreases parasitism by easily **eliminating males with defects or parasites**. Male DNA is expendable. Any defect and you are out. Women choose. Sorry boys! The future doesn't want you.

Hermaphrodite animals—possessing both male and female parts—do **not** posses this advantage: ***Male expendability***. Hermaphrodite animals are

WHY CIVILIZATIONS FALL: CAPITAL DEVELOPMENT AND ENTROPY IN NATURE

more susceptible to parasites. Hermaphroditism loses its trendiness among more sophisticated party organisms.

Now we *know*, males are put on earth only to be expendable in every possible way. Women have suspected this all along. Women choose the winners. Losers disappear. By guys! Incidentally, by-by parasites!

However, chasing sex and profit, the numbers game, does not actually improve the *quality* of life. At this point in pre-human history, quality has no meaning. In the biological struggle, only life **quantity** is important—with an (n).

In other words, sex was not derived to make life qualitatively better or more enjoyable. The function of sex is to allow life to achieve more competitive **numbers** against parasites. Big numbers are important because big numbers overwhelm small numbers to win the future over *competing cultures*. Big numbers survive; small numbers disappear. Sorry boys and girls. Quality has no part in the equation.

Numbers rule.

To repeat--the *quality* of life at this time is of no import. Numbers rule; and thus, only quantities count—that's quantities with an (n) like in numbers, not an (l) like in love or life or quality or sex.

There is no 'l' in sex. Oh, right. I guess we're wrong then.

WHY CIVILIZATIONS FALL: CAPITAL DEVELOPMENT AND ENTROPY IN NATURE

AN EARLY CAPITALIST ON HIS ESTATE

Climax populations hoard capital and stop the flow to everyone else sometimes for eons.

Important capital resources continue in dead bodies lost to the depths; these resources re-appear in currents or disappear sometimes for millions of years or forever.

Abrupt disruptions in circulation cause depressions and recessions no one can explain. "Why?" citizens cry. "Why *me* and not *you*?" *"I like me better than you."* No one knows the answer. But the questions are still familiar today. **Numbers rule totally without brains.**

Sounds like our government.

LIFE VALUE VS NUMBERS
Affectionate relationships have yet to be invented, but if they existed, the numbers would overwhelm them.

Quantity stifles quality EXCEPT IN ONE AREA:

N. THE FLOWER-FRUIT ECONOMIC EXCHANGE 200 MILLION years ago: *Cooperative Capitalism*

We mentioned earlier that in nature capital exchanges between unrelated individuals are ***always*** violent. This statement is not totally accurate. Long before the arrival of humans, nature designed a system of capital exchanges that were mutually beneficial. These trades take place on the floor of the *flower-fruit exchange*, and the organization is incorporated worldwide.

Of course, we are referring to how flowering plants exchange profits with pollinators and fruit-eaters for mutual benefit. Depending on one's religious affiliation, we can attribute this economic system to nature or God. It works remarkably well. Thank you God.

Plants have difficulty moving, not having arms or legs. So reproducing together and spreading seeds can be problematic to plants. Early plants devised many intricate systems for dispersal, and these worked well enough, but somewhere between two hundred and two hundred and fifty million years ago, a new concept materialized—**cooperative capitalism**.

The system involved trading **profits** for **work**. Plants could provide a small amount of food value to insects and in turn these insects would (unwittingly) provide pollination services. By encasing their hard seeds in pulpy fruits, plants could encourage fruit-eating animals to also distribute their seeds.

The system worked well, and continued to be improved for millions of years to the benefit of the businesses involved. Plants created a **profit**, and traded this profit for needed **work**. Everyone benefited. This is the way *cooperative capitalism* should work.

WHY CIVILIZATIONS FALL: CAPITAL DEVELOPMENT AND ENTROPY IN NATURE

Bare in mind, the entire cycle depends on the plants first creating a **profit**, a profit these plants can trade to promote their own family objectives. Without a **profit**, the system breaks down and capital can only be exchanged violently, a step backwards—except to those bullies who prefer violent exchanges rather than peaceful ones. *"Violence is fun!"*
Cooperative capitalism *requires tradable* **profits.**

O. LIFE EVOLVES NEWER AND NEWER TECHNOLOGIES THAT FAIL TO EVER ACTUALLY SOLVE PROBLEMS

Over millions of years, life continues to evolve new technologies to change, but never solve its persistent problems--population wars, toxicities, and constant violence.

New tech includes horns, teeth, thick skins, huge sizes, feathers, fur, better brains, etc.—these and other new **technologies** only change the calculations briefly; the wars continue without end.

The point is: **Cultural warfare** continues to de-value all life no matter how **technologies** change. **New technologies** only allow survival wars to grow more vicious! The violent premise does not change. Is this still true today…? Hm.

P. THE END OF THE DINOSAURS--The Dead Zone: 67 million years ago

TIME PASSES: Five major extinction events and over a dozen minor die-offs occur. **COMPETITIVE CAPITALISM, also known as survival of the luckiest, staggers back each time.**

Stable environments create larger and larger sizes.
Big **numbers**, big sizes, overwhelm small numbers and smaller sizes in constant number wars.
Technologies evolve; millions of years pass; but the wars continue uninterrupted.

THE DINOSAUR DIGEST
– Only 67million years ago

SIZE WINS AGAIN: In this fall edition, the reporters would like to thank all our many dinosaur subscribers. You have survived many untimely events over the last hundred million years.

When times are stable, big sizes win the numbers competitions. And you, fellow behemoths, are the champions: You are structurally and technologically superior. You have grown larger, and larger, and larger every eon.

WHY CIVILIZATIONS FALL: CAPITAL DEVELOPMENT AND ENTROPY IN NATURE

> All of you have eaten and killed and mangled your way to the very top of the food chain. You have survived many close calls to be the giants you have become. Out of hundreds of small siblings, many of whom you have cannibalized, only you have risen to the top. Congratulations! Take a bow, graduates!! Nothing can stop you now!!
> Surely, a great year lies ahead.
> Oops! What is that in the sky???

CLIMAX POPULATION CRASHES!!

Game Over!
Meteor 1 zillion / Dinos 0

Most scientists agree, a fiery meteor ended the dinosaur's game. Capital exchanges stopped; earth's capital economy collapsed; the status quo group—who mistakenly thought they owned the entire planet--got literally cremated; and almost everything else, predator, prey, and plant, died also.

And perhaps, we are all very lucky the dinosaurs died. If they hadn't died, none of us would be here! Dinosaurs were well designed for every environment. The dinosaurs were the **climax population** of their time. They owned the world for nearly one hundred million years. Against such beasts, our ancestors stood no chance. **Climax populations** can be deadly to diversity.

After the dinosaurs, however, the same cycle of deadly population wars started again, and again—but now, dinosaurs were not around to always win the battles.

Had no catastrophe occurred, mammals might still be hiding under ground? Or will hiding underground also be our future? Better keep a flashlight handy.

"DÉJÀ VU: IT ALL HAPPENED BEFORE!"

This is an--
IMPORTANT CHAPTER CONCLUSION: *Nothing happening today is truly new!! Everything happening today is repeating over and over again!!*
Cultural divisions, selfish aristocrats, **prejudice,** homelessness, **economic inequities**, toxic waste, unfair ownership, overpopulation,

WHY CIVILIZATIONS FALL: CAPITAL DEVELOPMENT AND ENTROPY IN NATURE

cultural **intolerance**, violent **extremists**, terrorists, lazy parasites, unbridled sex, **world wars**, apocalypses, and violent gangs—every social and economic problem we now experience also occurred long, long, long before humans.
 "*You can't blame us! We have an alibi. We did not exist.*"

<u>Most important, the forces that created these problems still silently command the table today.</u>
 Warring random **numbers,** obedient to the forces of cultural **entropy**, control human societies; and this control is exercised over **large *time* spans** that make the changing situation difficult for humans to understand.
 Technologies may change, but the **conflicts remain the same. Competing Numbers** and **cultural entropy** control human economies. Human reason does not. So why should we care???

 The problem is this: Numbers contain no ***qualitative*** element. Numbers are only numbers. If we allow battling **numbers** to win the future, the *value* and *quality* of human life will not be in the equation.
 If big numbers continue to win, the future of life will be just as irrational and violent as the past. The **numbers** don't care.

 Thus without changes, the past will repeat and repeat in the future. "*Déjà vu, all over again!*" Yogi Berra.

 If humans wish to increase the ***value*** of human life—rather than the numerical ***amount*** of human life—we need to understand the specific forces of **cultural entropy** that actually control economic and cultural capital development. Let us discuss these forces, next chapter.

WHY CIVILIZATIONS FALL: CAPITAL DEVELOPMENT AND ENTROPY IN NATURE 22

CH 2. WHAT IS CULTURAL ENTROPY?

Cultural Entropy opposes Capitalism and Capital Sharing Systems.

<u>Cultural Entropy:</u> For most of human history, bacteria remained invisible to human eyes. Humans attributed the diseases caused by bacteria to evil spirits and ignored real cures.

Today, by recognizing the once-invisible effects of bacteria, humans have found actual cures to diseases. Humans now live healthier lives.

The forces of CULTURAL ENTROPY, over long time periods, invisibly destroy and divide human cultures and families. Since these forces are invisible, we attribute the effects and diseases caused by cultural entropy to human evil or imagined monsters; in so doing we ignore actual cures.

Entire civilizations have perished without knowing why.

By understanding the destructive forces of cultural entropy, humans can live more joyful lives and perhaps find real cures to human problems.

Cultural entropy works over long, long time periods to divide once-unified cultures into competing and **non-sharing** parts. These divided cultures battle eternally in violent cultural wars that can never end. New divisions continually create new wars.

An economy or culture is designed as a **sharing** organism. When the culture no longer **shares**, the economy no longer exists.

A. ENTROPY in PHYSICS

The **second law of** thermodynamics says that when energy changes from one form to another form, or matter moves freely, entropy(disorder) in a closed system increases.

It takes **work** to make the entropy of an object or system smaller; therefore without work, entropy can **never** become smaller – you could say, without work in the opposite direction everything slowly goes to disorder or chaos (higher entropy).

Entropy is a measure of molecular disorder, randomness, work-energy, or chaos in a system. The principal derives from the **Second Law of Thermodynamics**. The German physicist, Rudolf Clausius, introduced the concept in 1850.

RULES INCLUDE: *Free energy evolves to randomness.* Or also: *Free Energy forces will extend to equality.*

The entropy process is easy to envision: All active energy is some sort of movement. Heat is movement. Cold is simply less heat, less movement. Moving, heated, energized particles tend to push against each other. This push away creates natural **polarization**, movement away, from each other, among moving particles. So free energy particles move from high density, high heat, high push, toward colder, lower density, less pushback, to eventually equalize the energy push from all directions.

Heat (movement) repels heat (movement) and incidentally moves toward cold (less movement). Cold does not move to heat (unless heat pushes it) because cold is not movement; cold is the *absence* of movement.

Thus a gas in a vacuum will expand from its active center to fill inactive space evenly, so that every push is the same from every direction. Heat energy, either in a solid or gas, will distribute itself to maximum randomness for the same reason, bringing a solid object to a single temperature. Energy movement—also called **work**--will distribute itself until the push is equal from all sides, until the energy is evenly distributed. Only **work** in opposition will counter this distribution.

In a similar fashion, random movements will eventually stir separate gasses into a homogeneous state at a common temperature. This homogeneous state will possess relative maximum entropy—total randomness of heat and particle distribution for that system.

IMPORTANT LAW OF PHYSICS: **Only work in the opposite direction will keep the energy in a system from randomly increasing/working to maximum entropy (chaos).**

According to some physicists, **thermodynamic entropy** *will eventually create a homogenous universe, a universe that expands until it has a single temperature, and is endless, and lifeless—not a truly pleasant thought. But it may not occur for a while, so don't worry too much for now. Also bear in mind, contrary forces (working against entropy) may exist or be created.*

FORCES CONTRARY TO ENTROPY:

WHY CIVILIZATIONS FALL: CAPITAL DEVELOPMENT AND ENTROPY IN NATURE

We may, *incidentally,* view **life** as a force contrary to entropy. **Life** struggles to align energy systems by its *own* priorities. Life struggles (works) to create stable systems against the random forces (workings) of entropy/chaos.

Recall however: Life, or energy-capital is, itself, a type of confined **energy.**

"Work is necessary to diminish entropy." Thus *only* **work**, a measure of **energy**, can oppose the workings of entropy or chaos. The laws of physics state: *Without work, entropy will **always** increase.*

To continue existing against chaos, life must continue working. To continue working, life requires **energy**—either *new* energy (supplied by the sun) or *circulated* energy (from other life forms). This **creation and circulation of capital energy** is called **capitalism** (or alternately, the circle of life).

Capital movement requires continuous work/energy input.

WHY CIVILIZATION COLLAPSE – The Too-Simple Rule:

All economic systems (human or biological) require constant energy input and circulation to achieve stability or growth.

Economic capital systems that lose energy input and circulation will collapse.

B. LINGUISTIC ENTROPY IN HUMAN CULTURES

Human languages **randomly change** over time. In Paleolithic times, human tribes, separated by a few hundred years, had difficulty understanding each other. A thousand years of separation can make tribal languages mutually incomprehensible.

The variables of linguistic change depend on the degree of separation and exposure to other language groups, plus other **topographical factors.** The deep separation of dark jungles apparently foments extreme language change: The Maya of the Yucatan spoke apparently **70 separate languages**. [Read: Ch 8, Why Civilizations Collapse] Jungles and mountain ranges can separate languages over short distances.

Numerous mountains and peninsulas separate Europe. Each separate peninsula has historically developed language and cultural differences.

The diverse continent of Africa is home to one quarter of the languages presently spoken. African topography is quite divisive.

On the contrary, combining river systems and trade can slow the dissolution of languages when other trade capital is included. China is an example we will discuss later. (Ch. 8)

Recall: Language data is trade capital. **A conversation is a *capital exchange.*** [Read: Ch. 3, 4]

Language differences obviously increase human **intolerance** and interfere with the **sharing** of capital understandings between human cultures. [Recall *biological intolerance*, Ch. 1.] Throughout history, violent **cultural wars** often occur between nearly identical populations simply because they speak different languages.

Modern inventions, written languages, and dictionaries, can *slow* **language entropy**, but language change is still persistent over long stretches of time. Will humans a thousand years from now be able to read and understand today's languages? Probably not... To oppose entropy requires **work**.

Capital is life. CULTURAL ENTROPY divides capital systems (including language). Human cultures rely on capital exchanges to exist. Capital exchanges include, among other trade items—language, information, food, breeding, work, and tools.

C. EROSION AND CREATION

Random events create cycles of creation and erosion. Elemental materials, pulled together by gravity, randomly build stars, planets, and mountain ranges. These creations simultaneously erode due to other random movements such as radiation, wind, and water. Creation and erosion are intertwined.

Living organisms interject themselves into naturally occurring patterns of creation and destruction to grab energy and raw materials [Ch.1]. *The circulation of energy and raw materials between living organisms is called capitalism.*

Capital (living) patterns tend to resolve themselves over time into cycles of apparent stability. However, over longer time periods, all organic cycles change and evolve widely. In other words, over long time periods, natural cycles are not inherently stable. Permanence in nature is an illusion. Random forces of entropy act on all circulating capital systems to create instability and erosion.

Whenever humans interject themselves into naturally circulating living patterns, they create additional changes. Human activities can facilitate or oppose capital cycles. Thus, human activities can assist or oppose the effects of entropy (chaos) on capital systems.

Human activities, for example, can assist soil erosion and depletion or oppose the process. When farming extracts soil nutrients over long periods, the soil becomes depleted. In this case we may say human activities assist entropy to oppose and destabilize the capital cycle. Work in the opposite

WHY CIVILIZATIONS FALL: CAPITAL DEVELOPMENT AND ENTROPY IN NATURE

direction (against random entropy) is necessary (through fertilizers) to return the soil to fertility or to healthy capital circulation.

Entropy erodes the stability of capital cycles. Work is necessary to oppose entropy.

Many ancient civilizations unknowingly diminished soil fertility and increased erosion in their environments over time, particularly in fragile desert areas. When such depletions occur over long stretches of time, humans often do not understand these changes. They may accept the situation as natural and unchangeable and fail to work to ameliorate damages over time. In such situations humans unknowingly assist entropy to erode capital circulation (in the soil or environment) necessary for human survival. [Ch. 7, 8 – Why Civilizations fail]

Increasing populations stress resources. Small populations (of humans or animals) may access resources in a region repeatedly, without greatly interrupting patterns of circulation. Increasing populations (human or animal), however, increasingly stress resources and capital circulation in any region to and beyond capacity.

Farming practices increase capital circulation (profits) and thus increase the capacity of a region to support human life; but increasing numbers (human or animal), combined with soil depletion, in both ancient (and modern) civilizations, stress the capacity of resources to circulate and regenerate.. Population stresses can erode and diminish capital circulation over time and create famines. When numbers stress a region's resources and overwhelm capital circulation, human conflicts become inevitable. Conflicting numbers do not possess reason.

We may pause to wonder here why wars are so commonplace in human history. Historians generally cede wars to human angst. We are warlike people. We disagree on who controls the land. War is the simple solution forced upon us by numbers.

Without the stress of numbers, however, human wars would be unnecessary and impossible. When human numbers stress resources, humans are forced to fight over possession. The abundance of expendable soldiers, in addition, allows deadly wars to continue indefinitely.

Future human numbers can continue to increase even with the loss of significant males from the breeding pool. Thus increasing human numbers make wars both necessary and possible.

D. CULTURAL ENTROPY

Real—not imagined—natural forces work in opposition to ordered capital-circulating systems (assisting chaos or entropy). In so doing, these forces oppose the stability of human (and animal) cultures. The forces of cultural entropy include all random movements—physical, biological, or conceptual—that chaotically affect change over time.

The forces of cultural entropy ultimately devalue and erode living systems, including human life.

CULTURAL ENTROPY, like physical entropy, evolves from **the random movements of energy** *in the universe—gravity, radiation, time, chemical reactions, etc, primarily exercised on biological (living) organisms.*

For example: The random movements of water molecules will quickly dissolve salts and sugars. Over long time periods, water movements will decay metals and cement. Gravity and radiation constantly weigh on living organisms. The divisive effects of cultural entropy (chaos) in animal cultures include old age, decay, predation, and wars.

But we cannot think of **cultural entropy** *as evil. Entropy has no intent. And importantly, cultural entropy often leads to* **changes** *in life systems. Without change, life would not be what it is. Cultural entropy is simply something we need to understand without emotional judgment.*

The **monsters** *that arrive from the actions of cultural entropy are created from human fantasies (Ch. 9, 10). Only by understanding the real* **origins** *of human monsters—wars, intolerance, overpopulation, human predators, and resource stress--can humans hope to control these monsters.*

CULTURAL ENTROPY *includes* **linguistic entropy** *plus* **all** *other random, polarizing, dissolving physical forces—atomic movements, erosion, chemical reactions, wind, water, heat, cold, gravity, time, sunlight, plus biological and* **human** *additions [Ch. 3,4,5].* **Over long time periods**, *the forces of* **cultural entropy** *pressure capital-sharing,* **cultural** *systems— biological and human--to disassociate/dissolve into separate, competing parts.*

CULTURAL ENTROPY over long time periods places all cultures into mortal conflict to claim life resources. The invisible forces of cultural entropy divide united cultures into competing parts; these disunited parts then engage in competitive cultural wars with each other.

Inevitable random human changes occur **over time** *in language, skin color, religion, dress, breeding customs, culture tolerance, capital sharing, infrastructures, social structures, technologies, and common understandings. This book will discuss several random factors of* **cultural entropy** *and describe the divisive effects cultural entropy exerts on civilization and capital circulation in animal and human populations.*

WHY CIVILIZATIONS FALL: CAPITAL DEVELOPMENT AND ENTROPY IN NATURE

Recall from thermodynamics: "Work is necessary to oppose entropy."

Incidentally: **Besides language, <u>everything</u> associated with life or social systems is affected by similar random disassociations, entropy, or decay, including human lives.** Old age, cancer, and death are results of *random forces of entropy* that slowly over time interfere with the correct reproduction of our DNA.

IMPORTANT TO RECOGNIZE TIME AND INVISIBILITY

Cultural entropy works divisively on societies and cultures over long, long time periods—under the radar of short-lived humans--tearing apart coherent systems and unperceptively leaving behind, separate, antagonistic parts, **parts unaware they were once a single, united family.**

CHEMICAL FORCES: RUST NEVER SLEEPS

Oxidation is an *example* of many corrosive **chemical forces** that function, *over long, long stretches of time*, to corrode and dissolve human and natural capital items. Other **divisive forces** (random movements) include sunlight, wind, earth movement, gravity, chemical interactions, climate change, radioactivity, and water. These **entropic natural forces** act to divide and scatter natural and cultural systems. These entropic forces—all simple, random particle movements, without intent--assist **cultural entropy** to decay and dissolve all ordered systems over long, long, time periods.

Slow changes that occur over long time periods often escape the attention of humans with short lives and shorter attention spans.

FACTORS *OPPOSING* CULTURAL ENTROPY--ENTAIL WORK

Some obvious factors oppose the forces of cultural dissolution. These factors include the reasons cultures—organic or human—form initially. Cultures form for mutual support—to defend against predation; to assist reproduction; to better access resources; or, in particular, to oppose other cultures over time.

Focused **work** of some kind is necessary to *oppose* the naturally divisive forces of cultural entropy. This work is particularly necessary in human cultures, a fact we will discuss later.

Note: In order to rationally **work** to keep their cultures together, humans must recognize and oppose the specific forces tearing them apart. Over long time periods, these invisible forces can be unrecognized.

C1   CULTURAL ENTROPY (CHAOS) IN BIOLOGICAL CULTURES:

WHY CIVILIZATIONS FALL: CAPITAL DEVELOPMENT AND ENTROPY IN NATURE

The organic derivation of cultural entropy is quite simple: Random energy forces work divisively on cultural or capital-sharing systems in the same way random energy forces work on all other cultural systems. In quickly reproducing organisms, the effects may occur more rapidly.

For example: [see following pic] A colony of single-celled organisms, called A, divides and divides. A tolerates itself, because, well, all the A cells are exactly the same thing. A is in some competition with itself, but generally it shares natural resources and mating privileges without toxicity with other A's. A is only toxic and intolerant to far different creatures, for example, Z's, and F's, and T's.

But random things happen. Sometimes A cells do not divide correctly and mistakes are made. Some A bacteria are not all exactly alike. In nearly one hundred percent of division mistakes, the random results are unsuccessful. In unlikely events, however, mistakes can be improvements or simply make things different. Call these different cells, CA cells.

Differences become magnified: Small differences are not problems to most A cells, but some A cells are intolerant, call these cells BA cells, and BA cells are intolerant of CA cells, which are only slightly deviant A cells. BA cells will not share resources or mate with CA cells. BA cells are **intolerant** of CA cells. So CA cells eventually become **intolerant** of BA cells. [See following pic.]

We might think that the A, tolerant cells, being the majority, would dominate the ensuing argument between intolerant BA and intolerant CA cells. Unfortunately, once BA and CA cells become toxic to each other, A cells, the tolerant cells in the **middle**, are the first victims. Plain A cells have no defense, *avoidance*; or offense, *toxicity*, to help their survival.

A cells are in toxic danger from both sides, from both BA and CA cells. And so the middle becomes a ***no man's land***; the tolerant A cells are the first to disappear. BA and CA extremes are eventually left to battle each other in a devastating culture war.

WHY CIVILIZATIONS FALL: CAPITAL DEVELOPMENT AND ENTROPY IN NATURE

Most biological systems are not so simple. The above example is a generic model of interactions biologists recognize have many more variables. When predation, parasites, and food competition become problematic, systems grow more complex. But for now, please accept the simplistic model above **for *illustrative purposes*.**

WHY CIVILIZATIONS FALL: CAPITAL DEVELOPMENT AND ENTROPY IN NATURE

Cultural entropy benefits **intolerant** extremes. *Intolerant cultural extremes create a toxic middle. Intolerant extremes stop sharing. When the sharing middle of a culture dies (from toxicity), cultural divisions occur. Culturally separate divisions then compete in a cancerous population war against each other over resources. Cultural wars stress resources. The cycle repeats and repeats.*

The human cycle illustrated is:
1) **INTOLERANCE CREATES INTOLERANCE;**
2) **EXTREMES CREATE GREATER EXTREMES;**
3) **INTOLERANT EXTREMES CREATE SOCIAL TOXICITY IN THE MIDDLE; TOXICITY DIVIDES AND DESTROYS SOCIAL SYSTEMS.**
4) **DIVIDED SOCIAL SYSTEMS VIOLENTLY COMPETE FOR RESOURCES THROUGH WARFARE.**
5) **WARFARE CREATES GREATER INTOLERANCE AND DESTROYS RESOURCES FOR THE FUTURE.**

The most destructive product of cultural entropy is the ***self-recreating*** meme of **cultural intolerance**.

Cultural intolerance in the natural world combines ***avoidance*** and mutual ***toxicity*.** **Toxic** organisms actively discourage the growth of competing organisms through various, usually chemical, means. Organisms exercise **intolerance** to avoid parasites and predation. **Intolerance**, apart from purifying a social system, also creates polarization and greater intolerance. Mutual intolerance, further, creates greater ***toxicity***.

Parts of a culture, that refuse to **share**, must **compete**. **Toxicity (competition) within cultures is destructive of the sharing, tolerant middle.** And without a tolerant middle, ***population wars*** are constant with *no possibility* of peaceful resolutions. Population wars stress resources.

The stages include:

        Separation/ Avoidance
        Intolerance/Polarization/lack of sharing
        Middle destruction/toxicity
        Population wars/ Competition/Cancer

2. LONG TIME PERIODS:

Most important: The processes of cultural entropy can dominate biological and human systems over *extended time periods*; **and long time periods make corrosive entropy effects underline invisible to short-lived humans.** Over the following chapters, we shall revisit cultural entropy time and again in the history of **human** events.

WHY CIVILIZATIONS FALL: CAPITAL DEVELOPMENT AND ENTROPY IN NATURE

Recall: The forces of entropy and **cultural entropy** randomly oppose the structures (work) created by life. The battle waged is for the future; and the question is, will human understandings or the forces of **numbers and cultural entropy** control the future?

3. AVOIDANCE/INTOLERANCE/AND PARASITES

Most species naturally avoid close proximity to other species; and they also avoid close proximity to their *own* species. Part of the problem is parasites. Parasites benefit whenever victims congregate in large numbers and in close proximity. **To avoid being parasitized or preyed upon, most organisms avoid each other.** *Avoidance behaviors* or *intolerance* are common in nature.

However, some organisms also benefit from the safety of numbers—schooling or herding together to deter predators, thus creating a culture. ***The benefits of <u>avoidance</u> and <u>unity</u> oppose each other.***

Avoidance/intolerance is also common in human populations. The balance between forces of avoidance (to avoid parasites), and unity (to unite for offense and defense and love) can be determined by environmental factors. In areas with high levels of parasitic diseases, highly diverse, united, human cultures are difficult to maintain. ***Avoidance and intolerance assist the corrosive effects of cultural entropy in human societies***.

Social animals, like lions, humans, and apes are particularly vulnerable to major population declines due to parasites. In human history, parasites and disease kill far more humans than wars.

Many human moral values are dictated by the ***avoidance meme***. Diseases like AIDES, typhoid, measles, influenza, etc. are facilitated by human proximity. It isn't that we don't like each other; we just don't want to get sick. At least, that is what my wife tells me.

When farmers plant a single crop on thousands of acres, they provide parasites an opportunity to concentrate. Large planting areas can give parasites opportunities to adapt quickly to human-created toxins. Animal and human proximity creates similar effects. Ebola, and the swine and bird flues are examples. ***Parasites benefit from proximity.***

Proper hygiene in human cultures, and smaller farm plots, are partial solutions to the problem—but the problem is ongoing.

The point is: ***<u>Parasites and disease assist the forces of intolerance and cultural entropy</u> to divide and polarize (animal and human) cultures over time.*** Humans are hard-wired for a certain amount of avoidance/intolerance to each other and to those in dissimilar cultures.

To repeat: ***The avoidance meme makes humans <u>naturally</u> intolerant and racist; avoidance and intolerance are divisive to human societies.*** To oppose racism, prejudice, and intolerance requires **work**.

WHY CIVILIZATIONS FALL: CAPITAL DEVELOPMENT AND ENTROPY IN NATURE

Repeat: *To oppose racism, prejudice, and intolerance requires* **work**.

Of note: *The human concepts of beauty and ugliness are largely determined by predation and parasitism (a separate discussion).*

4. SPECIATION (In organic Cultures)
Speciation is a biological term that describes how a breeding species can separate into nonbreeding strains. The forces involved are the same as those that drive cultural entropy. **Speciation** usually involves three identifiable situations—**separation, adaptations, and breeding isolation.**

For example: A species separates into regions. The same organisms adapt differently over time. Eventually, the adaptations create separate species that no longer breed with each other.

Speciation can be a bit fickle. Some species, like brown bears, separated for hundreds of thousands of years, will still breed together. Other species, such as some bird and mice species will grow intolerant and culturally separate over shorter periods.

Food selection and predation play a large role in speciation. For example, wrens on large continents group into large and inconspicuous species. The same family of birds, on isolated islands with few predators and plenty of food sources, turn into exotic birds of paradise.

In other words, speciation sometimes happens because it can. On small islands, female birds can be very picky about their male partners. Males must engineer exquisite and showy feathers to draw female attention. When food and predation are problems—in other words, if females require males to help raise their chicks--female birds must be less picky.

In similar fashion, a human culture, when surrounded by common enemies, may solidify in fear. The same culture, when freed of obvious external enemies, may split apart, due to cultural entropy, intolerance, and civil separation from within.

WHY CIVILIZATIONS FALL: CAPITAL DEVELOPMENT AND ENTROPY IN NATURE   35

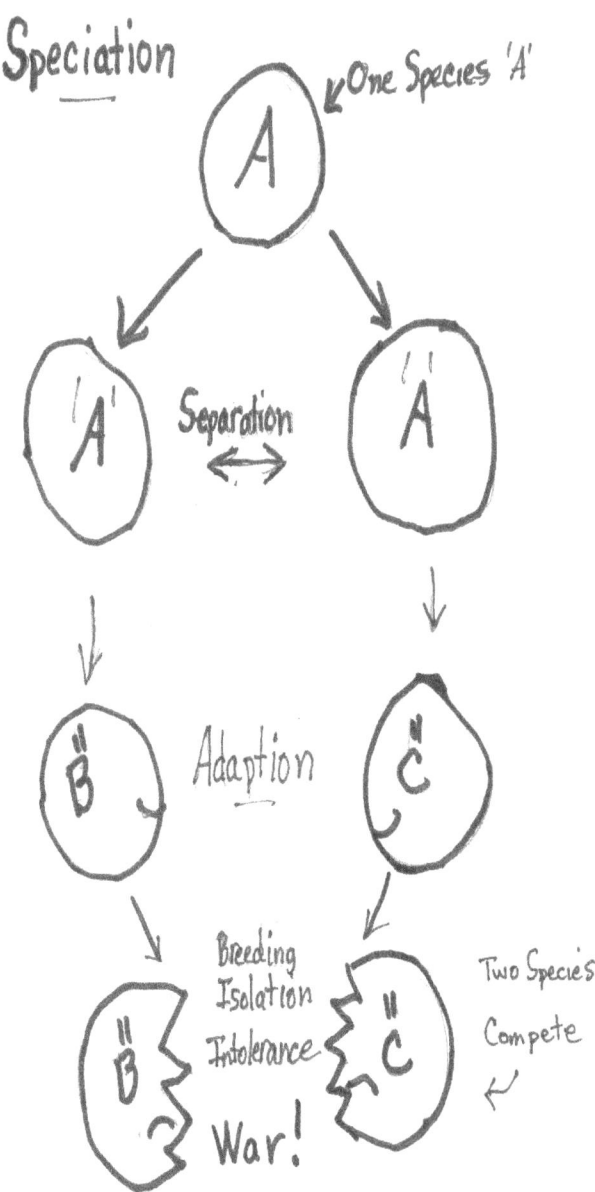

5. BREEDING INTOLERANCE

WHY CIVILIZATIONS FALL: CAPITAL DEVELOPMENT AND ENTROPY IN NATURE

In organic cultures, species become officially separate when they *refuse to breed together*. Usually, physical differences augment these breeding intolerances.

Cultures must **share**. Cultures that no longer breed together (share genes) become separate cultures.

***Human cultures that refuse to breed together distinguish their separateness.** Over time, these separations grow larger, often resulting in conflict.

A single culture may divide internally between separate intolerant religions (belief hierarchies); the culture may also divide vertically between economic statuses. These human divisions do not share capital with equity or breed together.

To various degrees, many religious cultures maintain their cultural separateness today by breeding restrictions—the Muslim, Catholic, Protestant, Jewish, Mormon, and Sikh religions, to name a few.

We may only wonder what conflicts will result in the future, if these divisions remain firm and grow larger. Conflicts between competing cultures are historically inevitable.

6. CANCERS IN THE BODY REFUSE TO SHARE EQUALLY

A single organism must **share** resources. Cell reproduction, beyond accepted bounds, takes excessive amounts of nutrients and interferes with community **sharing** activities. When sharing activities can no longer function, the organism dies. **Entropic forces** interfere with the chemical devices that control an organism's different cell divisions, thus random **entropic forces** create cancers.

Divisions within a larger culture (society) can also assume cancerous properties; when these divisions reproduce out-of-control they can demand excessive amounts of cultural nutrients and interfere with sharing activities in the larger culture.

Extreme cultural divisions can eventually destroy the larger culture.

IN CONCLUSION:
ENTROPY (chaos) erodes and divides all natural creations.
CULTURAL ENTROPY functions to divide living cultures and disrupt capital sharing and capital circulation within cultures.

WHY CIVILIZATIONS FALL: CAPITAL DEVELOPMENT AND ENTROPY IN NATURE

Divisive human products of cultural entropy include linguistic entropy, extremism, and polarization—all contributing to greater intolerance

INTOLERANCE acts destructively (in animal and human cultures) to magnify small differences and create extremes. EXTREMES dominate cultural conflicts and grow TOXIC. Toxic extremes destroy (poison) the tolerant middle. Without a TOLERANT MIDDLE, re-unity is impossible.

Cultural entropy divides animal and human cultures over time. Population pressures increase the effects of cultural entropy. Human activities assist entropy otherwise by contributing to soil depletion, deforestation, and erosion.
Conflicts between competing (non breeding) cultures are historically INEVITABLE.

Entropy will always increase unless opposed by work

Ch. 3 CULTURAL ENTROPY

CHAPTER. 3

D. CULTURAL ENTROPY--
UNIQUE TO <u>HUMAN</u> CULTURES:

1. Emotions and extreme human emotions
2. Linguistic Entropy and topographic barriers
3. Shared understandings--Ignorance memes and the importance of Truth in Human Systems
4. Cultural Entropy creates NO MAN'S LANDS
5. CLIMAX POPULATIONS oppose capital circulation
    STATUS LEVELS divide human populations
6. OWNERSHIP OF RESOURCES and breeding intolerance divides human populations and assists cultural entropy.
7. Slavery
8. Breeding Intolerance
9. Human Cultural Wars
10. Competitive argument
11. Population wars stress Resources
12. Klieber's Law of distribution
13. Why humans can wage wars--expendability
14. What does God think?
15. Cultural Entropy in Human Relations
16. Cultural Entropy in Legislative Bodies
17. PURITANITY causes religious divisions

WHAT DISTINGUISHES A HUMAN CULTURE?
Biological cultures share DNA. Cultures or species that cease sharing DNA become separate species. When human societies cease sharing they can be considered separate cultures, even though they continue to be the same species.

The most important aspect of sharing is DNA. Humans can share aspects of survival—cultural norms, economic interdependencies, mutual defenses against invasions, etc. But sharing DNA, marrying together, is what differentiates human cultures or statuses *over long time periods*.

Many long-surviving cultures have strict prohibitions against marriages outside cultural norms. Jews marry Jews, Christians marry Christians, and Muslims marry Muslims. Within religions, sects develop that also differentiate--Mormons marry Mormons, Baptists marry Baptists, Sunnis marry Sunnis, Catholics marry Catholics, and Shia marry Shia, for example; such prohibitions separate once-united religions over time.

Without prohibitions against intermarriage, however, different ethnicities, language groups, and skin colors can unify in a single sharing culture. Adopting a shared language diminishes unshared understandings.

When humans possess common economic opportunities—freely living together in cities with diminished reliance on tribal and religious priorities--social events can create a **common culture**, a united culture. The USA is an example.

Forces of division, however, will simultaneously ravage this common culture as it forms. Some ethnicities and religions purposefully refuse to integrate. Sub-cultures develop and differentiate simultaneously within the common culture. Children of the wealthy often selectively marry only within their economic groups. **Intolerant** statuses develop over skin colors, languages, or ethnicities. Religions and political affiliations often deter marriages between opposing belief systems—republican generally marry republicans; democrats usually marry democrats; the exceptions are newsworthy.

Over long time periods, small divisions often become permanent.

Cultural Entropy functions in human cultures in the same manner as in biological cultures, randomly forming divisions, polarization, and **competitive** (non-sharing) **capitalism** over time.

However, human cultures feature **additional factors** that **magnify the effects** of cultural entropy further. In particular, since human possess unstable **emotions**, and **human cultures are based on *shared understandings***, the effects of cultural entropy can **magnify** misunderstandings and divisive consequences within and between human cultures.

1. HUMAN EMOTIONS CREATE CONFLICTS AND MAGNIFY INTOLERANCE.

Primitive biological systems can demonstrate ***basic intolerance***-- avoidance, and toxicity. Intolerance causes polarization, and divisions in ***biological*** cultures.

Intolerance is also hard-wired into ***human*** cultures. Intolerance (fear of parasites) demands we avoid anything that is not identifiable as, *us*. Intolerance will not diminish naturally. To diminish intolerance—to oppose cultural entropy--requires **work**.

Ch. 3 CULTURAL ENTROPY

Human social cultures, in addition, can magnify cultural **intolerance** through shared degrees of **emotion**.

Emotions are not stable. A man may approach a bear one day, and the bear flees. On another day, however, the bear may attack. Emotions are not absolutely predictable. Emotions possess a degree of randomness, particularly in young humans, based on somewhat-random *chemical reactions*.

Human thinking is also dominated by a degree of <u>necessary</u> randomness. Our abilities to project random thoughts and sift out appropriate choices are what allow humans to cogitate at all.

Many emotions in higher animals are instantly infectious. Herd animals, for example, will all flee in fear, if they sense fear in the animals around them. Anger in lions is infectious. Fear and anger are in lockstep.

Thus it is true to say of emotional humans: Fear creates fear. And further: Anger creates anger. Violence generates retaliatory violence. Hate generates retaliatory hate. Intolerance creates greater intolerance. Ignorance generates continuing ignorance.

Violent, unstable emotions, like random energy, **polarize** *human* systems, like the fear of parasites, pushing people apart, thus **magnifying the forces of cultural entropy.**

Many violent **human** emotions—since they are reflective--are also **counterproductive**: For example, if we act out in anger to protest a wrong, we may merely create more anger or fear around us, allowing others to react to our anger while ignoring the wrong we are protesting.

For example: Young people may march angrily and passionately to protest intolerance, but their anger terrifies the older population. The older population reacts (out of fear) to become more—rather than less—intolerant. Extreme emotional activities often create consequences **contrary** to what was desired. Emotions magnify emotions, often in contrary directions.

Humans must be careful with extreme emotions, since often, emotional outbursts **polarize** the issues and make every problem larger or insoluble, rather than smaller, as is often the given intent.

Also true, however: Love generates love. Understanding fosters understanding. "The love you take is equal to the love you make," according to John Lennon. John Lennon knew a lot.

Dr. Spock also knew a lot—both the Dr. Spock of children's medicine, and the Dr. Spock of Star Trek, the TV series. Dr. Spock of the TV series always felt human emotions were terribly annoying; however, he recognized they served as excellent motivations, spurring humans to inhuman acts beyond reason.

Love and understanding, tranquility and calm, tend to bring people together. Thus the scientific truth is: We need more love, sangfroid, and understanding, and less of all those *other extreme things*. We all know this, but it's nice to repeat anyway.

To repeat: Emotions magnify emotions. **Thus <u>human activities can and do magnify the intolerant affects of cultural entropy</u>.** Extremes are toxic. Extreme actions are often counter-productive. Extreme actions push rational human concepts to absurdities.

Intolerance and racism are hard-wired; they will not diminish naturally; they can only be opposed by work.

*We may be stretching to suggest erratic human emotions arise from the random flow of atomic particles, but the connection is worth consideration.

The Norse god, Loki, was the god of chaos and mischief, and also of **change. Does a god exist currently that represents such emotional extremes? Thor enjoyed Loki, at times, but recognized Loki could sometimes go too far and become dangerously self-destructive.

2. LINGUISTIC ENTROPY

Random events cause human languages to change over time. The process has been defined previously this chapter [CH. 2]. Suffice to add, when human languages change, the exchange of *shared understandings* becomes more difficult. Without **shared** understandings, or shared capital, a human culture loses its purpose and divides into competing units.

Human cultures depend on shared understandings. ***A sharing culture practices cooperative capitalism.***

Competing cultures practice competitive (antagonistic) capitalism. As in nature, competing cultures don't share; they practice competitive capitalism and devour each other's capital. Ouch! That is not very nice.

3. THE IMPORTANCE OF SHARED UNDERSTANDINGS OR *TRUTH* IN HUMAN CULTURES

Human cultures stay together by **sharing** understandings. Memes that interfere with social understandings can be particularly harmful in human cultures.

Memes of ignorance: In human cultures, memes of ignorance are particularly harmful, pervasive, and infectious, since human societies *depend completely* on **shared-understandings** and usually benefit from the presence of **verifiable truths**.

Actions based on truths are almost always more productive than actions based on ignorance.

Animal cultures are guided by instinct. General ignorance of anything outside instinctive knowledge is a given among animals. Animals invest most of their calories in growth, teeth and claws. So animals can grow to maturity very quickly.

Humans have a different strategy: Humans *invest* most of their calories in their brains, in learning language and common understandings. Humans sacrifice physical growth—power, size, and speed—in order to build their social skills. For this reason, **human growth is very slow** and may appear inefficient. If calories utilized in social investments are squandered, or not shared, naked, solitary humans cannot compete. We are not strong or big enough to compete without social cooperation, and our teeth and claws have not grown sharp enough. **We have wasted our calories if our shared understandings end up being untruths. Untruths lead to erroneous decisions.**

Again, the capital humans invest in their brains is a real item. This real capital does not simply disappear. Capital stored in human brains, like wheat in a granary, continues to be an *exchange* item that can and must move within a *sharing* culture.

In humans, **understanding** is a product of capital/language *sharing*. Without receiving language and other human capital, a human child is helpless. Thus human ignorance—or lack of common understanding--occurs when emotional and intellectual capital **fails to circulate** from individual to individual and society to society. The situation is similar to a human who fails to receive blood flow to the brain and body. Necrosis and infection soon occur. Entire **cultures** can suffer the same fate when **understandings** *fail to circulate*.

The circulation (sharing) of *all other* capital products—food, shelter, tools, social fostering, capital profits, and cultural understandings, usually accompanies the capital information flow; **capital items all move together**. The **total** is capitalism. Curtailing or **hoarding** the flow of one capital need usually means the curtailing of *all* capital needs.

In particular, tyrants and events can deny specific information flow to specific subjects by denying free speech, and movement, in the same way the flow of food and profit can be controlled and denied. The organism may weakly survive, but its life purpose is compromised.

In general, whenever any circulation of capital is denied, the body suffers or dies. Our mutual understandings and joys are the most important economic capital humans possess and circulate.

Denying free speech to a social organism limits the flow of verifiable truth. Without verifiable truth, societies must make decisions based on ignorance. Decisions based on ignorance are often catastrophic. [See Ch 7, Ch 3]

4. WHAT ARE NO MAN'S LANDS?

Bourne: Why Civilizations Fall and Cannot Rise Again
Ch. 3   CULTURAL ENTROPY

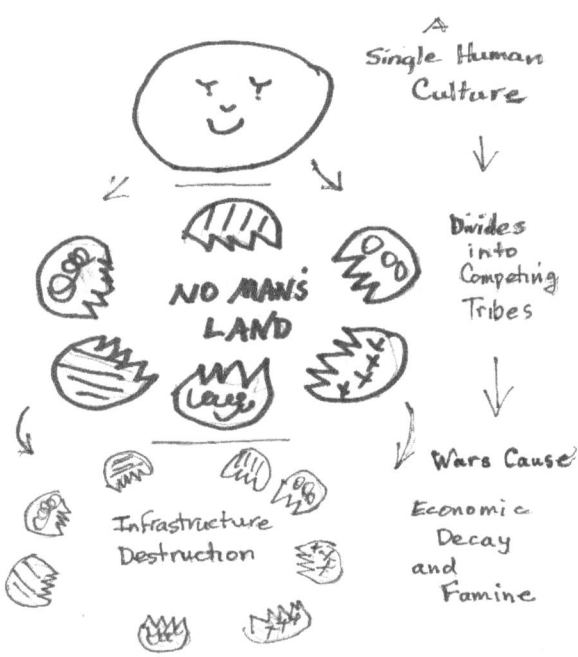

4. CULTURAL WARS CREATE <u>NO MAN'S LANDS</u>, CRIMINAL CHAOS, AND THE DESTRUCTION OF INFRASTRUCTURE AND THE MODERATE MIDDLE

The importance of **NO MAN'S LANDS** will become increasingly obvious when we discuss why civilizations self-destruct [Chapter 8]. However, when toxicities abound, the middle becomes a zone in which normal life cannot continue—this is true in complex civilizations, in cultures of bacteria, and in simple human relationships.

Capital is life. To prosper and create capital profit, humans require certain stability. Farmers cannot farm in an area if they know their crops will be stolen; neither can merchants sell wares or traders trade. Such lawless areas, or **no man's lands**, are too violent to be inhabited. **No man's lands** often must be abandoned completely even if they provide ample resources. Only small areas that can be forcefully defended are practical for habitation. [Ch. 7,8 – Why Civilizations Fail]

Important also, civilization cannot long survive without **infrastructure**—roads, bridges, aqueducts, schools, farming, trade, and storage facilities. To protect, maintain, and repair such infrastructure requires central power and profit circulation. When central power disappears in a chaotic **no man's land**, and no **profit** is created to circulate, no one is around to maintain infrastructure and life becomes ever more difficult.

Besides plagues, **NO MAN'S LAND'S *infrastructure destruction* is the single *most deadly force* to diminish human populations**, far more deadly than simple warfare. Recall, males are expendable [Ch. 2, 3], so wars can be fought with little effect on total populations as long as women are well-fed and free to breed. But when infrastructures decline, famine is the result. Famines, like diseases, starve breeding *women and children*—everyone—and so **entire *populations* disappear**.

When the Roman aqueducts ceased working, Rome ceased existing as a power. No infrastructure; no toilets; no toilets; no advanced civilization. Without aqueducts, extended farming areas had to be abandoned. Desperate conditions and population pressures increased soil erosion and depletion. Without farm produce and trade, populations starved.

The problems were not barbarian invasions. The problems were poverty created by slave states, divided government, polarization, and **no man's lands** that destroyed profit circulation and infrastructures. Without a flow of capital to continue aqueduct repair, the water to Rome stopped flowing.

Capital flows together. Capital flow requires **profits** from human labor. Slavery steals the profits of human labor.

Water is a type of capital. Capital is life. Capital (like water) must flow (requiring exchanging profits) to be effective. A common culture that ceases sharing (or cannot share because human labor creates no profits) is no longer a common culture.

The Roman elites turned their backs to central government and eventually embraced nationalism as separate state hierarchies. **No man's lands** diminished common infrastructure and trade between states throughout the Mediterranean.
[See Ch. 3, 4, 7 – Why Civilizations Fail]

Cultural Entropy: The City of Rome represented central government on the Italian peninsula for a thousand years. Central government, however, came to be widely despised by other Italian states due to political polarization. And the more central government weakened, the more it was blamed and vilified.

When semi-barbarians (actually northern Christians) sacked Rome, competing Italian areas—Venice, Florence, and Ravenna—offered little assistance. They kept their troops for their own defenses. Why should they offer aid to a rival?

The controlling families throughout Italy reviled central government and the state of Rome; they felt central power competed with their own

Ch. 3   CULTURAL ENTROPY

authority. The enslaved masses had no voice. The middle class had long disappeared due to the practice of slavery.

Cultural entropy divided the Italian peninsula into non-cooperating states. These states eventually engaged in cultural wars with each other, **competitive capitalism**. Disastrous and negative changes occurred over long time periods; these time periods were too extended for short-lived humans to understand what infrastructures—water, trade, prosperity, security, toilets--they were all *losing* by turning their backs on central government.

IMMIGRANTS: People today often blame immigrants for society's problems. Romans, 1600 years ago, also blamed **Immigrants, religions, pagans, and barbarians** for their social problems. The blame was probably misplaced and counterproductive.

Most barbarian invaders, by the fifth century, were Christianized. Soldiers, from immigrant stock, were the primary force keeping The Roman Empire's central government *together* its final centuries.

Some align the fall of Rome with the rise of Christianity. [Gibbons -- "The Rise and Fall of the Roman Empire."]   However, most historians now agree, Christianity served to palliate human despair at the time without greatly leading to a downturn in economic conditions.

The **polarization** and division of the great Roman Empire occurred from within, slowly growing over time without heeding philosophies or religion.

Slavery, intolerance, and the loss of a middle class disabled the Roman military, the primary force keeping Rome violently united. Ancient Roman families, not outsiders, squabbled to destroy and minimize their once united economy. Eventually they succeeded.

A common culture that refuses to *share* is no longer a common culture.
[See Ch. 8 – Why Civilizations Die]

Barren **no man's lands** are prevalent whenever civilizations begin to die, and they originate whenever cultures fracture/polarize into warring parts. Large swaths of productive territory must be abandoned. Entire populations decline in numbers or suffer famines and increased poverty, sometimes for hundreds of years.

We will later discuss [Ch. 8] how great civilizations in Asia, Europe, Africa, and the Americas turned into vast **no man's lands** due to the affects of **cultural entropy** and warfare over great stretches of time. And today, we can see entire continents, and inner city areas even in wealthy countries that have all the characteristics of lawless **no man's lands.**

5. HUMAN CLIMAX POPULATIONS OPPOSE CAPITAL CIRCULATION: STATUS LEVELS DIVIDE HUMAN POPULATIONS. OWNERSHIP DIVIDES HUMAN POPULATIONS

CLIMAX STATUSES—DIVISIONS WITHIN A SINGLE CULTURE, and BREEDING INTOLERANCE, oppose capital circulation.
Within any single culture, be it bacterial or human, status levels often develop. We can see such status levels in slime cultures, with films of the same organism in different degrees of productivity, depending on their proximity to food sources, the sun, oxygen, or toxicities.

Yeast films in beer produce a top status climax film in the area closest to food resources; these organisms contrast with low status films away from food sources and closer to toxicity, toxicity being the byproduct, alcohol, humans enjoy—unless the brew is stirred into greater homogeneity.

And, similar to past stories of overpopulation, the yeast is eventually killed at all levels of status by its own toxic byproduct, alcohol—quite symbolic.

HUMAN CULTURES also form into horizontal levels of differing **status**, and between these **status levels**, capital is unevenly allotted. Ownership customs cement status levels, particularly when laws validate ownership distinctions over long time periods. Land ownership, religious control, military control, ownership of professions, hierarchical ranking of free labor, and slavery—all these **status levels** allow human cultures to be divided into multiple intercultural groups.

In general, each status group controls—or is controlled by--different capital resources, and thus the flow of capital resources between status groups may become stifled. Capital often congests in the climax elite and stops circulating widely through the extended culture.

Interbreeding and shared understandings are often banned or limited **between** status levels, so the statuses grow biologically and culturally more separate over time.

Wars between statuses (**within** a culture) are as common as wars between nationalities (between **different** cultures).

Climax statuses can control resources over many years. Without resources, competing statuses cannot grow. Climax statuses can keep wages low while limiting opportunities, intentionally or incidentally. Economic circulation stagnates in climax areas.

In many rural areas around the world, populations are diminishing. Humans in these areas may be choosing to have fewer children due to poverty. Other young people in these areas may choose to migrate to find better future opportunities.

Ch. 3 CULTURAL ENTROPY

Climax statuses often occur in areas connected to no man's lands; together, such situations act to diminish human value and disturb human populations.

Forces of entropy motivate mass migrations worldwide.

6. LONG-TERM OWNERSHIP OF CAPITAL RESOURCES OPPOSES CAPITAL CIRCULATION

Ownership of capital resources can have positive economic benefits, by providing capital resources management and protection over time. *Simultaneously*, ownership of capital resources can have negative, and very divisive effects on human populations over long time periods. **Ownership irrevocably divides human families**. The division, of course, is between those who own resources and those who don't. Divisions occur also between quantities of resources owned by divided families.

Time **magnifies** the differences between owners and non-owners over extended time periods, particularly when socially restrictive laws back ownership.

PROPERTY OWNERSHIP and breeding intolerance assist the forces of cultural entropy to divide human populations.

7. SLAVERY AND STATUS DIVISIONS:

Slaves, often (but not always) the lowest status, can create no capital **profit** for themselves (their owners **steal** their labor), and thus slaves exist as a status with zero capital circulation. Slavery, and ***subsistence work***, also undermines capital circulation among free laborers, since **free labor** has difficulty competing with slave labor. Slavery de-values **all** human work. Humans forced to work at subsistence (nearly profitless) wages are enslaved.

Eventually, due to slavery, the economy of a larger, encompassing culture may weaken and die; an enslaved society creates limited **profits** (to share); without sharable profits the totality may be held together only by the force of tyranny. Human workers (most of humanity) are left out of the capital loop. The situation reoccurs often throughout human history. [Read Ch. 8 - Why Civilizations fall].

Capital is life. Capital circulation is capitalism. **No profits; no profit capital circulation; no civilization.** Human slavery limits capital circulation. Without proper capital circulation all living organisms die.

Nearly every civilization has been *negatively impacted* by slavery (stolen profits from human labor). We will later review the effects of slavery on western civilization, Greece, the fall of Rome, and the USA [Ch 4, 7, 8.].

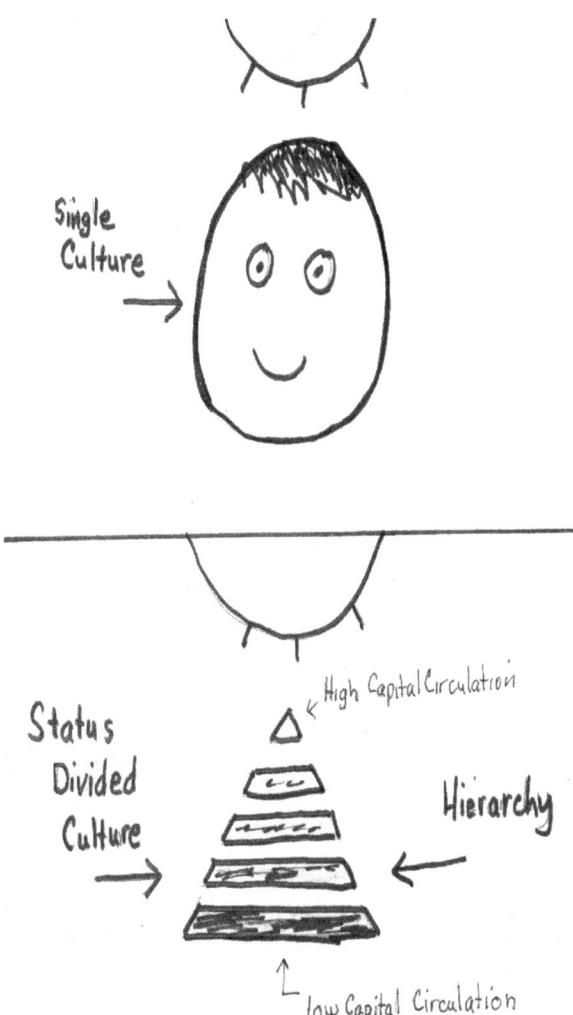

8. BREEDING INTOLERANCE IN HUMAN CULTURES

In organic cultures, species become *officially* separate when they refuse to breed. Usually, physical differences augment these breeding intolerances.

In human cultures, breeding is often banned between status levels. Interbreeding is also discouraged between income levels or groups speaking divergent languages. Many religions also ban or severely punish those members who dare to breed with those outside the faith. Such bans further isolate cultures over time and polarize cultural understandings.

Ancient sects, like the Jews, have remained separate for thousands of years, even while living within larger societies. **Breeding intolerance** creates **social intolerance**; and the Jews have paid dearly for their separate beliefs.

The blacks, Hispanics, and white races in the United States are now apparently breeding together. We can (arguably) assume in a short geological time period, these—now distinct—cultures *may* blend into an American pie with fewer and fewer ethnic distinctions. (?)

On the contrary, several sub-cultures still severely punish or isolate members who stray. If this continues, hundreds of years from now the Amish, Mormon, Orthodox Jews, Sikhs, Muslims, and other such sects, will be as separate as ever from an American melting pot.

What kind of final situation this lack of breeding unity will create is anyone's guess. Hopefully, everyone can live together. However, historically, **breeding intolerance inevitably creates social intolerance and conflict.**

WHAT SEPARATES HUMANITY??

Skin colors and language can create ethnic divisions. Many cultures advertise their differences using dress and activities—clothes, hats, turbans, hair-styles, shoes, aprons, flags, motor-cycles, tattoos, jewelry; all these things, and more, advertise our cultural belongings and also our cultural exclusivities.

If we wear a turban, we cannot be expected to interbreed with someone who does not wear a proper reciprocal headdress. Small decorative effects can create irrevocable differences. White power groups (aptly called skinheads) shave their heads. Sikhs are mandated by their religion to never cut their hair. Orthodox Jews sport hair locks and orthodox hats. Catholics often wear Saint Christopher medals or prayer beads. Muslim women must cover their heads. Ranchers often wear Stetsons. Hippies wear long hair and beads. Business executives wear suits and ties. Heterosexual women and transvestites often wear dresses and high heels. Nudists wear, well....

Small, puritanical, trivial items of dress can advertise our cultural preferences. Dress tells who we are and who we aren't. Dress tells who we can breed with, and who we must refuse to breed with.

Small, puritanical, trivial items of dress can separate us forever into warring tribes that must battle each other to the death. The forces of **cultural entropy** work over long time periods to divide us into irreconcilable adversaries engaged in endless genocidal conflicts.

POVERTY AND LACK OF CAPITAL RESOURCES

Many people are born into low status positions that have extremely limited capital options. These people don't possess adequate food, shelter, or profitable work. They don't possess skills that enable them to create profit. They may occupy a status level in which skills and movement are denied. Since the larger society cares about these people, some humane response is mandatory. But the choices are a bit limited.

The best choices increase poor individual's abilities to create capital through their own efforts (**work**). In other words, if these individuals join capitalism, if they receive reward **profits** for their **work**, the problem is greatly solved.

The solution, however, also depends on the *quality of work*: If a poor individual learns to sell drugs to make a profit, they have—to a certain extent—solved their own problem. They are no longer poor and possess profits to circulate. Unfortunately, the selling of drugs arguably creates greater problems of crime, disease, and homelessness. All products do not contribute *qualitatively* to the value of human life. The selling of illegal drugs—*debatably*—opposes capital flow by contributing to human death and disabilities. Other products--alcohol, drugs, fatty foods—also have mixed contributions to society. Total prohibitions against such products, however, tend to be counter-productive.

On the contrary, many occupations unabatedly facilitate capital flow--mechanics, farmers, producers, builders, teachers, caregivers, for example. Such skills add to healthy capital flow--and usually, increased capital flow is good for everyone.

Most experts agree: Increasing human job skills, social understandings, and halting cultural wars [Ch. 2, 4, 6], are the only solutions that yield permanent change to social inequities. Other solutions to poverty are piecemeal or counterproductive.

Simply providing capital to poor humans does not enable the human labor of these individuals. These people never become long-term **producers of profit**. They continue to be poor indefinitely. More important, poverty breeds poverty.

Hoarders will feed cats and dogs with no attempt to limit their breeding. The end result is a catastrophe of sick and starving animals. Obviously, to keep poverty from growing, some steps need to be taken to control the **breeding** of poverty.

Feeding poverty, like feeding wild dogs and cats, merely makes the problem worse. Cats and dogs cannot control their own breeding. Cultural entropy and numbers warring against other numbers control the populations of cats and dogs. Starvation and violence are *not humane, not kind* methods of population control.

Don't be fooled. Your cute little kitty is making population war against all other life forms. Unless stopped, kitty and dog genes will take over the world over time given enough food. Animal **numbers** battle each other savagely with no benign outcome. Rational humans, however, can make a difference. We don't need cruel and bloody population wars. We can control our populations in peace.

Kitties, and humans, and even dogs, can share the world in a rational and fair fashion. We merely need to act rationally and fairly. Oops! Maybe that is asking too much.

Population wars, which can't be won by anyone, can be halted. Just say no, and if that doesn't work, utilize the products of modern science. And if modern science won't help, the time-tested methods of plague, war, and famine are always dependable—though rather harsh.

Incidentally, the cultures and individuals that, clueless or not, utilize population wars to steal the future, must at some time be confronted. They are not innocent who take for themselves what they have not earned—the future of our united family. If rational humans fail to confront those who conduct population wars, then rational humans cede the future to those who may not be rational.

Ch. 3   CULTURAL ENTROPY

9.   HUMAN CULTURAL WARS –

FORCES OF *ENTROPY* PUSH HUMAN CULTURES INTO CONTINUAL WARFARE.
HUMAN *CULTURAL WARS (AS IN NATURE)* USE NUMBERS TO ELIMINATE COMPETING CULTURES.
CULTURAL WARS STRESS RESOURCES--
CULTURAL WARS CREATE TOXIC NO MAN'S LANDS.
NO MAN'S LANDS…DIMINISH POPULATIONS AND DESTROY CIVILIZATIONS.

We should not be deluded: All living populations are in competition internally and externally against all other life forms to claim the **future**. Cultural wars began with the first life and will always be with us. Population wars are ongoing, perpetual, and eternal in our biology.

Human cultures, like bacteria cultures, wage ongoing numbers wars against all other life forms, and each other, to compete for resources; this is **competitive capitalism**. Human DNA seeks to dominate all other competing DNA and overwhelm the earth. If we leave the situation to the **numbers**, one-day humans and not much else will cover the entire earth. Our DNA does not care much about variety or value. DNA has no brain. DNA does not seek understanding or God.

Cultural wars expand **numbers**. These numbers do not care about equity. **Numbers** do not care about other species, whales, dolphins, lions, forests, global warming, or the ecosystem. The forces of **cultural entropy** have no values whatsoever. They have no brains.

Simultaneously, **within** the human community, separate cultures vie for total power without real control or understanding. Each religion, each state, each community, each status level seeks to extend its own powers over all others by utilizing the power of overwhelming **numbers and capital control**. Much of this warfare in conducted *without the knowledge* even of the soldiers conducting the wars. **Numbers** make all the decisions; and numbers—we repeat again--have no brains.

All else equal: Big populations (sizes) win; small populations lose.

Breeding soldiers (women and children) may not recognize that their breeding purpose over time is to overwhelm the world and stamp out DNA, species, and beliefs that are not their own; but nevertheless the future aims of population wars are quite certain--the final resolution of breeding competitions lead directly to cultural dominance, not equity or peace.

Eventually the cultures that reproduce the most will possess overwhelming **numbers.** These numbers will dominate the **future**. Those who don't breed—with their beliefs--will be overwhelmed; they will disappear. **Numbers/0r size** trump beliefs. The war is ongoing.

We must understand: Population wars cannot be won; they can only be continued endlessly. Even if a single culture or religion one day manages to dominate the earth, the process will still continue. That winning culture will polarize and split into conflicting divisions over time, according to the undeniable rules of **cultural entropy,** just like the cultures before it. The process will merely repeat. The wars will go on.

The forces of **Cultural Entropy** force emotional humans to play the same game through eternity. The game has no final resolution.

"The only way to win is to not play."

10. THE ARGUMENT FOR COMPETITION/WARS TO ACHIEVE SUPERIORITY

Some may argue, the winner of any competition is certainly superior. Thus constant cultural wars are what we need to progress, to become superior—if that is what we wish.

If we are talking bigger numbers, the answer might be, yes. However, in qualitative terms, bigger numbers are only bigger numbers. A warlike, tyrannical culture crushing everything under its power is not what many humans envision as superior or progressive. Most of us don't wish to spend our lives opposing such a culture; and most of us would probably not enjoy being part of that culture either. We might want to do other things than wage constant war.

What does superiority mean anyway? Is the bully superior? Is the culture with the most powerful war technology the superior culture?

Bare in mind, the conflict for superiority cannot be won, not if the forces of cultural entropy are making the rules. The wars are eternal. The Romans won 1200 separate wars and still ultimately lost their civilization.

And today, the tools of war are far more deadly than spears and rocks. An atomic disaster could easily reduce human societies to extinction. Like the dinosaurs, our time would be over.

And most important, the forces of chaos took billions of years, violent, agonizing years of deadly competition, to bring the world to where it is today. Right or wrong, humans can go to the future more quickly and efficiently without the guidance of conflict and chaos. Humans, as opposed to other organism, have brains.

Human beings do not need to play only constant-sum games. They can use their brains to design different strategies. Humans can design societies that emphasize other pursuits, rather than violent wars. And these other pursuits should lead us to less despair and more joy.

The solutions (to halt population wars) are not rocket science; they don't take geniuses to recognize. The solutions merely take communication and mutual understandings. Violent emotions and ignorance are counter-productive. Love, understanding, and empathy are quite helpful.

To get out of boiling water, however, we must first recognize we are in boiling water.

11. POPULATION WARS CREATE RESOURCE DEPLETION

Population wars **naturally** create resource depletion. When two cultures compete via **numbers** to out populate each other—which, together with violent confrontation, is what population-wars entail—the result places terrible stresses on resources and all other species. Grabbing resources—and keeping them from others--is the primary purpose of population wars.

Equally important, societies involved in population wars are too busy fighting in the present to maintain infrastructures that might benefit future resources. We see this story repeat often in the Roman, Khmer, Anasazi, Maya, Easter Island, and other early civilizations. [See Ch. 7 Why Civilizations Fail]

12 KLEIBER'S LAW OF (DISTRIBUTION) CIRCULATION AND SOCIAL GROWTH:

Size of transport system vs size of life. (Dawkins The Ancestors Tale - 514)

They've discovered is a simple equation: $q_0 \sim M^{3/4}$. Termed Kleiber's Law (named for the Swiss biologist Max Kleiber), the equation states that an organism's basal metabolic **rate** -- the amount of energy it consumes at rest -- is roughly equal to its **mass** raised to the three-quarters power.

Larger organisms have lower cell metabolism than small organisms. Kleiber's law holds true from protozoans to elephants, and the **reason** cell metabolism *must* be slower in large animals is based on transport systems. As organisms grow large, the bulk of the animal necessary for distributions increases disproportionately. The weight necessity for circulation grows *larger proportionately* as the animal grows larger. Single cells are exposed on all surfaces to oxygen sources, for example, while the oxygen supplied a cell in a large animal must be piped in through via an ever more complicated circulatory system.

Circulation includes **foods** in, **waste** out.

Ch. 3 CULTURAL ENTROPY

A circulation system to keep an elephant's cells supplied at a high metabolism would take up too much **weight** in the elephant's body. The solution by nature is that cells in large animals metabolize more slowly. These cells are thus satisfied with a slimmed down transport system (require less oxygen and foods and produces less waste). They don't require as much servicing as highly metabolizing cells, and so everyone is happy.

The situation is somewhat similar in human systems. As societies grow, the need for transport to supply all areas grows in relation to the entire system, but transport requires a larger and larger percentage of the whole to be equally affective.

The problem can be solved in two ways: Humans can lower their metabolism requirements. Or humans can develop **technologies** to facilitate capital circulation at increasingly higher and higher energies per capita—this is, in fact, what human societies have done.

A person living in a high rise today requires more relative transportation service than a person living in more native conditions. Food, waste disposal, information, heat, movement—all must be carried long distances to the living spaces of individual families. Energy for this transportation is largely supplied by fossil fuels.

So—*assuming efficiencies stay the same*--to supply increased future populations equal amounts of capital goods will require geometrically **increasing energy intensity per human family**. If N is the human population:

$$Energy\ for\ Circulation\ Waste \sim N\left(1 \div N^{\frac{3}{4}}\right)$$

Thus, future technologies must increase faster than the human increase in population to maintain the **value** of human life at the **present level**.

Or, families could seek ways to lower their requirements (metabolism), the method used by cells, to lessen the impact of increased population.

In recent years, *transportation efficiencies* have increased exponentially—thanks to increased use of fossil fuels and digital technologies--to provide humans increased capital value, but when these efficiencies finally maximize—or fossil fuels disappear--the value deliverable per human will diminish with increasing population.

The point is: Increasing populations require disproportional increases in energy use for equal circulation. All living economies depend on capital circulation. **Thus, increasing population <u>numbers</u> eventually decrease population <u>value</u> unless opposed by ever increasing**

efficiencies. We can't depend on technologies or energy sources to continue to improve forever.

To repeat: The circulation/pollution needs of an organism increase geometrically faster as size increases. Thus the human problems of environmental, plastics, food, and water actually increase more rapidly than human numbers. If the human population doubles in the next twenty years, for example, the problems of pollution will increase by 3 or 4 times. The solutions are **relative**, not necessarily exact, though in animal populations the relationship is amazingly precise.

Assuming technologies solve the problem of pollution by half over the same time period—a great step forward--pollution will still continue to accumulate at the same unsustainable rate as today.

Ultimately, we do not have a pollution problem; we have a numbers problem.

Pollution has **no solution** as long as numbers continue to increase. Similarly, problems of water, hunger, ignorance, conflict, intolerance, hatred, etc., have no practical solutions whatever, as long as **numbers** continue to rise.

To repeat: According to Kleiber's law, human problems—pollution, hunger, conflict, intolerance, etc.--**cannot be solved** by mere behavioral changes, moralities, government initiatives, or even technologies. Numbers can thwart all such stopgap solutions. The only permanent solution is to control population wars.

13. VERY IMPORTANT: WHY HUMANS CAN WAGE WARS WITH LARGE CASUALTIES—Males are expendable.

Female mammals control lactation and so are uniquely necessary to raise infants to maturity. Male mammals do not lactate, so nature can use males for other tasks to improve species health.

By competing with each other for breeding rights, male struggles can increase genetic health and decrease parasitism. Males with defects can be discarded from the gene pool with little penalty, since plenty of healthy males are available to fill the breeding void.

The point is, **only numbers are important: Male lives are expendable.** (Male deaths do not affect the final numbers.) Female lives are not expendable. When it comes to maximizing population—a situation necessary to conduct a proper **population war**—women are the *important* sex.

The situation is less true if men are expected to fulfill child-raising duties—such as most bird species. In the case of birds, the lives of both male and female parents are often necessary to raise chicks to maturity, so male lives and female lives have more equal importance.

To conduct large-scale warfare with significant casualties, an expendable population is absolutely necessary. Besides humans, only insect species can conduct large-scale wars. Ants and wasps, for example, create soldiers out of non-breeding females. These females do not contribute to the future. So such soldiers can be sacrificed without regard to the future. As long as their sacrifices contribute to the success of the queen, they are totally expendable. The lives of worker insects mean little or nothing. But we probably suspected this already.

What may come as a surprise, however, is that human male lives mean little or nothing when it comes to the future population. Human societies can sacrifice significant percentages of male lives without any population penalty, as long as women remain well fed and child-rearing tasks can be re-distributed.

If the rewards of warfare are increased resources or captured women, the **numbers** payoff for any warring tribe is positive. In other words, a warring tribe can increase its population and resources without real penalty, even if significant young men are expended in the process. These men, like warrior ants, can easily be replaced, as long as women keep breeding. And so, constant population warfare unfortunately makes **number** sense in early tribal systems—and has for thousands of years. [However, this is not as true today. See Ch 10: Modern wars make no number sense.]

We will discuss tribal warfare in greater detail later; but suffice to conclude, male expendability makes the bloody history of civilization *possible* and allows human population wars to be eternal and bloody.

14. WHAT DOES GOD THINK ABOUT POPULATION WARS?

Some among us may think, if God created the universe, then God created the forces that push us towards population wars. Thus we would be wrong to pursue any other course besides total subservience to our DNA, to **numbers,** to **cultural entropy,** to **competitive capitalism,** to **chaos.**

In the contrary argument, God—or nature, if preferred-- provided us with brains. We would be ignoring God's purpose not to *use* our brains. Violent emotions my urge us to actions we know to be counter-productive—abusing children, for example. We *could* argue abusing children is okay because that is what our violent emotions are urging at the moment. But most would agree: God does not wish us to abuse children any more than God wishes us to pursue **population wars** that lead to mutual annihilation. God provided us with brains to lead us to *better* alternatives than those provided by blind **numbers** and **extreme emotions.**

Most important, those who believe in a unifying and beneficial God *must* believe God wishes us to live together in peace and understanding and not constant violence. The alternatives would be ridiculous and would project a God that is Satanic. Most of us—in fact, **all modern faiths**—totally reject such a concept.

The conclusion is: God—or nature--provided humans with brains so humans could seek **qualitative** growth and enlightenment and not be dominated, like animals, by **numbers and ignorance and conflict**.

15. CULTURAL ENTROPY IN HUMAN RELATIONSHIPS

We would be derelict not to mention at some point, that the corrosive forces that work on human societies work exactly the same in simple human relations.

Extreme emotions can be toxic to common understandings and to feelings of oneness and togetherness. When the common middle ground of a relationship becomes a **no man's zone**, uninhabitable, the relationship has no way to recover. By retreating to extreme emotions, men and women destroy their abilities to relate and communicate. Extremes minimize similarities and maximize differences.

So, even when a relationship contains wide areas of agreement, those areas are made invisible by toxic extremes.

In addition, by diminishing physical attraction over time, the forces of entropy act to diminish the forces keeping relationships together. The forces of **cultural entropy** encourage human attraction to divisive partnerships—all to increase human **numbers**.

Over long time periods, the natural forces of cultural entropy oppose monogamous relationships. To combat the forces of cultural entropy tearing us apart, **work** in the opposite direction—to oneness and calm and mutual understanding--is continually necessary.

16. CULTURAL ENTROPY IN POLITICAL SYSTEMS

Cultural Entropy promotes **extremes**. Entropy works to divide political systems and human tribes. We will address the process in greater detail, but **time** and **extreme** positions (creations of cultural entropy) are toxic to moderation and consensus and create polarization in political systems. **The process (in both animal and human cultures) increases with the passage of time.**

Extreme emotional positions, further, encourage ignorance memes (by stifling consensus human understandings). Ignorance is particularly destructive in **human** cultures, since human cultures (as opposed to animal cultures) depend on information circulation for survival.

Extreme political positions are usually emotionally simple and easier to enunciate than emotionally complicated truths, so extreme positions have innate advantages over complicated (truthful) positions.

We can easily see the effects of this process in modern assemblies and democratic systems. The random forces of cultural entropy assist intolerant extremes to dominate and destroy the tolerant middle. Without a tolerant middle, the legislative process divides irrevocably. The ensuring chaos is an invitation for a tyrant to take control.

To oppose such divisions (entropy) requires **work and understanding**. Divisions will not naturally cure themselves.

17. PURITANITY causes religious divisions

We will talk of *puritanity* again and again. Puritanity is based on the human assumption that more *purity* is always better; humans who practice puritanity allow small, divisive differences to be magnified, while similarities are ignored.

Puritanity, or the extreme desire to purify a religious or social belief system, has acted repeatedly throughout history to divide belief systems and discourage common consensus. Puritanity can act to enlarge cultural divisions based on *increasingly smaller* differences.

The early Christian and Muslim religions were repeatedly split over issues that most modern scholars would consider trivial. Jihad is a call to purify the Muslim religion. The Spanish inquisition was a call to purify Catholicism. Puritan sects were attempts to purify Protestantism.

Puritanity encourages separation and intolerance and assists the divisive forces of CULTURAL ENTROPY.

Puritanity in social systems evolves from **intolerance** in bacterial cultures, in which organisms avoid all other organisms seeking to avoid parasites, diseases, and predation.

DNA IS NOT EVIL

DNA is not evil. However, in the words of Richard Dawkins, "DNA is extremely selfish." DNA has no brain to conjecture moral concepts. DNA is programmed only for its own reproduction. DNA does not consider other DNA in its plans. DNA considers nothing; we reiterate: DNA has no brain.

The point is, DNA is programmed to continue reproducing, without regard for consequences. It is a simple viral meme that brings with it, life. But that life is in competition with other life forms. War between all DNA, all life, is the rule. Wars devalue life.

Life—or DNA—is a **number** product. Only humans have brains to think beyond numbers to consider qualitative issues.

If humans wish to extend value to life and include all humanity, then humans must control their DNA and their numbers.

Ch. 3 CULTURAL ENTROPY

CH. 4
CAPITAL ECONOMIC INNOVATIONS IN HUMAN CULTURES

CHAPTER 4 -- WONDERFUL HUMAN ECONOMIC INNOVATIONS THAT GREATLY <u>ASSIST</u> CAPITAL EXCHANGES: These economic inventions emphasize <u>cooperative capitalism</u> over <u>competitive capitalism</u>.

Capital is life. Capital circulation is capitalism. Without capital circulation, (sharing) complex life cannot survive.

HUMAN TOOLS OF COOPERATIVE CAPITALISM:
A. SHARING OURSELVES (EVE)
B. LANGUAGE,
C. HOME CONSTRUCTION AND TOOLS
D. COOPERATIVE HUNTING,
E. FIRE,
F. HERDING, FARMING,
G. THE FLOWER-FRUIT EXCHANGE,
H. FOSSIL FUELS AND FIRE,
I. COMPLEX SOCIETIES, INFRASTRUCTURES,
K. TOKEN CURRENCIES,
L. CENTRAL GOVERNMENTS,
M. BANKS AND STOCKS,
N. HUMAN EDUCATION, Circulated understandings
O. TECHNOLOGIES,
P. THE INTERNET,
Q. THE GREEN REVOLUTION—

**ALL THESE HUMAN INNOVATIONS
ASSIST CAPITAL CIRCULATION
WHILE BEING OPPOSED BY
CULTURAL ENROPY AND TIME.**

SHARING

Cultures of herbivores may graze together, **sharing** the resource. Herbivores may also assist each other by watching for predators. Families of lions can share their catch.

Many animal couples share childrearing duties. Otherwise, sharing is rare in nature.

Humans use the **sharing** process to grow beyond their animal roots. Humans pass foods from family to family, build on past accomplishments, and share common responsibilities. Early hominid cultures were uniquely **cooperative** in design.

Humans redesign **cooperative capitalism** to meet their unique needs. Human societies move away from **competitive capitalism** (mutual predation) in many areas.

Humans develop tools and technologies to assist their use of **cooperative capitalism**.

SOME TECHNOLOGIES MULTIPLY *SHARING*—THESE TECHNOLOGIES MULTIPLY HUMAN VALUE

*The more we **share**, the more we all become. The less we share, the more we diminish ourselves.*

A. SHARING EVE (A NEW TECHNOLOGY)

Humans are not really very smart; certainly not as smart as we think we are. We aren't terribly strong or athletic. Our morals are suspect. Our choices are generally wrong. Our memories are fallible. Compared to all other animals we are physical failures. However, we excel all other species in our abilities to share. Sharing is what makes us successful.

Language, of course, helps the sharing process immensely, as long as we are sharing truth. Sharing lies, we will realize again and again, opposes human survival.

And the most important capital product humans' share is *ourselves*. In particular, scientists suspect an early woman, called Eve, and her progeny, by sharing *themselves*, made civilization possible.

Eve liked to circulate. She was very pretty and was particularly attracted to young men in other troops. Humans have the same predilection today. Young people raised together in Kibitzes, Jewish work units, generally seek romance outside their group. Young people worldwide naturally avoid their siblings and cousins and seek mates outside their immediate families.

By circulating herself, Eve also circulated human culture. Recall: *Female choice is what makes heterosexuality work*. Troops that shared Eves also shared common understandings and traded technologies. Recall also: Cultures (species) differentiate themselves when they cease sharing DNA. Sharing brings us together and pulls us apart.

In fact, we can probably blame Eve, not hairy-chested men, for the demise of the Neanderthals. Neanderthal ladies probably did not circulate as actively as Eve. The reason is probably nature and not fashion choice. Neanderthal ladies, like almost all primates today, were likely interested in romance, at best, a few days every year. This estrus strategy worked through years of hard times to keep Neanderthal bands within their abilities to feed themselves. But later, since Neanderthals did not trade or mate widely, their technologies, spear making for example, remained limited to primitive materials immediately at hand—Neanderthal trading technologies did not improve over time.

Eve, like modern women, could choose a mate whenever she wished. By seeking mates outside her troop, Eve allowed early humans to gather in larger numbers and to trade language, tools, and understandings over wider areas as an extended family. Re-united after extended times, troops, sharing Eves, could rekindle familiar family bonds and dissipate suspicions. This small sharing difference between Neanderthals and Cro-Magnons may have made all the difference. It was not hairy-chested violence or war that sank the Neanderthal's ship, but a pretty smile that circulated.

Back to the model: Think of Eve as capital. Eve's children were capital growth. The more capital circulates, the greater the mutual benefit. Eve generated cooperative capitalism.

B. SHARING LANGUAGE: LANGUAGE is the human race's most fundamental invention (technology) for creating capital circulation (or sharing capital). When we converse together, we are actually sharing capital knowledge, like food, stored in our brains.

Young animals place most of the calories they consume into growth—teeth, claws, muscle, and bone. Most animals are much more efficient at growing physically **large** than humans.

On the contrary, young humans place most of the calories they consume into their brains, learning language and skills. Human growth otherwise—teeth, claws, strength, and size—is neglected.

Humans need to understand--the energy they put into their brains does not simply *disappear*; this energy continues to be tradable capital. This capital must be **shared** and *circulated* to increase human value (otherwise it will be lost).

Humans cannot compete with animals in growth, claws, teeth, or physical abilities. We use our capital calories elsewhere, in learning. Humans can only survive by **sharing** stored capital skills and creating capital **profits** through skillful work. If we share our *stuff*, we survive. If we don't share our *stuff*, particularly our intellectual capital, we die.

It is fundamental to recognize that learned language is a type of stored capital, stored *energy*, real stuff. Sharing language profit (truth) is circulating *real* energy capital. Capital is life. Capital circulation is capitalism. Language (knowledge) is a type of capital (life-energy).

THE IMPORTANCE OF TRUTH

We might also pause here to emphasize the important of **truth** in language circulation. The circulation of language does no good (does not assist survival) if the information circulated is untrue. ***In fact, the circulation of non-truths leads a human society the opposite direction totally--to failure and apocalypse.***

The random (by chaotic/entropic forces) or purposeful (by human malice) circulation of untruths negates the positive values of language in human progress and impedes human survival.

This concept is examined in greater detail in [Ch. 2, 4, 5, 7, 8.].

C. HOME CONSTRUCTION AND TOOLS

Gorillas and chimpanzees often make sleeping nests. Our ancestors probably possessed similar skills. Utilizing branches and leaves to create comfortable habitations was a first step in creating and manipulating tools.

Manipulating wood and rock products was a first step in creating weapons and permanent tools.

C. TOOLS AND MORE *STUFF*:

Tools are capital items. *Carrying* capital items, tools and *stuff*, helped early hominids *stand upright* and grow successful. Using tools and *stuff* allowed humans to revalue our self-definitions and remake our environments.

Many animals also use tools—crows, otters, apes—but an upright gait allows humans to *carry* tools with them at all times with two hands. So humans can carry tools into areas in which tools cannot be quickly manufactured. Female's wide hips are well designed to carry children while walking upright.

Hominids created tools; and carrying tools created upright humans.

When wielded by those who have hands and walk upright, large sticks and rocks provide defense; these tools can also access nuts, small prey, and underground tubers.

African herdsmen today carry long staffs. They know, predators respect height. Predators are likely to back off without contest from something, they perceive as very tall, coming their direction. Early hominids may have found the same advantage.

A hominid carrying a club could easily dispatch a larger unarmed hominid. Survivors enjoy greater reproductive success than those who do not survive; so club-carrying (upright) genes might quickly proliferate.

Having tools (technology) constantly available is a great survival advantage in many ways. Tools or technology or language **multiply human value**.

If a human walks naked in the wilderness, that human has a certain (rather low) value consistent with survival. However, if that human is clothed and carrying a spear, the survival value of that human is **multiplied**. In addition, if that human is walking with friends, (in a culture), and they all carry tools, and they all exchange survival information; the value of *everyone* in the group is multiplied along with the ability to survive.

Technologies and sharing multiply human abilities and thus multiply human value. Language capital and carrying capital items, or *stuff-we-can-carry-and-exchange*, changed human society and allowed the spread of humanity.

NUMBERS RULE

In sufficient numbers, hyenas can push lions away from food sources. Lions generally recognize when they are grossly outnumbered and outweighed, and they are smart enough to back off. Human ancestors benefitted from the same strategy.

A single hominid gatherer had little power, but dozens in close proximity—perhaps carrying spears—could be intimidating even to lions and hyenas (and are today). Most animals recognize when they are outnumbered and outweighed and will concede the territory.

(Numbers) times (technology) = Total Power
(Humans) times (spears) = Total Power

The **number** of humans multiplied by the amount of their **technology** (spears) equals their total power. Lions generally recognize when they are overpowered.

The point is: To function, as a large group, requires language skills (sharing technology) and social coordination. Living on open grasslands requires more language skills and closer social cooperation (both being **sharing** technologies) than living in trees.

To repeat: **Numbers** rule; this is true between species, and within the same species in **cultural wars**. The culture with the higher numbers (total power) wins over weaker cultures. Technologies multiply the power of human numbers. **Numbers rule in cultural or species wars, in human cultures as in competing bacterial cultures.**

D. HUNTING SKILLS ASSIST CAPITAL ACCUMULATION

Sites have been discovered dating back nearly 2 million years in which human ancestors apparently carved up prey animals. Perhaps they speared or stoned unsuspecting herbivores from trees and took the meat to protected sites **to be shared.**

Sharing is *cooperative capitalism*.

Eating meats requires less digestive specialization than eating plant material. Hunting skills opened up larger regions for human habitation. Cooperative hunting required greater social, **sharing** skills than simple gathering.

Hunting and gathering skills allow humans to gather more capital profits (skin, horns, bones, meat, grain, etc). Profits can be traded (for foods, mating privileges, tools, etc.) to facilitate cooperative capitalism.

E. FIRE UTILIZES CAPITAL RESOURCES

Use of fire dates back at least 400,000 years. Some research suggests a date even earlier, or perhaps even 1.4 million years ago. Fire use separated our ancestors from all other animals. On a capital basis, fires release the pure capital energy stored in organic materials. Our ancestors could not digest the capital energy of wood, but they could burn it. No other animal controls fire or fossil fuels.

Fire use, and later, fire production, required many shared social skills and enabled our ancestors to move safely into open areas. Cooking allowed access to many otherwise indigestible foods and killed bacteria and parasites.

Gathering around fires must have encouraged language development and social understandings. Think how safe our ancestors must have felt when **sharing** the protection and warmth of a roaring fire.

No other technological advance (other than language) can match fire use in moving our ancestors forward in the struggle for **shared** survival.

F. HUMANS ORIGINATE HERDING AND FARMING:

Herding, domesticating animals, and farming enabled humans to vastly increase the amount of **food capital** available to assist human development. Both herding and farming require extensive **sharing** of responsibilities and harvest.

Ants tend aphids to collect a sweet calorie payback. Otherwise, only humans apparently herd other species. Many herbivores naturally form herds. Humans took advantage of herbivore's herding instincts to exercise control. Some might argue, the herded animals took control of humans. Today, domesticated animals far, far outnumber their wild cousins.

If numbers are in control—and actually, they are—domesticated animals have won the game by far over their wild cousins.

Modern Homo sapiens skulls have been dated from 150,000 years ago. So humans have been wandering around for at least 150,000 years. Farming only began roughly 11,000 years ago. Why the lag in time?

Our early ancestors were adapted to hunting and gathering. They were reluctant to change until they were forced by hunger to do so. According to *An Edible History of Humanity*, by Tom Standage, early gatherers were larger of stature by quite a bit than the later farmers they became.   The point is: Early gatherers ate *better* than later farmers. Farmers took over because of **numbers**. Farmers could raise more children to maturity than hunter-gatherers. (But they probably had to **work** harder than their hunter-gatherer ancestors. *Work opposes entropy.*)

Farmers work is wasted if their crops are stolen by others. So farming communities were forced to evolve *social structures* of ample power to guard their crops and herds.

The diets of early farmers may have been less varied than that of earlier traveling bands, but farmers could grow consistent amounts of food over long periods to create larger and larger populations. We have discussed **population wars** before.   (And we will discuss such wars later in more detail.)

The hunter-gatherers were overwhelmed by greater **numbers** of farmers. Humans did not necessarily choose farming to improve the *qualities* of their lives. **Numbers** made the decisions, not *qualitative* choices.

Farming, however, once adopted, allowed human societies the luxury no other animal possessed, control of the growth of capital resources. All other animals must *chase* food-capital resources or locate them where they might be sporadically growing. Only humans—and perhaps some insect species—can nurture and grow their own produce near where they live.

By creating profits in food, human societies could transition from **competitive capitalism** to a more **cooperative capitalism**. Food **profits** allowed trade. Trade enabled human specialization.

By weeding out undesirable plants and cultivating desirable plants, by providing nutrients and protecting plants from harm, humans revolutionized the ***production of capital***. In a small area, they could produce a heretofore-unimagined amount of food. By domesticating animals, humans also gained access to a wide range of *alternate food sources*—grasslands for example—human stomachs could not utilize. Besides food sources, animals provided horsepower far beyond human strength.

The embrace of new farming technologies, however, did not necessarily improve the *quality* of human life, although it vastly increased the *numbers* of humans. Farming practices placed much more capital into circulation, but the amount of capital allotted to many humans continued to be small or even to diminish over time due to population (number) pressures.

Domesticating animals provided an immense step forward in manipulating capital resources. Horses could run far faster than humans and carry lots of stuff. Men on horseback could overwhelm foot soldiers. The horse was the primary technology (tool) that allowed Europeans to overwhelm native populations worldwide.

Farming technologies vastly increase the need for **sharing technologies** in human cultures.
Still true: Human cultures, that cease **sharing**, cease existing.

G. THE FLOWER-FRUIT CAPITAL EXCHANGE – Cooperative Capitalism
We discussed previously how, long before humans, nature devised a humane, **cooperative capital-exchange** between flowering plants and animals. Plants created extra **profit.** Plants were able to trade their extra profits for work they required, work spreading and fertilizing their seeds.
Like employers, plants paid their workers with enough energy capital to keep their workers working.
Like normal employers, however, plants are not overly beneficial. They don't like paying more than the minimum wage if they can help it.
Humans participated in the cooperative-capital exchange from the beginning, as fruit eating primates. Later, humans revolutionized the entire process: By purposefully spreading the seeds of plants whose profits they enjoyed, humans encouraged the plants to create more profits.
Viewed differently, by encouraging the success of fruit eating primates, plants created a self-fulfilling economy of **cooperative capitalism**. Plants now have a flexible and intelligent population (humans) dedicated and enslaved to their (plant) productivity. In the same way, domestic animals are now manipulating a separate species (us) to protect and increase *their* numbers.
Cooperation means more profits, and more **profits** ultimately mean more plants and more humans. **Profits** also give humans new levels of

trading opportunities for mutual benefit and peace. Recall: Without **profits**, capital exchanges are violent and usually deadly.

Profits allow plants and humans to place stuff in capital circulation, stuff that is not their own precious lives. Whew! **Profits** allow it all to happen. **Profits** are nice! *Don't disrespect (reasonable) profits.*

Note also: By domesticating humans, certain animals have astronomically increased their own populations—dogs, cats, farm animals far outnumber their wild cousins, and most have an easy life.

Note in addition: The differences between **competitive capitalism** and **cooperative capitalism** are not absolute and inalterable. There are few absolutes in nature.

H. HUMANS DISCOVER FOSSIL FUELS (like fire) ARE HIDDEN CAPITAL RESOURCES

Discovering hidden energy resources, mislaid by billions of years of living activities, greatly expands inexpensive capital resources available to all humans. These resources (peat, coal, oil) provide energy to increase the horsepower we once utilized from animals.

And note: Nitrogen fixation discovered by Faber in 1908, assisted by fossil fuels, today allows humans to increase harvests up to four times what was once possible. Hybrid plants provide many times the return of ancient plants. And so—because of fossil fuels, technology, and hybrid plants—the world can support huge population **numbers** today. But how long can the technology continue improving? We will surely find out soon. **Numbers** put great **pressure** on **resources**.

Without fossil fuel energy, fertilizers and pesticides created from fossil fuels, and hybrid plants, experts estimate eighty percent of the human population today could not survive.

The dark side: Fossil fuels create toxic byproducts and the supply is limited. Would we rather starve? Or will new technologies and population control be better solutions?

(?)

I. HUMANS INVENT SOCIETAL SYSTEMS THAT SHARE CAPITAL RESOURCES

Human societies, that **share** capital resources, organize precisely like individual animals; in other words, both solitary animals and social systems can specialize due to the internal *sharing* of capital profits. Capital circulates like blood to nourish the total organism.

By sharing resources, cells can specialize into bone, muscle, digestive, and many other specialties in a single animal organism. Human societies, by **sharing** capital, can share work, and specialize into hundreds of different artistic and creative skills for mutual benefit. Specialized occupations can create greater profits. Greater profits allow greater capital circulation—a more healthy blood flow to society.

Early gathering societies cooperated against the threats of predators, protecting children and sharing dangers. Sharing chores of hunting, gathering, meal preparation, tool making, and childcare also meant sharing food resources and language capital (information) widely.

The **capital flow** through society, (or **sharing**), is the most important tool of human progress. Sharing capital flow (profits), or the practice of **cooperative** *capitalism*, allows a society to grow as a single organism.

However, as specialties grew in larger societies, the circulation of capital began to vary, overfeeding some areas and starving others. [See ***Status levels*** Ch. 4,5] When the flow of capital diminishes throughout a society, the health of the society diminishes concurrently. An organism dies or suffers necrosis when circulation (sharing) does not reach all parts of its body.

J. BARTERING, SHARING, TRADING—A HUMAN INVENTION THAT SIDESTEPPED VIOLENCE

Trading capital profit items for other capital profit items allowed capital items to be fairly exchanged without the need of violence. **Note: With the exception of the fruit-flower exchange, all capital exchanges in nature are violent. Ouch!**

Yes, it's true—before humans, if you needed some of your neighbor's capital, you generally needed to kill your neighbor. Humans took a step forward in **cooperative capital exchanges** in creating *profits* and discovering trade. Your neighbors appreciate this.

Note: To have something to *trade*, a **profit** is necessary.

Sharing language profits, or truths are the most important tools of human survival. Untruths lead to conflicts and chaos and non-survival in human civilizations.

K. HUMANS INVENT TOKEN CAPITAL AND TRADE

Token capital--like dollar bills, and tradable items--assists the exchange of capital items for value without the need to shed blood—amazing, no bloodshed! (This is probably disappointing to some humans.)

REMEMBER: Before human trade, every exchange of capital between unrelated individuals was through force and death.

Token capital is arbitrarily given token value, or the value of some real commodity, to be utilized in exchanges. In early Egypt, wheat was utilized as payment. Farmers who placed their wheat in government granaries received clay tablets, tokens with marks indicating how much wheat they held. These redeemable tablets were later traded as commodities for whatever the owner desired. These tokens held real value in wheat.

Later, since clay tablets could be easily forged, humans substituted metal coins. Coins, and later, paper money and credit cards, were and are simply easier to carry than baskets of wheat.

The point is, token capital receives its value from some actual capital source. When society created gold coins, humans assumed gold actually was the source of value. Using a semi-commodity, like gold, with scarce availability, places stresses on capital circulation and can cause economic stagnation.

In medieval times, people hoarded gold; this hoarding stifled the flow of capital of all types and made difficult economic times even worse. Today's societies do not tie their currency values to commodities, but rather, to the integrities and stabilities of their governments—a rather questionable but malleable concept.

Economists don't seem to know wherein the real commodity value of currencies comes from anymore, but since all currencies trade against each other, it doesn't matter. The values of currencies are **token**, not real. Token value gets into currencies somehow; and this value can easily and fairly circulate. Dollars can turn into pounds; pounds can turn into rupees; rupees can turn into yen; currencies can be traded for products. Value is simply mutual agreement, **token**.

Plenty of currency is available, because governments can print money as they see fit.

Traders can make money when they correctly predict how currency values ebb and flow. Governments use central banks to enter the trading arena to make certain their currencies are properly valued. But all currency values are relative, relative to other token currencies, not necessarily (or only indirectly) to real capital items, like wheat.

This house-of-cards situation seems as if it would be unstable, but on the contrary, it seems to work better than any previous method to keep capital profits flowing easily. Terrible things would still happen if *everyone* decided to keep their capital in their mattresses and capital ceased circulating, a situation that has happened in the past. On the other hand, rampant inflation and government instability can make a token currency valueless.

Recall: Capital **sharing** (including food and information) is the most important tool of human progress. But a future Armageddon may prove the technicians wrong; we might all want our baskets of wheat back.

Crypto-currencies are a new capital concept; these work without central banks. Crypto currencies carry values buyers are willing to bid that moment on the Internet—presently an even more malleable and volatile situation.

Some people still wish to return to commodity-based valuations for greater stability—a dollar might equal a basket of wheat—but those are in the minority. Most economists fear stagnation more than free flow. Today's common currencies may one day disappear.

We are all today dependent on massive amounts of token capital circulation immediately from all areas of the world. The flow of token value allows the equal flow of real value, real capital, *stuff,* to wherever it has a purpose. Anything interfering with this flow—trade barriers or hoarding, for example—will have serious consequences.

(Without flow, no show.)

Note: This book is being published in 2019 in the middle of a growing trade war between the world's largest countries.

*The more we **share**, the more we all become. The less we share, the more we diminish ourselves.*

L. HUMANS CREATE CENTRAL GOVERNMENTS—CENTRAL GOVERNMENTS CAN CREATE AND MAINTAIN INFRASTRUCTURE

Central governments have the power to create and defend infrastructures; infrastructures offer wide assistance to capital **sharing**—financial systems, roads, canals, protection from violence, food dispersal, bridges, trash collection, and so forth. We will include some negative reports on central governments later.

Let it be known: **Central government is neither evil nor always beneficial.** "We all benefit from effective government. We are all hurt by ineffective or tyrannical central government."

No one wants government to control all life; but we all want government to deal with our *sewage*.

*"The question is not government, but the **quality** of government, and sewage."*

M. HUMANS CREATE BANKS AND STOCKS

Banks and stocks allow capital that might be imprisoned in unusable locations—like sacks of gold--to be **re-circulated**. The feudal ages were made far darker due to the lack of circulating capital. The gold standard congested land ownership and capital in the hands of an elite.

Repressive religious laws forbid lending money for a profit. Repressive societies diminished the value of human labor. The creation and circulation of profit capital diminished to a trickle.

When humans put money in banks rather than in their mattresses, that capital could be lent out and re-circulated. Imagine that capital is energized blood. If it is stored in a distant place—like oil underground or gold in a mattress--it serves little purpose, but if it circulates through the organism, it can feed growth wherever it goes. Banks today release capital to circulate widely. Greater circulation generally creates greater prosperity.

Of course, when banks or stocks goof up, we all suffer. Too much circulation may create toxic effects—like fossil fuels create--or blood pressure that is too high. If banks lend out money too freely, the pipeline may rupture. Like slicing through a blood vessel, capital losses may endanger the health of the entire organism. If banks go insolvent, innocent victims may lose dangerous amounts of their important capital.

If numerous banks go out of business, the entire economy may suffer serious harm. The situation is akin to a bubble of air in the circulation system. The patient may die.

In similar fashion, if stock values suddenly plummet, the vacuum of lost capital can affect every part of the economy, even parts that seem to have little to do with banking or stock trading. In a modern economy, everything is connected through capital flow to everything else, just as in a single organism.

Modern economies can grow quite complicated, but the basic process is quite simple. Thousands of economists worldwide watch capital items intently to try to gauge where we are going and what we should be doing. The numbers can grow endless, dull, and confusing. We need economists willing to pursue this thankless task.

Moving away from absolute specifics, however, and viewing capital circulation from a comfortable distance, allows a more unified and less limiting vision. Such is the purpose of this book.

We will leave current dollars and sense issues to the real economists in government and education. They get paid more than we do.

Suffice to repeat: When a majority (percentages may vary) of human workers in a society can create **profits** from their work, and those profits can circulate equitably, the economy can progress. Without profitable work, however, the process falters badly.

*"**To succeed, we need to share.**"*

N. GENERAL HUMAN EDUCATION

Education is a capital **sharing** process in human cultures. Even if education has no economic purpose otherwise, its benefits to humanity to facilitate **shared understandings** make education ***the most important***

human commodity. By sharing understanding, a human culture achieves its cultural identification, defines its **self.**

A common culture without a common cultural understanding is not a culture. We might argue further, our common cultural understandings are what we amount to, are how we grow as humanity.

Education can also provide specific skills, skills that assist humans to participate in economic circulation. **Skills** are extremely important, but ***shared human understandings*** are what make humans humanity.

[Read Ch. 9 – The human self]

O. ENERGY AND TECHNOLOGY INCREASE HUMAN VALUE

Technologies increase the human ability to **share** and perform work. **Work** can create tradable profits. Machines use cheap energy and leverage to replace what was once slave labor. Machines—like the spear, the automobile, and language—multiply ***human value***.

Humans, who control machines and capital, possess much greater capital value than other humans who depend strictly on their labor and are without technological advantages. Technology can thus magnify human **differences** based on differences in the technologies different humans may possess.

Technologies help human societies to **share;** but they can also be used to **limit sharing**.

The ability to move vast amounts of energy through pipes or through wires at nearly the speed of light, and the further ability to manipulate that energy through technology to accomplish work—these innovations have pushed human progress to great heights.

Technologies, however, are often blind to ***qualitative*** consequences—whether technologies increase or decrease understanding and sharing in a society depends on human usage.

Language, for example, can be used to bind a culture together or to tear it apart. The spear, fire, the Internet—all technologies can be used to bring together or destroy.

IN OTHER WORDS:
TECHNOLOGICAL OR CAPITAL INEQUITIES (WHEN THEY OCCUR) CREATE SOCIAL INEQUITIES.

In more other words: **If you have more capital than me, you have more human value than I do.**

If you possess a smartphone and an auto, and I do not, then your human capital value is a good deal more than mine. You can literally socialize with anyone in the world, while moving at seventy miles an hour;

while I can only go as fast as my own feet and I must socialize only with those in close proximity. The farmer with a tractor can plow many more acres than someone with a pointed stick. The soldier with a club has no chance against an opposing soldier with a machine gun. Educated people are assumed to possess more value than uneducated people. Those with experience in any field are generally more valuable than those who have no experience. Technology makes ironman superior to other men in every way. [Well, maybe he's not so good at cuddling or reading stories to children, but...]

Those who possess capital or can **buy technology** have a great advantage over those who don't. So, while laws may *try* to treat humans with equality, capital advantages separate us and isolate us from each other. None of this information is terribly complicated or much of a secret. Most people recognize that wealthy people have great capital leverage in continuing to get *ahead* compared to non-wealthy people.

The point is: The forces of *Cultural entropy* help create and enlarge economic divisions; in other words, random factors help the rich get richer and the poor get poorer, particularly over long time periods. Social divisions create economic inequities; and economic inequities create status divisions. And finally, social divisions and economic inequities usually create conflict.

What is true for individual humans is also true for integrated cultures. A culture possessing a great deal of capital technology has an advantage over other competing cultures possessing less capital technology. And technological differences can grow over time, rather than diminish.

Thus: **Cultural entropy (forces of chaos) tend to enlarge—rather than diminish--economic differences between cultures.**

Thus we can clearly see why some cultures—those that possess the most capital assets--feel they are superior to other cultures. The possession of capital is the possession of value. The possession of capital resources, moreover, is usually the possession of power.   Capital can finance technologies, the police, and the military.

European powers overwhelmed much of the world in imperial times. European technology was superior at the time. European humans, however, were no different than other humans; they simply possessed more powerful **technology**—horses and guns.

The illusion of European (White) superiority is still apparent today in some cultures. With the spreading of capital technologies throughout the world, this illusion is diminishing, as it should.

Cultures that fail to share resources grow increasingly divided. Capital is life. <u>Cooperative capitalism</u> assists life to prosper. Cultural wars lead to <u>competitive capitalism</u> and conflict.

P. INTERNET COMMUNICATIONS GREATLY ASSIST CAPITAL FLOW, WHILE <u>ALSO</u> GREATLY ASSISTING POLARIZATION, EXTREMISM, AND DIVISIVENESS

The greatest innovation in modern times, we all realize, has been the Internet. The Internet allows the spread of capital information and facilitates the buying and selling of capital goods in ways no previous civilization has experienced. In addition, games and entertainments cheaply fulfill dreams of the young and old.

Information storage and circulation has differentiated human societies from all other life forms. The full realization of the Internet's potential upside and downside has yet to be realized. So strange to realize, the capital flow—that once moved slowly through primordial forests on human shoulders—can now move through wires and space at the speed of light.

Bare in mind, for all its hoopla, the Internet does **nothing new**. ***The same rules still apply regarding circulating capital, cultural entropy, and everything else***. What the Internet does is circulate everything much, much, much, much more *quickly* than was ever possible in human history. Thus we ignore the basic principals at our own peril. Capital is life. Verifiable truth is the most important tool for human survival.

Cultural entropy (chaos) can now move faster than ever also.

THE INTERNET ASSISTS EXTREMISM AND POLARIZATION IN HUMAN SOCIETIES

No better forum has ever existed to assist extreme views and political polarization than the Internet. The reasons are rather simplistic: Intuitively, memes, opinions placed on the Internet, political websites, are extreme in nature. In other words, people don't use the Internet to express normal, unemotional, moderate sentiments. Normal, unemotional sentiments are, well, boring, and not worth writing about.

On the contrary, dramatic, **extreme** feelings are what draw attention. Attracting attention is what the Internet is all about. The circulation of truth is secondary and minimized compared to the circulation of memes that attract attention of viewers. Dramatic, extreme clicks ***finance*** the Internet.

The attentions of U-tube viewers are often manipulated by quick views of female cleavage and cute puppies; these views draw attention to whatever irrelevant concepts the designer wishes (often having nothing to do with sex or cuteness). Even though annoying, these videos persist because they work to draw attention. Advertisers have been using similar methods for decades, selling everything from autos to cigarettes. They aren't just selling their product; they are selling enticing beauty, a scene of nature, or joyful moments. The point is: Human attentions are easy to manipulate.

For many political pundits, the creation of **extreme** emotions and angst are far more important that the search for verifiable truths. Pundits are aware, viewers are not interested in consensus or complicated human understandings—these things are too much work. On the contrary, most humans seek an easy emotional catharsis, a symphony of righteous indignation and intolerance, an easily consumed view that does not require the hard work and complications of human understanding, love, consensus, and the difficult search for God and meaning.

As in legislatures, and cultures in general, the forces of **cultural entropy** favor extreme views over moderation. The moderate majority (those capable of consensus) are often unaware they are being minimalized, subverted, and forced into meaningless conflicts by those at the extremes.

We repeat: Human civilizations are totally dependent on circulating memes of truth to survive. Memes of untruth lead contrary to the survival of human civilizations to entropy and catastrophy.

IN ADDITION—DUE TO TECHNOLOGY, AND THE INTERNET, THE IGNORANCE MEMES ALSO CIRCULATE FASTER TODAY

When information capital (verifiable truth) *fails* to circulate, **ignorance** appears in the form of superstitions and lies. This is not rocket science; it is simply true. **Ignorance multiplies and grows exponentially without the opposition of verifiable truth.** Extreme views nurture ignorance.

Human society depends on the circulation of honest capital (verifiable truth) and stagnates in the presence of dishonesty or when capital in general cannot circulate. Untruths generally lead to conflicts; superstition and lies have led to warfare since the beginning of human history.

SPEED CREATES ILLUSIONS: The speed of the Internet allows the dissemination of information (often lies) faster than any controlling agency can act. Decisions, based on lies and misinformation, are generally bad decisions. Verifiable truths generally lead to fairer decisions.

People should recognize the ignorance meme for what it is—cultural necrosis in the absence of proper circulation (sharing of verifiable truths). Any body part will suffer gangrene in the absence of blood flow, and that gangrene infection will quickly spread.

The slow decline of Rome, and other civilizations, into increasing levels of darkness and ignorance, is symptomatic of the disease of degenerated capital circulation. Infrastructure destruction, warfare, crime, ignorance, and terrible poverty are symptoms of this same disease. **We cannot jump to the conclusion that all verifiable truths lead to peaceful resolutions, but we know from experience, misunderstandings and lies cause bad things to happen.**

The modern circulation of capital via Internet and natural channels greatly facilitates growth and common understandings. However, excessive circulations of false concepts and trivial memes have the same affect as the consumption of junk food. The human race can become ignorant, mentally shallow, and psychologically unhealthy on this diet.

Most wise people agree, however, governments should not attempt to make decisions on information flow for entire populations. The assumption of value in human life depends on that human's realization of his or her own belonging and direction, not on the direction they are forced by government or religion to pursue. Those who ***must accept*** a direction forced upon them by government are—by definition--enslaved.

More important, creative thinking is what allows societies to progress and improve. Governments that enslave the understandings of their populations may doom those populations to eternal stagnation. Think what boxes would encircle the present if we were limited by the ideas of bureaucrats and the ideas of perfect thinking that originated a thousand years ago.

The status quo is not sacred. For the good of future enlightenment, it must be susceptible to change.

The hope is: Verifiable truths will lead to enlightenment.

On the contrary we know from history: Deceptions lead to further deceptions and darkness.

Q. THE GREEN REVOLUTION

We would be derelict not to add the green revolution to the list of human **sharing** accomplishments.

Normally, a certain amount of vegetation can grow on a certain amount of land. The amount is limited by several factors—sunlight, water, and available soil nutrients. Early farmers found repeated crops could deplete the amount of nutrients in the soil, and thus their crops declined.

At the turn of the century, scientist recognized that the nutrient in soil that most quickly diminished was nitrogen; plants require nitrogen for growth. Nitrogen is plentiful in the atmosphere, but only a few varieties of plants can utilize it. Atmospheric nitrogen is tightly bonded. Microscopic organisms can unlock the nitrogen bond and create nitrates, which are useful to plants. Plants, which contain these organisms, include the (legumes) clovers, and alfalfa, and such.

Scientists realized, nitrates (and other fertilizers), added to soils, could make unproductive soils worldwide very productive. The problem was making these fertilizers cheap and available.

German chemist, Fritz Haber, developed a process for creating ammonia nitrates in 1909, which was later commercialized. We all need to thank Fritz Haber for the foods we now eat, and the massive population these foods can support. We might mention, the nitrates created also are used to manufacture dynamite and explosives; these killed millions. Haber was also instrumental in creating mustard gas, which killed and maimed thousands in World War 1. Well, no one is perfect.

Haber's overall contribution (and that of other scientists) allows billions of people to live on this earth. Otherwise, we could only exist in our millions.

In addition, the green revolution is greatly assisted by the development of productive, genetically engineered plants, irrigations techniques, antibiotics, pesticides, fossil fuels, tractors, and fast growing domestic animals. Without these technological economic developments, human population numbers could not approach present levels.

Scientists estimate (natural) farming techniques without pesticides, artificial fertilizers, and genetically designed plants might feed, at best, approximately 50% of the modern population. That leaves the other 50 percent of us, well, starving. If we also leave out fossil fuels, the percentage of people starving would approach 80 percent of us all. Humanity has begun a cycle that cannot easily be altered without significant despair, assuming the population continues to rise.

Human farming in the sea, plus utilization of heretofore-unproductive land areas, is still possible in the future. The human population might increase and increase to twenty or thirty billion if all present technologies pan out and we continue to stress land and resources to the max. If new technologies don't succeed, then the story will be different, best not presented to young audiences.

FUTURE POPULATIONS

"The Population Bomb", written in 1968 by Ehrlick, failed to recognize how quickly technologies would develop, and thus predicted a quick disaster would soon overcome the human population. The predicted apocalypse and famine has yet to appear, but the conclusions in "The Population Bomb" still loom in the future. At some point, population numbers will stress resources beyond the ability of new human technologies. When this tragedy will occur, no one can now say.

The forces of **cultural entropy** (chaos) are quite patient. They can foment human disasters through vast time periods. We might be well advised to not test the farthest reaches of our resources. Living within our means (and not hoping to be rescued from disasters by new technologies) might make human life more valuable and less stressful to all living humans.

CONCLUSION: Human activities (technologies) mentioned in this chapter allowed capital creation, circulation, trading and sharing in ways vastly improved from natural capital circulation. In particular, capital exchanges of profits in human societies, or <u>cooperative capitalism</u> no longer required violence and could be mutually beneficial.

Forces of cultural entropy, however, work against all cooperating capital-sharing systems. Population pressures (numbers) consistently increase the erosive effects of entropy and cultural entropy and stress resources.

Many negative results occur over long time periods, invisible to normal humans—these include wars, language entropy, soil erosion, the circulation of memes of untruth, economic statuses, human polarization, and extreme emotions—all of which work against human unity. To oppose the forces of cultural entropy requires a great deal of focused <u>work</u> towards unity.

The speed of the Internet creates a storm of conflicted information, good and bad. The Internet emphasizes extreme and polarizing views over consensus.

Recall: Non-truths lead human systems to make catastrophic decisions. Healthy societies depend on the circulation of truth and understanding.

From the invention of the spear to the invention of the atom bomb, new technologies make population wars more deadly and magnify social differences. *<u>Better technologies (without social understandings) do not necessarily improve the quality of human life. As long as human cultures continue to practice violent competitive capitalism (wars), the future value of human life may be as diminished as in the past.</u>*

CHAPTER 5 --
SOME HUMAN ECONOMIC INVENTIONS THAT GREATLY *IMPAIR* CAPITAL CIRCULATION OVER TIME, AND THUS ASSIST THE CORROSIVE AND DIVISIVE EFFECTS OF CULTURAL ENTROPY:

These random distortions, increasing over time, and unwise strategies (effects of cultural entropy) push human societies *away* from <u>cooperative capitalism</u> back to <u>competitive (predatory) capitalism</u>

A. LINGUISTIC ENTROPY
   1. Linguist Entropy
   2. Lies and Distortions
   3. Symbolic Language Considerations
B. CULTURAL WARS—Population wars stress resources.
   1. Human advantages in War
   2. Mideast and African Examples
C. SLAVERY: Slave states and Status Levels stop capital circulation
      Greeks and Romans examples:
D. IGNORANCE results during times of stifled capital flow
E. NO MAN'S LANDS and infrastructure destruction cause famine and population declines
F. CLIMAX POPULATIONS stifle capital circulation
G. PURITANITY and extreme human emotions assist Cultural Entropy
H. Why Do Killer Bunnies not Exist?
I. FAMILY VALUES decay over time unless opposed by work.

A. LINGUISTIC ENTROPY DISTORTS LANGUAGE AND ADDS TO CULTURAL ENTROPY:
1. LINGUISTIC ENTROPY

Humans invented language and learn it naturally; however, **linguistic entropy** distorts languages over time.   Human languages are quite malleable. A culture separated by several hundred years may find communications difficult. A culture separated by a thousand years may find communication impossible. The human family may divide into separate, antagonistic cultures over language differences.

Since language is the most important technology humans use to share capital resources, when a culture's language loses its connectivity, the culture may also cease to connect, creating intolerance.

Historically, most wars are between antagonists speaking different languages.

Extremist leadership can disunite combined societies along linguistic lines, based on the assumption that those who speak different languages are, indeed, different. The truth is—humans are humans no matter what languages they speak. And if any tribe goes back enough generations, they will meet at the same language and family.

Time is a problem to short-lived humans. **Linguistic entropy** distorts human language and understandings over long, long time periods, so humans fail to comprehend their mutual origins.

Today, some leaders assume that sharing a unique language gives their particular population uniqueness. And so, reviving tribal languages is today popular. However, being separate is a mixed blessing—particularly when separate languages generate **intolerance** (as usually happens) while discouraging the circulation of cultural oneness.

Single language pubs, popular in some areas—English only, Gaelic only, French only, Spanish only—are actually being exclusive, creating new cultural divisions, rather than encouraging cultural togetherness. Such innovations may be backwards steps in human relations.

Well-meaning parents often send their children to ethnic schools. Such schools teach ethnic languages—Armenian, Arabic, Hebrew, Greek, for example—and provide religious educations in various Catholic, Jewish, Muslim, Sikh, or Mormon concepts, to name a few.

Reviving and maintaining our differing cultural heritages is very important; however, we must accept such activities simultaneously revive, maintain, and enlarge our cultural differences.

World population wars have slaughtered millions of innocent victims. Generally such wars occur between populations separated by linguistic or religious differences, leadership, and very little else. Human emotions and puritanity magnify small differences. The point apparently is: The better we communicate, the easier it is to solve our problems. Cultural linguistic differences often hinder cultural communications and blind us to our common human family.

Modern technologies, such as written languages, dictionaries, and now the Internet, can help keep languages whole; but on the contrary, some groups seek unique identities by purposefully using digital methods to shred language into parses only they can understand. **Technologies** can also act divisively when commanded.

The struggle for mutual understanding is ongoing. Only by recognizing our **single human self-identity**, can humans avoid the violent divisions of the past.

2. HUMAN LIES AND DISTORTIONS ASSIST THE FORCES OF CULTURAL ENTROPY TO CREATE CHAOS: THE IMPORTANCE OF TRUTH FOR HUMAN SURVIVAL

The sharing of language capital greatly assisted early humans to survive. However, the positive benefits created by language do no good if the information circulated is untrue. Early humans lived or died by accurate information.

Verifiable truth is the most important tool of human survival.

Language allows the circulation of information and also misinformation. The circulation of untruths, either caused by random errors or human malice, can disrupt totally the ability of a sharing culture to survive, like spreading poisoned food through a colony of ants. Untruths result in bad decisions, and in early human societies, bad decisions would have often resulted in death or failure to survive.

In early cultures, misinformation often brought immediate failure. In modern societies, memes of untruths can circulate for longer periods because consequences are more difficult to understand. But the final results are consistent: Erroneous understandings lead inevitably to erroneous actions and conflict. This is certainly not complicated rocket science.

Such thinking, in fact, may seem quite elementary—and it certainly is—but it leads us to directly recognize the absolute importance of **truth** in human existence. Without truthful understandings, human progress—indeed, continued human survival—is not possible.

We should probably distinguish here between normal truth and TRUTH with a capital T. Socrates taught us that Truth with a capital T is illusive. Socrates taught that Truth is a living, growing, changing thing, and we are misguided if we think we can possess this thing, Truth, totally. Great Truths, like God, are not necessarily finite or changeless, and we can't own them or put them in cement or even in the pages of a book. But, while Socrates pointed out the illusiveness of Great Truths, Socrates--like Buddha, and Jesus, and Mohammed—did not free us from the need to pursue and seek Truth. In fact, all these prophets are in total agreement, seeking Truth, or God, or Joy, or Oneness, is the purpose of human existence.

Some say, the human soul only diminishes when it stops seeking Truth.

But back on earth, human souls must still find ways of living together. To live together, humans must share—and the most important thing humans can share is *understanding*, the understanding of verifiable truths about ourselves with a small t.

To repeat: When we share untruths, these untruths invariably lead us to decisions that compromise our survival. Untruths evolve directly from the chaotic forces of **cultural entropy**, and, of course, some humans have learned to circulate memes of untruth to give themselves unfair advantages.

We may be stretching things to insist untruths always lead to catastrophes. Untruths, like random actions, may ***accidentally*** lead us to somewhere nice, but the preponderance of wrong actions, like random actions, most often lead to places we do not want to be.

Ignorant memes are inevitably destructive to human understandings, whether these memes come to us through history, from the Hitler's of the world, through Hollywood imaginations, or through the Internet.

To belabor the analogy, untruths, circulated by language in human societies, act precisely like viruses/parasites in the human blood system. Human blood however, is designed to seek out imposters and eliminate them. Human societies may be less advanced than our own blood in recognizing what is true and what is false.

When governments try to control information flow, they tend to impede all capital flow. Governments tend to allow only information that is complementary to their own government positions. Those in power tend to oppose any change that endangers their positions of power. Government actions, by impeding the flow of understanding, act in tandem with the powers of **cultural entropy** to limit human joy and unity.

The irony is: Government powers, by seeking to control capital flow and create stability, can constrict understandings and create conflict and self-destructive chaos. [Ch. 5, 6, 8 – Why Civilizations Fall]

3. SYBOLIC LANGUAGE
THE CHINESE have suffered through thousands of years of revolutions and rebuilding cycles. Though their spoken languages have split according to the same factors as European languages, they uniquely evolved written symbols that remained stable for a thousand years. Thus, though Chinese and Japanese cannot understand each other's language, they can understand each other's writing. The word meanings remain over time.

Symbolic, written language may partially explain why rebuilding cycles in China include a far wider area than those in Europe. The populations share a written language even if they can't easily speak to one another. This written language, though archaic to new technology, may be a unifying factor over time that is absent in other areas of the world in which phonetic spellings and pronunciations dominate.

China is admittedly an anomaly to the rules of cultural entropy. Stable central government, cycles of rebuilding and divisive, and civil wars occur over much longer periods than in other areas of the world. Topography may be a reason; China is controlled by two closely aligned river systems; and a single ethnic group, the Han, dominates 90% of its population. Other possibilities—none conclusive—will be discussed in Chapter 7,

The possibility of creating a **pictorial language** that utilizes modern computers and printers might actually benefit future societies, particularly future historians, and those many teenagers who spend much of their lives texting.

Malleability is the major benefit of phonetic writing; however, to control a style of infinite variety is difficult over time. A common pictorial language might provide a *unifying* technology for the future human race.

B. CULTURAL WARS: THE HUMAN ADVANTAGE

Population wars are ongoing eternally between all organisms. All cultures must maximize their populations to compete with other populations.

Children are the primary weapons in cultural wars. Cultural wars stress resources.

We feel it bears repeating: Human populations have a unique advantage when it comes to waging population wars with large casualties. Since males are not absolutely essential to raise children (women exclusively control lactation) males can be expended without necessarily affecting childcare or the numbers of babies being born. If men are lost, other men are happily willing to deliver sperm to fertile women. Given the opportunity, a single man can fertilize dozens of women, so the loss of dozens of men can theoretically be minimized, if **numbers** are the only criterion.

Unfortunately, when Cultural Entropy controls human societies, numbers **are** the only criterion. So wars make excellent sense in human cultures, even with severe casualties, if those wars win adequate resources to keep fertile women well fed, and enough young men survive to maximize female fertility.

In the animal world, only wasps and ants can wage protracted wars with major casualties. In the case of insects, the warriors being sacrificed are infertile females. Like human males sacrificed in a war, these females are not necessary for the hive to maximize its fertility, so they are expendable. The queen can produce hundreds of eggs each day to make up for any loses. **Numbers** make the decisions.

Fertile, solitary bees will not sacrifice themselves in mass attacks; because, if they die they are sacrificing their next generation, their own children; besides, they aren't crazy. Fertile females are too valuable to sacrifice themselves.

Human males are biologically, and unreasonably hard-wired for tribal warfare, and many human cultures have structured themselves around constant warfare. In today's world, these **war-structured cultures** have particular problems dealing with peace. They breed too many young men without access to non-military jobs and peaceful activities.

Expendable men, war-structured societies, fertile women, and the stresses of cultural entropy explain most of today's conflicts.

The Mideast, as an example, has been an area of **tribal** warfare and strife for several thousand years. Tribal, **population wars** are symptomatic of war-structured *social* organizations.

The Palestinians and the Israelis are presently engaged in a **cultural war**. Though the Israelis have won ground wars with technological superiority, the Palestinians continue to fight using their growing **population**, their army of children. The **numbers** of Palestinians continue to increase exponentially, doubling every few years with the help of food supplied by international sources.

The final outcome points to continued conflict. The Israelis have lost the population war. Palestinians have an excess of unemployed young men with little purpose but to continue antagonistic pursuits.

Given enough food, and no employment, the Palestinian war-structured culture cannot stop fighting. If they destroy the Israelis, they will, given enough food, begin to fight each other. The forces of **cultural entropy** are in control. Human reason is on the sidelines.

Also on the sidelines are the major religious. Both Jewish and Muslim belief systems (mostly peaceful) are being ignored or twisted to suit the **extreme** views created by competitive capitalism and war-structured societies. Clueless **extreme** leaders encourage the conflict. The moderate middle has been destroyed.

THE AFRICAN DILLEMA (A CULTURAL ENTROPY EXAMPLE FOR THE FUTURE)

Some scholars have described the African continent as being resistant to civilizations. Proponents of slavery even claimed Africans must be less intelligent than other races since no great civilizations apparently appeared in the continent's entire southern regions.

The rules of **cultural entropy**, however, tell an entirely different story. Africa is by far the *oldest* cradle of human society. The random forces of human division have been active in Africa ***far longer*** than on any other continent.

Human cultures in Africa have been ravaged and **polarized** by the storms of **cultural entropy** for hundreds of thousands of years, far, far longer than on any other continent.

Concurrent with the **polarization** of human populations over great spans of time, virulent parasites and animal populations developing in synch with hominids had ample time in Africa to develop particularly virulent controls against hominid development, much more so than the clueless big game in areas visited by later human migrations.

The result in Africa is close to what would be *predicted* in the single area of the world in which the forces of **cultural entropy** and **extreme emotions** have been active on human cultures *for the longest period*--an extraordinary variety of polarized **linguistic and cultural divisions**, separated by lawless, violent, and uninhabited **no man's lands,** and interspersed with wastelands controlled by sophisticated parasites and fierce animal species.

In the absence of large central governments, and opposed by the effects of an unpredictable tropical climate, plus **extreme human emotions**, human infrastructures quickly decay.

Far from being *undeveloped*, Africa provides extraordinary instances of how human development polarizes and stagnates under the influence of divisive **cultural entropy** over *long, long spans of time*.

Far from being a reminder of the past, chaotic Africa gives us a glimpse of what a *future* world will resemble, if the divisive effects of **cultural entropy** continue to act worldwide without opposition from human understandings.

NOTE: Technological advances have radically changed the African experience both to the positive (better living standards) and to the negative (more deadly conflicts in cultural wars).

Cultural wars, waged in Africa and elsewhere, pose THE primary stress to world resources.

.....

Bourne: Why Civilizations Fall and Cannot Rise Again
Ch. 5 THESE HUMAN INVENTIONS DIMINISH CAPITAL CIRCULATION

C. Human inventions that impair capital circulation: SLAVERY

C. SLAVERY—A HUMAN ECONOMIC INVENTION CREATED TO <u>DIMINISH</u> HUMAN VALUE
I. The Slave State: Or HOW we can stop capital circulation, diminish the value of human life, and destroy civilization, all with a single institution, 101 --
Persia, Greece, Rome, China, Africa, and the USA

"Many people view slavery simply as immoral. Slavery **is** immoral, and always has been. But we should not be blind to the terrible **economic** consequences of slavery that over time affect **all** social levels."

Slavery severely diminishes the circulation of free capital (sharing) within a society by diminishing the value of free human labor. Slavery devalues **all** human life. **Profits** are absolutely necessary for capital circulation. Without profits, nothing is available to circulate. Without profits, **free** organisms cannot grow, including humans. Even elite slave owners suffer from the weakening of their larger societies—although, of course, less than other statuses.

When elite owners restrict resources and **steal the profits** from the labor of their slaves, they diminish the ability of all capital profits to circulate in their society.

Cultures with diminished capital circulation, like biological organisms, grow weak. Weakened cultures with diminished capital flow grow increasingly susceptible to the ravages of **cultural entropy** over time.

The effects of cultural entropy include polarization, ignorance, lack of understanding, control by violent extremes, militarism, no man's lands, the rise of competitive capitalism over cooperative capitalism, and complete cultural dissolution.

1. THE FALL OF GREECE

We use Greece for illustrative purposes, but similar **enslavement stories** occur throughout the world in *every* large civilization without exception.

Some history: Ending a time of polarization and uncertainty, Alexander the Great united the Greeks. Later he conquered much of the known world. When Alexander's conquests ended, the Greek world experienced a momentary flush of prosperity.

Trade greatly increased throughout the conquered area. Persian and Egyptian goods flooded the shelves of Greek merchants.

The most valuable commodity, a flood of newly-conquered slaves, poured into wealthy Greek cities from every conquered province. Cheap labor became cheaper. The price of ***free*** Greek labor, however, quickly *diminished*, eventually approaching zero. Slavery destroys *all* human value by diminishing the value of free human labor.

The human labor of *free* Greeks, who did not own slaves, *lost* value. *Free* middle-class farmers or common workers could no longer create a capital ***profit*** through their own labors. Without circulating **profit,** the entire society weakened.

When small, family farms could no longer compete, or could survive only at subsistence (profitless) levels, large slave estates took over. Small Greek communities serving family farmers, once prosperous, began to disappear.

With the disappearance of small farms, and the associated support system, the human capital of young free men to stock Greek militaries declined severely.

Capital resources to support military activities also declined in line with the decline of capital profits throughout the empire.

Urban commerce suffered as well, because the majority of free Greeks, over time, possessed less and less **profit capital** to buy merchandise. Free labor could no longer create a **profit**. Slavery sucked up profit and gave it to the elites. Slave owners steal the profits from human work. This profit does not evenly circulate (is not shared).

Capital over time congested in the hands of the rich. Slaves could not be tapped for military service, because they would have turned their weapons first against their masters. Children of nobility refused to serve as foot soldiers. A century after conquering the known world, Greece began to lose its preeminence as a military and economic power; **it possessed diminished soldiers and diminished economic, capital resources. Slave states must expend significant resources to keep their enslaved in line.**

An elite Greek climax population opposed change, negatively controlled resources, and upheld a narrow status quo. Capital energy that had once flowed freely through the empire, dried up.

Slavery sapped the energy of the middle class. Without a middle class, the flow of capital slowed to a trickle.

In the Hellenic age, Greek philosophers and mathematicians opened new avenues of human understanding, but they had no idea of the *real* **numbers** confounding capital flow in their civilization. High levels of slaves meant Greece had little human **profit** capital left to defend lofty ideals, or to maintain the average *value* of human life. Capital is value. When capital stops circulating, the value of average human life diminishes. Capital is life.

In the 1840s southern, confederate writers, Senator Calhoun among them, defended slavery by citing the Greek model. The value of slavery, the argument stated, was to provide an elite with the opportunity to pursue "societal and artistic enlightenment." "What would Socrates have accomplished had he been required to work in his family's cement business?" Calhoun wondered. The institution of slavery allowed the human race to move forward. A hierarchical society provided peace and stability.

Of course, nothing could be further from reality. Keeping an entire population in darkness in order to provide short-term shortsighted enlightenment to a few does not move society forward. Such activities shove society backwards and ultimately limit any perceived enlightenment. Put more obviously: **Enlightenment that is not circulated is not enlightening.**

Human tribes have always lived by the same rule: A skill that is not circulated (**shared**) has little benefit. Like an isolated flame, the skill will soon disappear. Human language allows skills to *circulate.* When it comes to human progress: Circulation is everything. Without circulation, investments in understanding are wasted.

Human geniuses, those who actually move humanity forward, rarely occur in the top elite. From Ben Franklin to Einstein, brilliant achievements inevitably come from hard **work** and a prosperous, large working class able to create and circulate **profits**.

Back to Greece: Capital is life. Enslaved humans are enslaved capital. Grand slave estates confounded the need for trade or small businesses. Because of slavery, **the labor of *free* people created less and less profit**. Slavery devalues free human life. All forms of *profit circulation*, including education and understanding, slowly diminish in unison.

Cultural entropy creates **polarization, population wars,** and **elitism.**

Society ignored the few philosophers—Socrates, Diogenes, the Cynics and Stoics (We could also include Buddha and Christ here)--who spoke against elitism, polarization, slavery, social inequities, and capital sequestration.

The demands of society—harshly criticized by Stoic thinkers at the time—made strict male and female roles obligatory and population wars **unavoidabl**e. (They still do.) Diogenes pointed out the problem in 400 BC, but no one apparently understood. Population wars devalue human life. They still do.

Diogenes in 400 BC felt social dictates pushed humans away from joy and communion with the gods. He chose, instead, to live joyfully nearly-naked in an abandoned wine cask without servants or the comforts of wealth. According to myth, when Alexander the Great visited the great teacher, he asked Diogenes what he could give him. Diogenes replied—to the world's richest person—he had no needs Alexander could fulfill. Diogenes then added, "Alexander's shadow was interfering with his (free) sunlight."

The mythical meeting between Diogenes and Alexander—if it occurred—compared monumentally different philosophies. Diogenes owned nothing but his freedom, but needed nothing. Alexander (a competitive capitalist) owned most of the world but yearned to violently grab more.

POLARIZATION AMONG THE ELITES

Alexander's conquests were counter-productive for his homeland. **Climax populations** throughout the Greek empire divided and fought against each other after Alexander's short reign. Status levels and slavery increased. Local powers opposed and refused to support central control. The weakness of central power diminished common infrastructures, roads, trade, and common economic prosperity. Alexander's vast conquests polarized into feuding parts. Far from uniting the world, Alexander's conquests eventually divided the world further.

And of course, no one knew why the crisis constantly grew worse. Greek politicians at the time blamed the decay on cultural impurity, lack of respect for the gods, lack of fighting spirit in the young, immorality, or philosophers like Socrates (who had the nerve to point out society's flawed incongruities). **Addressing such perceived problems achieved nothing, since these were not the real problems.**

2. THE ROMANS:
SLAVERY: AND the fall of the Roman Empire

The Roman army took over as the Greeks faded. The Roman civilization eventually died from the same progressive diseases as the Greeks: *Slavery* destroyed the middle class; and cultural polarization, and the lack of profit circulation eventually destroyed infrastructure. Without infrastructure—water, roads, education, soldiers, shared understandings, and trade—the capital **economy** of the empire could no longer stand.

The power of the early Roman army came from endless working-class men authorities could impress into service. These troops were not slaves or impoverished. They were young, healthy men from free farming communities.

Romans, like the Greeks, were proud of their farming heritages. Ulysses, a Greek King, was interrupted from plowing his fields to be impressed into the Trojan War. In 485 BC Cincinnatus was working in his fields when he was summoned to become dictator of Rome.

Early farms were quite small. When Romulus founded Rome in 750 BC, he divided the area into two-acre parcels, an area then considered appropriate for a family to support itself by hand. From these acreages, a family could theoretically support its needs and render some profit to trade for needed items, such as clothing, plows, or farm animals.

A farmer possessing an ox (technology) could double his production. Since farming was not year around, farmers could not only trade their produce, they could trade their free labor. In particular, farmers were available as soldiers when necessary.

Soil erosion and leeching eventually made larger plots necessary for survival. Wealthy men owning large tracts farmed with the aid of tenant farmers who divided the profits. Later, however, slaves (working for free) gradually replaced tenant farmers, and small farms disappeared altogether.

Many of the early communities beginning 1000 BC along the Italian peninsula practiced communal agriculture without individual ownership. Ownership arrived centuries later. In addition, many of these early communities did not necessarily consider themselves Romans. They spoke a variety of dialects, from Greek to Etruscan. But they faithfully served in Roman armies. They eventually created a common Roman state.

Much has been written about the Roman legion's fighting ability. Surely, Roman soldiers received prolonged training and had excellent fighting spirit. They were often rewarded for their victories with plunder from the losing states. So, in the early years of Rome, young men were often happy to serve.

But, fighting spirit aside, the sheer **numbers** of healthy Roman soldiers gave the empire its actual edge. The Italian peninsula possessed a nearly endless **number** of **free young working men**. And the Roman state possessed ample **profit** capital for new military campaigns. Older states, like Egypt, Greece, and Persia, had already lost their middle classes and were thus severely weakened.

Financially, the state generally expected to reward itself for successful campaigns at the cost of losing states. The rewards for Roman victories included new populations to enslave, outright plunder, and new tax revenues—all for personal and state enrichment. The Roman state could also control and tax trade across its conquered area. Widening Roman infrastructures also rewarded conquered territories.

So continual military campaigns made economic sense to early Romans; and the motivations were largely economic rather than heroic.

The Roman Genocides

Concurrent with an increasing population and decreasing crop yields (from slavery and erosion), Roman systematically targeted neighboring civilizations.

Marcus Porcius Cato recognized Rome's power rested on its ability to feed its soldiers. He urged war on Carthage in order to control the vast produce created by regular Nile floods. In the Third Punic War (149-146 BC), Roman armies torched Carthage, slaughtered and enslaved her inhabitants, and claimed her farming fields to feed Rome.

By this time, the two acre farm had disappeared economically. Wealthy individuals created larger and large acreages which they worked with tenant and slave labor. Eventually, tenant farmers were replaced completely by slaves. The changes left many free Romans without means to support themselves and hungry. Nile wheat was necessary to keep free Romans fed.

Incidental to common understanding, the Roman armies under Julius Caesar annihilated in a single decade nearly a million Europeans, and totally exterminated dozens of northern European tribes over many years. These tribes—forefathers to populations that eventually re-settled Europe and the new world--ceased to exist. Other Europeans died from famine and tribal wars when they were pushed from their native lands. Over a half million prisoners—mostly women and children—were taken as slaves by Caesar alone.

All this booty made Caesar very popular with most Romans, but not with the Senate—since he conducted many of these campaigns without permission. Most Romans considered northern Europeans to be filth, and thus Roman sensibilities were not upset by massacres.

Since Caesar ended up on top, only positive descriptions were possible of his genocidal efforts, and his heroic position has not eroded over time. Hitler was not so lucky, but he had the same idea—enable one status in society by murdering and enslaving another.

The fall of Rome began, not in defeat, but in excessive victory. In particular, the many victories enjoyed by Julius Caesar brought over a half million new slaves into the Roman system, a half million slaves into a system already glutted with slaves from other conquests—that is a lot of slaves.

With cheap slave labor, *free* Roman labor rapidly began to lose value; **free** family farms (not depending on slaves) began to disappear. As in Greece, small, **free**, family farms could no longer make a **profit**. At best they could survive at subsistence levels; at worst these free Romans were forced to sell themselves as slaves to *improve* their prospects. And when small family farms and small family businesses began to diminish, the middle class and the human capital needed to stock Roman legions strangely disappeared also.

To stay healthy a society must **share**, circulate-its-profits (**profits** created from **work**), an economic requirement about which Romans had not a clue. Slavery diminishes capital circulation; slavery does not allow a free middle, working class to **profit** from their common labor.

[Recall: Work (**profit**) is necessary to oppose entropy. Without work in opposition, entropy **always** increases.]

Eventually free workers were forced *to join in status* with enslaved workers, since neither status could reasonably **profit** from their labors. Without profits, profit capital is not available to circulate. A slave state ensues, consisting of a tiny super-wealthy elite and a population of workers in varying degrees of slavery.

Slave states over time are vulnerable to the polarizing forces of **cultural entropy**. Polarized cultures self-destruct into feuding states and undefended islands of lawlessness or **no man's lands.** *Entropy can only be opposed by focused work*; and when the **value of human work diminishes**, the forces of cultural **entropy** naturally dominate.

Strong **central governments** generally oppose the **polarizing** forces of entropy, but central governments depend on healthy capital circulation. Tyranny and militarism—the forces most often used by central governments under duress—generally **oppose** conditions necessary for healthy economies, so the negative conditions cycle downward.

When the profits from family farms disappear, the farms disappear as well. Soon after, once prosperous small towns built around prosperous family farms, diminish with their industries. Self-sufficient slave farms owned by the nobility increasingly dominate poorer rural areas. Capital ceases to circulate. Free labor, lacking resources, can no longer produce a capital profit; at best, small farmers exist at *subsistence*. The middle, or free, working class disappears, and the entire population is economically enslaved.

If family businesses make no profit, how can families: Educate their children? Grow their business? Stay in business? The answer is, without **profit** you can do none of those things; and when all the small businesses in a society go out of business, the society is soon out of business too. Oops! Bad business.

Those who took notice at the time could see the slow dissolution of their, once-great state--but Romans, like the Greeks, had difficulty focusing on the real **reasons why**. Time dimmed their understandings. They accepted a constantly diminishing **status quo** as perfection and opposed all progressive change.

Politicians made impassioned speeches against Rome's phantom enemies—immorality, disrespect for the gods, the decadent younger generation, racial mixing, immigration, lack of military courage, and religious discord. None of these had any real value. They were not the real problems. These arguments, however, made excellent political rhetoric and diverted from actual solutions. Does this sound familiar? It should.

The pagans blamed the Christians. Later, when the Christians took over, they blamed the pagans. And later yet, when the pagans were eliminated by **intolerance**, the Christians blamed each other. Bloody civil wars erupted between intolerant Christians over differing interpretations of arcane scriptures, scriptural *differences* even wise men did not understand.

Had the Romans taken the trouble to actually count their diminishing resources, they may have noticed the real problems—capital hoarding, a disappearing working class, land erosion, resource depletion, lack of capital creation or profit circulation, no man's lands, infrastructure degradation, cultural polarization, unfair laws to protect the status quo, population wars (causing excessive populations), **numbers**, and the disease of slavery were the common causes.

The great harvest taken from the Nile allowed Rome to feed the excessive number of its peoples and continue defending itself long after it population and economy would have otherwise crashed due to the accumulated erosions of cultural entropy.

Capital, or profit, the life-blood of *a successful economy*, no longer flowed. Sequestered in the hands of a few, the lack of circulating capital and the competition of slavery denied free men a profit from their labors. Without profits, nothing was free to circulate. Free men could not find jobs even at subsistence. Does this sound familiar?

With the value of skills of low value, capital values of education and enlightenment could no longer circulate. Lacking *common cultural understandings*, the Roman *culture* dried up.

Foreign invaders did not destroy the Roman culture; greed and the forces of entropy created slave states; slave states placed most of the Romanized population in such desperate poverty, the common culture divided into warring tribes and disappeared.

To repeat the story: Over time, capital profit filters up, not down, and *stays* at the top. Climax populations enjoy positions that allow them to limit resources to others and to accumulate additional capital for themselves. Soon the elites, assisted by repressive laws, accumulate nearly everything—yes, everything, all the land, all the capital. This **everything** does not **circulate** (is not shared).

Capital is life. Without circulating capital profits, civilizations cannot prosper. Without blood flow, the patient dies. The story is actually quite simple.

To repeat again and again (sorry, but it seems important):

When capital congests in slaves and when climax populations dominate resources, when population numbers stress resources, the value of *free* human labor falls to zero, profit disappears, capital ceases to circulate, the middle class dies, the few free individuals remaining have **no profits** to educate their children or themselves, commerce diminishes, knowledge capital stops circulating, and central power slowly withers. Traders and trading towns die out because they find no one to buy their goods, no **profits** to trade, and no central power to protect needed **trading infrastructures**.

Education and human understandings are expensive in time and calories. Recall, humans use most of their calories in social, not physical, growth. Free Romans had no profit capital to educate their children.

To continue to circulate, knowledge or intellectual capital must continue to create a profit--even if that profit is merely emotional security or increased understanding—in other words, to complete a healthy cycle, all capital, like blood, must **circulate**, particularly **understanding**.

Truth and change are the enemies of slave states. Lies and superstition are the pillars of slave states. Climax populations on the top *must* commit to the status quo, because the status quo is the climax population's reason to be on the top. If the status quo—whatever it is—is perfectly right, then all other arguments must be absolutely wrong. To protect the perfect status quo, all other arguments and the truths they contain, must be squashed.

D. THE CIRCULATION OF IGNORANCE:

If understanding is the most valuable human capital, then the opposite of understanding, ignorance, occurs during capital blight, when authorities halt the circulation of information capital.

The greatest human-caused disasters occur when human understandings are overcome by the blight of ignorance. Without circulation, the organism dies.

HOW IGNORANCE IS THE DIRECT RESULT OF CONGESTED CAPITAL CIRCULATION:

The belief in lies and superstition, **ignorance**, is a self-replicating meme that grows exponentially in the absence of circulating truth and understanding. Note: Human understanding is a capital item. Human language is the primary technology of cooperative capitalism. (Recall: Cooperative capitalism, as opposed to competitive capitalism, does not require we violently eat each other.)

We must emphasize: Truths and understandings are **real**, capital items that elevate humans and allow human societies to grow and prosper. Humans put most of their energy calories into constructing human understandings. These **understandings** are *real* items of value; they represent significant calorie investment; and these invested calories do not simply disappear—they function as **real** tools to allow human societies to survive. The circulation of these capital tools for survival is of extreme importance.

We can't argue that only good things happen when truth freely circulates, although the hope is strong. But we can seriously maintain: Terrible things nearly always happen when truth **fails** to circulate—wars, famines, ethnic cleansing, civil misunderstanding, and inquisitions, to name a few. Such human horrors result from human beings over-reacting to extreme feelings based largely on **ignorance**.

Building a house based on ignorance and errors will likely create an unsafe situation for those needing a home. Ignorance also leads directly to situations that waste the value of human life and destroy the future.

Most important, ignorance festers and grows most strongly in **extreme** situations wherein **extreme emotions** dominate—such as **no man's lands** and population wars in which verifiable truths cannot reasonably circulate.

So extremes create ignorance and vice versa, and the results lead directly to *the terrible chaos and despair most humans perceive as **evil***.

Thus, the origin of most evil is not an invisible Satan, but a visible **ignorance**. This is not to infer that some sort of pure evil does not exist in human society. Sexual predators and sadistic murderers apparently enjoy the suffering of others. Monsters, slave owners, and predators steal the capital of others without compassion. Egotistical humans will happily sacrifice all others to advance their own desires.

Are these people evil? Or are they simply ignorant, selfish, thoughtless, or themselves victims of extreme, crazed emotions common people cannot understand?

In the end, the argument is without an easy solution. But if we look for Satan to fight against, we seek something impossible to find. On the contrary, ignorance is all around us, ignorance is easily identified using verified truth, ignorance is real, and we can all take a stand against it.

NOTE: TO EXIST, A SLAVE STATE DOES *NOT* REQUIRE TYRANTS OR VILLAINS; IT MERELY REQUIRES THE ABSENCE OF PROFITABLE WORK AND CAPITAL BLOOD FLOW TO A SIGNIFICANT PERCENT OF ITS POPULATION. THE LACK OF CAPITAL PUTS EVEN FREE INDIVIDUALS INTO A STATE OF SLAVERY TO WHOEVER CAN FEED THEM.

E. NO MAN'S LANDS - INFRASTRUCTURE DESTRUCTION: DESTRUCTION OF THE MIDDLE, INTOLERANCE, POLARIZATION, GANGS, AND LAWLESSNESS.

Until the first century, Roman cities, like early Greek cities, experienced *prosperous* growth and growing capital circulation. Bubbles of **profit** from free human labor moved up the hierarchy; these capital bubbles moved throughout the empire and stimulated and funded the growth of infrastructure and central government, the Appian Way and the Roman aqueducts.

In the first century BC, reading grew increasingly common among free Romans. Free Romans could afford educations for their children.

By the forth century AD, however, reading throughout the entire Roman Empire began to grow uncommon. The problem was poverty. Each generation grew less able to feed itself. Funding education was not possible.

The control of resources and property fell from a large working class into the hands of a small elite. <u>The labor of free Romans had no value</u>. Romans had no profit or understanding to circulate. In the absence of shared understanding, the meme of ignorance dominated Roman civilization.

Over the years, the Roman way captured the bordering states around it. Tribes that had once thrived as free peoples adopted the Roman *slave* state as their own. The vise tightened throughout Europe.

After the third century, Rome was forced to hire mercenary troops from northern Europe and Asia to defend itself. Rome's middle class disappeared. Individual slave states grew less dependent on Roman central power. Without central power, without jobs, lawlessness and **no man's lands** grew, and trade diminished further. Rome fell slowly bit-by-bit into chaos, without anyone realizing why.

Some inner cities today may be defined as NO MAN'S LANDS. Criminal elements prey on the cycle of capital and limit circulation and the creation of safe infrastructures.

THE BARBARIAN HOARDS

Many historians *still* blame the fall of Rome on barbarian invasions. But a Roman state with a healthy middle class had no difficulty repelling barbarian encroachments. During Rome's growth period, Rome was the aggressor, and barbarian tribes were the unfortunate, hapless, eventually enslaved victims.

Bare in mind, many barbarian invaders, by the fifth century, were actually Christians; and many invading leaders had previously served the Roman army. In its final years, *immigrants and immigrant armies were what primarily kept Rome together.*

The true story is: Rome disintegrated internally with little outside help. Many city-states sought independence; they vigorously opposed fellow states and central government; they feared Roman imperial power far more than foreign invaders.

Barbarian hoards largely consisted of middle-class farmers, free men, not slaves, possessing family assets. They generally possessed their own family weapons and livestock and fought for self-enrichment.

Far from destroying Rome, **immigrant** communities and immigrant generals were the heroes who **sustained** Rome in its final centuries. In the final hours, when Rome was under siege, neighboring Italian states of Florence and Ravenna were unable to cooperate in mutual defense. Under Alaric (a Christian) Visigoth, a force of, at best 40,000 soldiers—nearly half, recently freed slaves—was able to pillage an empire of up to ten million Romans (about half in slavery) and much of Southern Italy (existing in terrible poverty) without common opposition. States feared, if they sent forces to assist other states, they would suffer, themselves, slave rebellions. And after the fall, polarized Italian states did not take steps to re-create common Roman infrastructure. They possessed inadequate capital.

The population of Rome plunged from 800,000 to 500,000 in 410, and later to a few hundred thousand in 455.

In the following centuries, the Italian peninsula and much of Europe reverted to **tribal slave states**. Attempts by later emperors to reunite the empire met with recurrent failures. The common Roman family (common **sharing** economy) disappeared.

Cultural entropy, ignorance, poverty, polarization, and slavery destroyed imperial Rome. **The final Barbarian invasions were an anticlimax.**

SELL YOUR CHILDREN HERE (CHEAP):
With the value of human free labor at zero, free Romans sold their own children and themselves into slavery to keep from starving. Slaves had more value than free people. (Slaves had access to resources through their owners. Free men, who owned nothing, had access to no resources.) By the forth century, the practice of accepting slavery over freedom became common.

All free humans who held no resources were eventually enslaved to their poverty, whether they sold themselves outright or not. Freedom means nothing without resources to make human labor valuable—this is still true today. The human capital that had once led Rome to world dominance no longer held worth. Julius Caesar, the greatest Roman hero, with the intoxicating lure of cheap slaves, shares much of the blame.

Ch. 5 THESE HUMAN INVENTIONS DIMINISH CAPITAL CIRCULATION

Note: Slavery was never officially **abolished** in early Europe; slavery simply became ***unnecessary***—those without capital were physically **bonded by their poverty.** *Capital enslavement created human enslavement throughout the entire society.* The point was made and did not require emphasis.

The situation is still true today.

<u>**Social development may be divided into epochs as follows:**</u>
Early development and settlement
Working class growth with capital profit circulation
Mature growth and social stratification
Middle Class diminishment
Climax populations drain capital flow
Slave states divided by no man's lands
Economic and philosophical stagnation
Warfare between divided States

A society may be stagnated or cerebrally dead even if it has not yet abandoned its population centers and community icons.

F. HUMAN *CLIMAX POPULATIONS* CREATE GROWING STAGNATION

Elite climax populations took over as Rome aged, but these began to shrink as well, to ever smaller, isolated, and polarized elites. Eventually, the darkness of ignorance and poverty moves upwards, overwhelming even those at the top.

For many years during the dark ages, travel between Italian cities was no longer safe. The lack of connecting infrastructure added to cultural polarization and economic inactivity.

The truth is: Even populations that *own* everything suffer when the body weakens—the rich see their assets constantly diminish in value; and they are entrapped in constant battles simply to stay where they are. Wars erupt over disordered pieces of a constantly diminishing pie.

Realize that even middle class Romans enjoyed bathing, indoor plumbing, and relaxing spas in the first century. But even kings in the Middle Ages seldom bathed, and pests that spread cruel afflictions tormented their lack of hygiene.

The point is: When infrastructures disappear, the plumbing also disappears.

Climax populations of privileged aristocrats became trapped in immobile positions--parasites, ignorance, and enemies continually harassed them. Warfare was constant; but victories were shallow and of short duration.

Consider Hamlet. He was not a happy prince. The life of a privileged aristocrat merely gave him torment. His elevated position constantly demanded unremitting defense and conflict. He reasonably found the struggle senseless and vain; he realized the endless struggle led nowhere.

Hamlet might have preferred the enlightened life of a scholar and freethinker, but that life was not possible. He was stuck in a box that gave his mind no alternative except to play the same violent game his ancestors had all played, a **no-sum game** of competitive capitalism (human conflict) that could not be won by anyone (as Shakespeare's play brilliantly illuminates).

The downward struggle eventually twists a vise around every level of society. Everyone loses.

Entrenched hierarchies can often withstand substantial blows that decimate the peasant stratus below them. In time of food shortages, the elites, if they control the military, can command the foods they require and survive while masses of peasants perish. Aristocrats may historically stay safe in their castles, while surrounding peasant villages are burnt and looted by invaders.

After such catastrophes, the hierarchy may reestablish control; thus the continuity of top hierarchies may commonly be greater than the bottom of society.

Hierarchies, however, are still vulnerable, and during times of economic strife, those vulnerabilities are greatest. A city-state is most apt to be attacked by a competing tribal state when it is weakened by food shortages or military setbacks.

Even more common, the forces of cultural entropy work on weak hierarchies in time of strife to create feuding divisions *within* the hierarchy. Cultural divisions can further weaken a culture and keep that culture from maintaining the necessary infrastructures—roads, canals, and protection of trade routes—to allow capital to flow successfully.

Again, capital is life. Without successful capital circulation, the quality of human life diminishes. Untruths diminish the successful circulation of capital.

The same story repeats again and again, from China to the new world. When the elite come to own too much, capital profits cease circulating. Without access to resources, human labor loses its value.

Increasing populations (cultural wars) put increasing pressures on *resources*. Without resources, human labor can create limited profits. Darkness grows from the bottom and eventually encloses the top. The central culture splits again and again into antagonistic, hierarchic states that engage in population wars against each other.

Without central power, infrastructures disappear and lawless *no-man's-lands* dominate. No toilets for anyone.

Constant warfare and cultural intolerance may dominate for centuries, devaluing all human life. Eventually, a tyrant appears to violently conquer all opposition and reinstall central government. This tyrant may recreate lost infrastructure or not.

Plagues and no man's lands can severely diminish populations with sick infrastructures. Then the divisive processes of cultural entropy begins again. The process repeats and repeats. This is human history.

G. __PURITANITY__ assists Cultural Entropy

We will encounter ***puritanity*** often in human cultures. From emotional human extremes evolves the concept of purifying a culture by exclusion of all elements deemed *less than perfect*.

The exclusion process is somewhat similar to organic systems that exclude by **intolerance**, any organism they deem inferior or different. However, in human systems, the puritanity exclusion process grows more subjective.

Some religions and cultures exclude those adherents who do not *strictly* abide by perceived codes of understanding. Puritanical systems can exclude others on increasingly smaller degrees of difference. By encouraging **puritanity**, leadership isolates their adherents under very specific authority, their own—those able to differentiate these increasingly smaller differences between other sects.

By magnifying differences and minimizing similarities, movements can **polarize** their adherents. Jihad is an attempt to unify religion under a single code; but when utilized, the puritanity of jihad creates polarized states, creating a situation counter to the stated purpose of unity.

In Christianity, one religion has divided into dozens of religions largely due to regional differences and the concept of **puritanity**.

In legislative systems, ***puritanity*** divides opinion and makes consensus impossible.

In human relationships, *puritanity* inflames conflict and creates separations. Each party assumes an extreme, puritanical view that cannot be reconciled.

PURITANITY ADDS TO THE FORCES OF CULTURAL ENTROPY TO DIVIDE CULTURAL AND FAMILY STRUCTURES.

H. WHY DO KILLER BUNNIES NOT EXIST?

Often the reasons things don't happen may be as meaningful as the reasons things do happen. But science usually has difficulty addressing non-happenings. In fact, when non-observed things fail to happen, science can sometimes be stubborn and uncomprehending.

Many important non-observed happenings come to mind, but one, in particular is especially pertinent to the evolution of life—the killer bunny problem.

The fact is, bunnies have been around for millions of years, but killer bunnies have not developed. Even considering the slow movement of evolution, these bunnies have had plenty of time to evolve into killing creatures, capable of defending themselves and going on the offensive. What are they waiting for? Are they just lazy? Bunnies are not noted for progressive thinking. They continue to allow themselves to be killed and eaten by creatures even smaller than themselves. Evolving a single deadly claw or a poisonous bite would solve the bunnies' problem, but it hasn't happened.

And bunnies are not alone regarding their lack of initiative. We might also consider shrews. These little beasts have the potential to overwhelm all other creatures, but they desist. Shrews possess one of the most powerful physiques in the animal world, a remarkably strong backbone, razor sharp teeth, a very poisonous bite, and even, yes, echolocation. With fast metabolisms, shrews in captivity can eat one half to twice their body weight in prey daily and have ten litters in one year.

Wake up shrews! The world is yours! You merely need to grow a bit larger—not a difficult task—and take over. But for millions of years shrews have chosen to remain small and hide in burrows or sleep under leaf litter. There is no excuse for such indolence.

Even Hollywood has noticed the problem. In a 1959 movie, directed by Ray Kellog, scientific experiments on a small island cause shrews to grow to wolf-like proportions (strangely resembling Doberman pincers and German Shepherds with wild hair does). These stylish shrews destroy and terrorize everyone, even the humans on the island; these humans make a last stand in Bermuda shorts and high heels as shrews rip through the walls of their laboratory. The howling horror only ends when, lo and behold, the hungry shrews have eaten everything edible on the island and thus starve themselves to death. The shrews solve their own problem. They are a self-annihilating species. Total dominance is self-destructive in an environment that depends on diversity.

Perhaps Hollywood has thus solved the problem of killer bunnies. Bunnies don't evolve as offensive creatures, because to do so—to eliminate their predators—would only lead to bunny starvation. Killer bunnies would be a self-annihilating species. Bunnies have chosen to die quickly from predation, rather than slowly and painfully from starvation and disease. They have chosen life quality over life quantity. Smart bunnies.

But after some thought—something not common in many Hollywood films—we must recognize the Hollywood answer, like most Hollywood answers, is only vaguely representative of truth.

Starvation might act quickly on a small island. But on a large continent, even killer shrews might take decades to consume everything. Evolution does not take quality of life in mind when changes occur. Numbers only are important. Nothing can actually prevent self-annihilating beast to evolve.

In the millions of years of evolution, life may have been devastated or pushed to the brink on many occasions by self-annihilating species. Scientist often suspected destructive viruses and pathogens as extinction events, before the more visible effects of falling meteors stole the show. Dinosaurs were overwhelmed by the sudden dominance of mammals, possibly in bunny form; this was a theme seriously considered in past centuries.

But reality has intervened. Apparently the many diverse interdependent cycles of nature are sufficient to skew the numbers against the common appearance of self-annihilating bunnies on *most* occasions.

Species evolve, not to establish greater individual dominance or personal perfection; rather, evolution works independently of individual members to maintain raw numbers at maximum and stable levels. Numbers stability has common value to living organisms. Any self-annihilating species is stifled in its quest for total dominance by its own need for general capital circulation and stability; otherwise we would see the situation occurring more often.

The algorithm of life must depend on many mutual balances. A too dominant species generally skews the balance to its own annihilation and nature returns to normal. But simply because self-annihilating species are rare does not mean they can't occur or haven't occurred in the past.

And that brings us to humans. Oops. Humans are far more dominant than killer bunnies would be, even if they slashed out with the vicious claws they don't possess. Humans have overwhelmed all our predators. Only pathogens and self-destructive warfare keeps killer humans from eating everything on the planet and starving to non-existence.

Humans have become a self-annihilating species. But unlike the shrews, we are not living on a small island. The human island is the entire world, and it is taking some time for us to consume everything here. Humans may be slow to the table, but we are on our way.

Humans have thus proven, nature's balance is not inviolable. Self-annihilating creatures are possible.

Now, how about killer bunnies? Perhaps carnivorous bunnies will arrive late in the day to save the world from us. Or perhaps humans will evolve to control themselves. Both scenarios are possible.

I. FAMILY VALUES decay over time.
The theme should now be clear: The forces of cultural entropy decay family values over time. Family values—sharing capital and

capital understandings—are the glue that keeps human families united. When such values decay and disappear due to the pressures of entropy and time, eternal warfare pushes disunited humanity to Armageddon.

The human species is an annihilation species. Nothing can stop us but ourselves. To survive we must make reasonable decisions as a single family.

Family values decay over time unless opposed by work.

The time story:

The story goes--If cruel people toss a frog in boiling water, it will instantly leap out without damage, but if these same cruel people leave that same frog in water and gradually increase the temperature, the frog will remain motionless until it dies.

Whether the story is true or not, it serves as a lesson. Often, we fail to react to slow changes because we simply do not understand anything is changing. Even if we are bound in misery, we accept the status quo as inviolable and protect the system that imprisons us--even as that system makes life more and more unbearable.

Older people become more and more bonded to whatever status quo they have learned to accept. Young people can be less fearful of change and less invested in the old. But change is always difficult.

Religious and cultural norms usually favor the status quo. Why? By definition: Religious and cultural norms are what the status quo is.

Most humans find it simpler to stay in scalding water than to take a leap of faith into an undefined future.

So how do we get <u>out</u> of the boiling water? Before anything else, we need to realize we are <u>in</u> boiling water.

Ch. 6 HOW CULTURAL ENTROPY DECAYS HUMAN FAMILIES

CH 6 –
How Cultural Entropy Decays Human Families

ENTROPY WORKS UNIQUELY IN HUMAN ECONOMIES TO STIFLE CAPITAL CIRCULATION, POLARIZE POPULATIONS, AND ASSIST FORCES OF CHAOS AND CONFLICT: CAPITAL IS LIFE. CULTURAL ENTROPY OPERATES DIFFERENTLY IN HUMAN CULTURES THAN IN BACTERIAL CULTURES. REASONS INCLUDE:

A. STATUS LEVELS
B. HUMAN EXTREME EMOTIONS: CHAOS, CONTRARY CONSEQUENCES, EGOTISM,
C. PURITANITY AIDES CULTURAL ENTROPY TO DIVIDE RELIGIOUS BELIEFS
D. HOW CLIMAX POPULATIONS: OWNERSHIP LAWS CAN OPPOSE CAPITAL CIRCULATION
E. HOW CULTURAL WARS/POPULATION WARS CREATE WAR-STRUCTURED CULTURES
F. HOW CULTURAL ENTROPY CORRODES DEMOCRATIC INSTITUTIONS AND THE LEGISLATIVE PROCESSES
G. THE IMPORTANT OF TRUTH FOR CAPITAL CIRCULATION
    The Soviet Food Crisis

    Cultural entropy works in simple, biological cultures to create intolerance and divisions. **Cultural entropy** works similarly in human cultures.
    However, due to human emotions, ego, human cultural organizations, biased laws, and language changes, the effects of cultural entropy ***magnify*** in human societies.

A. CULTURAL ENTROPY CREATES STATUS LEVELS

In the same way cultural entropy works over time to divide cultures into antagonistic, competing hierarchies, cultural entropy works **within** a culture to divide that culture horizontally into separate, status levels.

Yeast and slimes form films of different statuses. Some elite films are close to resources; other films are close to corrosive forces. The mutual films share some resources and gain some advantage from specialization and cooperation. Elite films, however, gain more than low status films. Low status films may be little more than dead-end sacrificial structures. The differing films do not cooperate and share capital like a single organism.

The human capital story is similar: Capital flow between status levels or between feuding states can create inequities. At times, the elites hold capital out of circulation, starving those below them. Intolerance and violence between status levels occurs in the same way as when a society splits into intolerant, separate, feuding states.

The results in both cases include economic necrosis, class warfare, infrastructure destruction, lack of understandings, and greater intolerance over time.

India is an area in which human status levels have been entrenched over many years. In early-history, status levels simplified social organization into specialty occupations. Over time however, status levels grew more and more restrictive, both of human desires to progress, and of the flow of capital throughout the society.

Status levels act much like legalized slavery by enslaving humans and capital within confined limits. Social limits deny capital circulation and dampen creation of capital profits. Capital is life. Limits on capital flow devalue all life.

Slime films may not mind being devalued; humans often do.

Humans may often think, by devaluing others they make themselves rise up to a higher status. "I may not be much, but I'm better than you!"

Historically, however, status levels, like slavery, act with some uniformity to devalue the profitability of *all* human life. When free labor has little value, free laborers cannot receive profit from their work—so not only labor, but human freedom, loses its value.

Those who enjoy elite status may *appear* to benefit from the cheap labor of others, but economic-stagnation and infrastructure-decay historically permeate even the rarified levels of society—as experienced in the dark ages and in many areas of the world today.

When infrastructures disappear, so does the hot tub. Large enslaved populations leading lives of low value create societies in which *all* human life is of less relative value. The central problem is capital circulation: Societies, in which human labor cannot create profits and capital fails to circulate, are societies in which human life has diminished economic and human value.

B. EXTREME HUMAN EMOTIONS FROM CHAOS, ADD TO ENTROPY EFFECTS, and CREATE CONTRARY CONSEQUENCES

1. Emotions from Chaos

Human emotions are often (described as) unpredictable, quixotic, and self-destructive. Emotions evolve from semi-chaotic chemical reactions that can be volatile in young humans. In mature adults, emotions are not completely random, but neither are they completely governed by logic or reason or even consciousness.

Random human emotions relate to randomness in nature. This apparent randomness in human thinking may greatly assist human cognitive abilities and human survival.

Our dreams and imaginings throw up wild possibilities for future actions. We can sort out from these possible actions, particular activities that may give us survival advantages.

Without random, somewhat chaotic thoughts, we might not be able to think at all. So we should be grateful to the forces of entropy for our abilities to cogitate, and at the same time we must keep vigilant to control the chaotic, emotional forces within us that would lead us into eternal chaos and conflict.

Sleep is necessary in all animals. Some feel the primary reason for sleep is to allow our brains time to (chaotically) regenerate. We are paralyzed during sleep so these chaotic activities will not cause us or others harm. Denied sleep, humans will grow emotionally unstable and eventually sicken and die.

Chaotic human emotions evolve directly from entropic forces in nature and contribute to the divisive powers—from the same origins—that destroy human civilizations and human relationships.

Songwriter, Bob Dylan, exclaims, "If my thought-dreams could be seen, they'd probably put my head in a guillotine." Thought-dreams come from chaos, and may appear evil. We all see an array of random possible actions before us, and some of them may cause pain to others. We are not evil to possess extreme thoughts; we are only evil if we allow extreme thoughts (evil or ignorance) to control us.

Some psychotic individuals have extreme difficulties controlling their chaotic thoughts. To survive, humans have suffered the gantlet of wild thoughts for millions of years. The process (from chaos to reason) is not always easy. **Extreme** emotions can sometimes gain control (Hitler) and lead to terrible conflict.

2. The Theory of Overreaction and Contrary Consequence:

Extreme emotions often create consequences totally opposite to those expected. Human emotions can have Ping-Pong effects, spewing out reactions at random angles.

For example: A father reacts in extreme anger to his daughter's low grades. The daughter reacts emotionally to her father's anger by abandoning her studies totally—the unforeseen consequence is the opposite of what was hoped. Often extreme emotions and extreme actions simply cause extreme actions in opposition.

Revenge cycles, of extreme actions and extreme reactions, can grow like cancers in human events without any hope of resolution. The *Iliad*, by Homer, written 2500 years ago is such an event. [See Ch. 9, 10 – The Absurd Movement in Art].

Well-meaning human legislators often draft legal resolutions with consequences exactly opposite to those intended. Laws banning alcohol and drugs historically have contrary effects. Prohibitions can make drugs more—rather than less—attractive and available to users. Excessive profits from illegal sales, in the hands of criminals, can corrupt all parts of government. Removing drugs from distribution only increases the profits for remaining products; greater profits motivate renewed and continued illegal activities.

Contrary consequences are often the result of well-meaning individuals seeking to create *puritanity* in their social or religious systems. [See **puritanity** Ch. 3, 5]

EXTREME EMOTIONS IN HUMAN LEADERS

3. Egotism is an **extreme** emotion. Extreme violent emotions uniformly lead to human antagonism and polarization. Few humans reach positions of great power without great egos. Millions upon millions of humans have perished in clashes between **extreme** egos.

Check online: According to *all* major religious beliefs, **ego** is the primary obstacle that separates humans from God and our search for nirvana. Unifying emotions, on the contrary--love, humility, caring, tranquility, contentment, calm, and the desire for common understanding—these lead us away from ego and violence and *toward* God.

Moderation, however, is the absolute key. ***All emotions grow toxic in their extremities.*** Extreme emotions lead us from reason to blind ignorance.

Ego, however, will always be popular in the human consciousness. Egotists possess an abnormal need to make themselves feel important and to place themselves over the selves of others; so egotists are uniquely drawn to **positions of importance and authority**, politics and the ministry. In listing their own faults, ministers place egotism, along with lust, as major impediments to their relationships with God. Politicians apparently have no faults.

Is Heaven a place we have matured beyond ego? Some think so.

Modern times are filled with examples in which **the extreme emotions of egotism** lead to catastrophes and in the opposite direction from God.

If ego has so many painful effects, and is disproved by all major religions, why is ego so persistent in the human soul? Well, the answer is quite simple: Ego, the need for importance, is a primitive survival mechanism that cannot be easily set aside. Capital is stuff that is important to life. If life did not consider itself important, it might choose not to keep living. Ego, like lust, is a part of the human body, like arms or legs; these cannot be severed without serious penalty otherwise.

We are capital. Capital is important stuff. To continue living we must feel we have *some* importance. But if we seek tranquility and social unity, we must avoid the ego **extremes** that push us away from God and peace and other humans.

Our *sense of self* develops into our sense of ego. We will discuss in greater detail how the sense of self assists survival in organisms and can be beneficially extended to family and society. [Ch. 8 – The Sense of Self]

C. PURITANITY: CULTURAL ENTROPY CREATES PURITANICAL INTOLERANCE AND DIVISIONS IN RELIGIOUS BELIEFS
THE CONTINUING STORY OF CONTRARY CONSEQUENCES AND COUNTER PRODUCTIVE ACTIONS:

Entropy works on all cultural *concepts* over time to dissemble and divide, particularly when these concepts are scattered topographically. Religious beliefs often suffer from the concept of **PURITANITY,** whereby the idea of cleansing or purifying the practice, can create isolated sects that are mutually **intolerant**.

Puritanity demonstrates the principal of contrary consequence, in which human emotions create consequences exactly opposite to what is desired.

In the years after its origination, Christianity changed from small informal practices within homes to highly ritualized theocracies. The leadership of these theocracies split often over dogmatic differences; the different Christian sects quickly characterized each other as apostates. Each competing sect was **intolerant** of other Christian practices, often more than pagan practices.

Central theological powers utilized maximum penalties to maintain control. Civil wars eventually split the Christian faith into eastern and western denominations. Numerous splinter groups separated topographically, finding safety in their distance from central power.

Central church authority struggled to put down violently any beliefs that opposed unified powers—these included both pagan beliefs and other Christian beliefs.

However, in the fourteenth century, the central church began to lose control, as the power of central governments in Europe grew. Splinter groups begun by well-known protestant reformers, Calvin and Luther, were now free to split the central church into sects that generally **conformed to nationality**. These groups, in efforts to re-purify themselves, split again and again into many of the denominations we recognize today.

The differences in these denominations are often quite indeterminate and difficult to understand by modern standards. Many denominations, like the several Puritan sects, made themselves stand apart by their greater and greater degrees of severity in dress and behavior. Such distinctions of what is best called, **puritanity**, allowed further and further separations of Christian denominations based on increasingly *smaller* differences.

Egotistic leaders insisted on strict interpretations of their own divisive (puritanical) views over compromises.

The many Christian religions we encounter today are products of time and cultural entropy, in which small differences, like random movements, continue to increase over time, unless forced together by a tyrannical center or re-united by **work** toward common consensus.

Puritanical human emotions combine with the forces of cultural entropy to create divisive social effects—these changes are random, not products of reasonable human planning.

The Muslim religion experienced similar splits due to **cultural entropy**, within the first few generations of its conception, into what we now recognize as Shia and Sunni denominations, plus numerous ethnic sects. The practice of *Jihad* originated out of desires by devout practitioners to *purify* the Muslim religion. However, like other practices of **puritanity** and intolerance, the results are often violent, divisive, and counter-productive.

As in the Christian religion, practices of *puritanity*, or Jihad, consistently produced more—rather that less—division and rancor. Jihad divided Muslims, while the crusades and the Catholic Inquisition divided Christianity. Extreme emotions consistently produce more extreme emotions, not consensus. Extreme emotions create **contrary consequences**.

Cultural entropy and **puritanity** divide major religions over increasingly minor dogmas and superficial differences. Such differences include language, dress, cultural affiliations, nationalism, and just about anything over which humans can disagree.

We might mention at this point that both Muslim and Christian religions would have split into many, many more schisms over time except for the tyrannical power of central theological forces; these forces worked ceaselessly to violently exterminate all forms of rebellion over thousands of years.

Simultaneously, central tyranny extinguishes many of the simple precepts, created by their prophets, which make religions meaningful and God reachable to their followers.

In general, central powers strive to stifle separations, both religious and civil. However, the forces of **cultural entropy** are persistent over many years and continue when central powers wane. So, while central power can extinguish schisms in the short run, the tendency-of-systems-to-randomly-split will outlive the reign of most central powers. So today, the divisions of all religions into ever smaller, ever-more i**ntolerant** sects, is greater than at any time previously.

Also important, cultural and religious divisions occasionally occur simply because they are easy. The Mormon religion, for example, a Christian split, experienced extreme central control in its infancy, particularly due to intolerance from the larger Christian society. When external intolerance diminished, central control in the Mormon religion also diminished, and schisms grew more common. The Hebrew religion, the Sikhs, Muslims, Christians, to name a few—all benefit to a certain degree from external intolerance; and they suffer entropy and internal divisions when *external* intolerance diminishes.

Read about speciation (Ch. 2).

D. **CLIMAX POPULATIONS—Trees in the Forest**
[See Ch. 1 – Climax populations diminish diversity.]

A climax forest occurs after many years, when the tallest trees take over. These tall trees can claim most of the sunlight; and they also possess deep roots that can access most of the available resources.

Most people walk into a climax forest, a forest of tall trees, and feel they are walking into an animal paradise, a place where bear, and deer, and rabbits, and all manner of animals can live in abundance. Actually, the opposite is true. A climax forest is a difficult place for many animal species.

In truth, a climax forest holds a dark, dark secret--beneath its tall branches, in the darkness, few plants can grow. And where few plants grow, few large animals can survive.

Most humans like to think of a climax forest as a beautiful and perfect paradise, but it often is a place of scarcity. Fortunately—with great drama—most forests burn regularly. After a fire, grasses and other plants return with food for rabbits and deer.

Ch. 6 HOW CULTURAL ENTROPY DECAYS HUMAN FAMILIES

The point is: A climax forest can tie up capital resources for hundreds of years, far away from hungry mouths, but eventually those resources circulate again, and a new cycle begins. Most forests are transitional—in other words, they are in differing states of crisis recovery before they reach their final, climax state. Transitional forests, not climax forests, provide much of the food for large herbivores to survive. And in nature, most climax forests are only momentary.

All economies, animal or human, depend on capital **circulation**. No healthy circulation; no diverse economy.

In human societies, climax populations can similarly tie up capital resources and leave the statuses below them in scarcity and darkness, particularly if they are unaware of the need for general capital circulation and regeneration.

PERPETUAL OWNERSHIP CAN STIFLE CAPITAL CIRCULATION

Legal ownership does not exist in biological systems. Ownership in nature simply means forceful possession. Thus capital in nature is in continual **circulation**; it belongs only momentarily to whatever organism can command the moment.

A water buffalo owns its *own* capital only so long as a lion or tiger does not violently take its life as food. A predator commands a territory only so long as its power is greater than other predators. An octopus owns its garden only so long as a larger octopus or shark doesn't drop by to claim the territory. A pine tree claims its dominion only until felled by disease, fire, or ax. Etc, etc...

So, in nature, all capital assets circulate continually; but this circulation is not voluntary or without conflict. **In nature, competitive capitalism is violent.**

Farmland is useless to human societies unless that farmland can be reasonably protected—possessed—by that society, and the harvest shared by those who **work** the ground. If farmers lose their harvest to thieves, the entire tribe may starve. So early human societies organized to protect common resources, to keep human capital from being grabbed by others. Most human laws revolve around ownership or claiming resources. **Cooperative capitalism** depends on laws that allow profits to be created and peacefully traded (**shared**).

No man's lands are areas in which properties cannot be defended. When people cannot farm, they starve.

Large tribes could defend larger resource areas than small tribes, first for hunter gathering, later for herding and farming. Tribes, that could not protect their resources, disappeared. A primary reason for humans to form larger and larger tribal units was that larger tribes could defend greater resources.

Recall: Large populations pay a price by inviting parasites. The reward must be substantially more than the price paid through parasitism.

Tribes of hunter-gatherers could wander widely. But those who planted fields had to guard those specific places against trespass, from planting through harvest. Sedentary living changed the dynamics of human societies.

Ownership is important in human development, since ownership laws mean humans do not necessarily need to *kill each other* to trade capital. Ownership establishes cultural continuity and limits violent capital exchanges.

However, land ownership by individuals, or private corporations, is not an ancient, undeniable right as maintained by some. The private property concept arrived rather recently in human societies only a few thousand years ago with the arrival of farming.

Before farming, humans spread across the world hunting and gathering for several hundred thousand years *without* land ownership. The first modern Homo sapiens skull dates to about 150,000 years ago. Homo sapiens communities with cave art and religious tokens date back at least 40,000 years. Farming only began to dominate around 15,000 years ago in specific areas.

We assume private ownership of land replaced communal ownership sporadically around 3000 BC as town boundaries stabilized. Cultures required armies to protect land from external encroachment and also required rules defining what clans controlled what areas of production and harvest. Early communal communities may have shared all resources and work somewhat evenly as a single family. But when communities specialized, new rules became necessary to fairly disperse and trade capital resources between separate families.

Land rules became even more rigid as cultures grew in size. Concurrent with ownership of land and stock, the ideas of owning other humans, professions, trade items, and status rights became acceptable. Humans designed laws to define and protect ownership conventions—but in so doing, they inadvertently created status levels limiting later capital flow.

Over time, ownership in human societies can progressively cause stagnation and inequity. When climax populations control resource assets indefinitely over hundreds, thousands, or tens of thousands of years, those assets may stop circulating for the common good.

When capital resources, controlled exclusively by a status of society, cease circulation, the lack of capital starves other statuses and limits economic or cultural participation. Assets commonly claimed by status levels include: Land ownership, pools of investment capital, and claims to intellectual, religious, professional, and artistic professions.

In the future, if a certain status were to gain exclusive control of the media, then that status would control the perception of truth and understanding, correctly or not, for everyone else. If all farmland were to be one-day owned by a single status, then that status would control all food production—not necessarily a happy situation for the hungry. In the past, government and religious control were the exclusive domains of specific elite statuses. Such statuses did not necessarily govern to the advantage of the entire populace.

The eventual losers are those born into low status populations or those in cultures overwhelmed by the **numbers** of competing cultures. Such low status individuals are pushed outside the flow of capital (or literally enslaved). Recall: Capital is life. Shared capital is shared understanding. ***Those outside the capital flow are enslaved to ignorance and poverty.***

Victims also include those born into upper elites, the "Hamlets" of society, intelligent enough to recognize the limitations created by confined social positions. Such victims have no choice but to defend positions and estates they may find vain, godless, and hollow.

But status levels can be persistent: Some social theorists fear elite and powerful statuses will control the future even more firmly than they controlled the past. Once elites grab climax control, they can be impossible to dislodge, particularly if their ownership is protected by long-term legislation.

Ownership is the status quo: The primary purpose, of human laws, is to protect the ownership status quo. Short term, these laws assist human development. However, over time, much time, such laws can grow extremely restrictive, favoring an ever-smaller elite, creating enslavement, restricting capital circulation, and suffocating human progress.

Time makes all the difference. A fortune will grow obscenely large without any work whatsoever, if it compounds (at rates greater than inflation) over an extended period. The consequence is, capital congestion grows larger and larger over time. The top 1% today controls more than 50% of the world's resources. This is obvious inequity, and because of the forces of cultural entropy, this inequity will grow larger and larger (not smaller) over time.

"The richer get richer; and the poor get children." Note: Children are a type of capital. Numbers can battle capital possessions.

Unless steps of some sort ensue, we can expect the situation must grow more and more unequal into the future. The situation will not alter without intervention or catastrophe. Taxing and otherwise limiting ownership rights can have both positive and negative effects short term. The solution,, long term, to spread greater fairness in capital dispersal, is somewhere in the reasonable consensus.

But we must repeat: The forces of time and cultural entropy continue to work to make the disparity greater, not less. Only **work** in opposition can oppose this increase in entropy (wealth inequity).

Capital is life. Capital circulation, capitalism, is necessary for all living systems to continue living. In cooperative capitalism, human labor must generate a profit that can circulate without the need for violence.

GREAT WEALTH

We have attempted to distinguish in this book the differences between **competitive capitalism** and **cooperative capitalism**. We might also attempt to distinguish the differences between associated concepts--**negative wealth** and **positive wealth**.

Negative wealth (due to ignorance) generally does not circulate. In addition, forces of negative wealth historically have taken steps to stop the circulation of capital generally by legal and military means. In the dark ages, aristocrats had little need to circulate capital—particularly to serfs—since serfs were obligated to do what they were told without compensation.

Wealthy aristocrats could keep all those beneath them—even lower aristocrats--at subsistence levels, since they literally controlled all resources. **Negative wealth** exalts itself by keeping other statuses down and by *limiting the value of free human labor*—either by design or ignorance. **Negative wealth** encourages memes of ignorance and discourages diversity and human social freedom. **Negative wealth** encourages tyrannical laws and governments that maintain elite statuses over those of common people

Negative wealth, moreover, inhibits the processes of **cooperative capitalism** and substitutes habits of **competitive capitalism**, cultural wars, and militarism.

We must emphasize, however, negative wealth is not necessarily evil. The evils associated with negative wealth stem from ignorance and not necessarily from evil intentions.

On the contrary, **Positive wealth** acts to diminish ignorance. **Positive wealth** circulates widely. **Positive wealth** creates industries. **Positive wealth** enables jobs that compensate human labor in profitable ways. **Positive wealth** invests in infrastructure and new technologies that provide future jobs and enable human enlightenment. **Positive wealth** invests in education, diversity, and science. **Positive wealth circulates**, energizing the **work** of the human family and the value of humanity. We repeat, "Only **work** can oppose the forces of **entropy**."

Much of the antipathy against wealth is a reaction against **negative wealth** and the tendency of negative wealth to be socially stagnating.

Taxing wealth is a very popular concept today. Some onus on wealth is probably inevitable. However, the dangers of too extreme or radical taxes are obvious when we view wealth from the view of capital circulation. Taxes on wealth have not been successful when attempted in several European states for this reason.

In the early Soviet Union, theoreticians assumed all wealth was negative. By eliminating both negative and positive wealth, planners eliminated most of their capital profit circulation. By seeking to control all capital production, planners managed to cause widespread stagnation and enslavement of the very populations they had promised to free. By controlling the circulation of capital understanding, they encouraged the circulation of memes of ignorance.

Today, if we wish to tax wealth, we should understand all wealth in not negative. Wealth that is invested and circulating is creating beneficial effects for everyone. We need to be careful to not destroy the innovators and capital markets that enable innovation, progress, and human understanding. We cannot, in outrage, attack profits everywhere. Bare in mind, the circulating profits of human labor are what allow cooperative capitalism to work. And **cooperative capitalism** is what enables human progress and economic wellbeing.

The wealthy, of course, should shoulder more than their share of the tax burden, bearing in mind they benefit greatly—far more than the rest of us--from the infrastructures and protections of the wider society. But great care should be exercised not to tax wealth to **extinction** and destroy wealth **circulation** and the economy in the process.

In addition, the idea that specific (human) owners should own property, earth's resources, **in perpetuity** is rather absurd if one thinks of earth, like nature, as something that cannot be owned in perpetuity. Perpetuity is infinite. Should no trespassing signs be forever?

Human ownership conventions are concepts time will one day turn to dust. Redistributions of capital and property resources by laws can work out badly, however, if attentions are not given to capital circulation, the need for capital diversity, and beneficial activities by some of those of great wealth. [Ch. 5, **6**, -- The Soviet Food Crisis.]

E. HUMANS INVENT WAR STRUCTURED SOCIETIES: TRIBAL WARFARE AND TERRORISM

Tribes with expendable young men are hard-wired for constant military conflicts. From the beginning of history, human tribes have engaged in constant population wars with each other. Fortunately, most ancient tribes did not possess modern weapons.

Today, the Afghani, Taliban tribes have literally been in **numbers** wars for a thousand years. During this time they were either fighting external forces over these years, or they were fighting each other. **Their military social structures mandate constant warfare.**

These warring tribal cultures date from thousands of years **before** the origin of the Muslim religion. The underlying military social organizations have actually changed little due to the influence of religion.

However, religious **extremism** adds to the violence. In addition, external political forces, today, provide capital for a nearly unlimited flow of weapons to these regions, weapons ancient tribal soldiers did not possess. Regions that have difficulty buying food for children apparently have no difficulty buying weapons for war. **The wide dispersal of war technologies greatly assists constant conflicts over peaceful resolutions.**

So warfare in such situations is not dependent on particular adversaries, or on winning or losing specific conflicts, or even on religion. Warfare is a social necessity in such societies regardless of real circumstance. **Numbers** fight **numbers** without rational thought. Military social structures mandate constant war. Motivations for conflict—religious differences, cultural differences, language differences, or economic differences—are superficial.

In more modern social structures, *when young men have career opportunities, and marriage is not dependent on placement in a military hierarchy, such young men might be more reticent to risk their lives in military campaigns.*

In addition, when woman's role is not limited to reproduction and child rearing, fewer expendable young men are born as fodder to instigate meaningless wars. Without an excess of young men, wars are difficult to conduct. With an excess of unemployed young men, wars are nearly impossible to avoid.

Thus, when women are forced to maximize their fertility, population wars are absolutely inevitable. Too many men are born not to have conflict.

GANGS ARE TRIBES: Young men, in military hierarchies and without career opportunities, create conflict whenever they enter the streets in large **numbers**. With adequate **numbers**, *any* intolerance—religion, cultural, economic—will suffice to divide a population into warring groups. Young men are hard-wired to desire action. Young men are enslaved by extreme emotions. Young men are attracted to cultural, tribal gangs, and have been since the beginning of humanity. Gang or tribal activity is what makes human society what it is.

Women enslaved as breeders and young men enslaved as soldiers have difficulty finding places in non-warring cultures. Cultures evolved for warfare over thousands of years have difficulty functioning in times of peace. The **numbers** are in control, not human reason or God.

Behind the conflict, the forces of **cultural entropy** and the meme of cycling **ignorance** control the action. Only through understanding these forces, as God surely desires, can many areas in the world progress to enlightenment and peace.

F. CULTURAL ENTROPY CORRODES DEMOCRATIC INSTITUTIONS AND THE LEGISLATIVE PROCESS OVER TIME.

Countless Roman's died in the civil wars that eventually made Caesar dictator of Rome. Was Caesar a hero or a villain to overthrow the Roman senate? Historians disagree.

Arrogant and ambitious men are *always* present everywhere. **Legislative entropy**--by destroying consensus--is what allows ambitious men to overwhelm legislative bodies. If the Roman senate had been powerful, united, and not corrupt, it might have easily deterred the ambitions of any one, egotistic man.

The forces of **Cultural entropy** divide legislatures over time into intolerant **extremes**; these extremes lose the ability to come to consensus or govern—exactly like the Roman senate.

In the presence of polarized and ineffective power, dictators are anxious to fill the void. The results initially may seem progressive and allow decisive decisions. And so, we can see why tyrants are so prevalent in human history and continue to be common today. Legislatures, democratic or autocratic, that dissolve into chaos, always invite despots. Despots are always waiting in the wings.

And in human groups, chaos is a natural product of time and cultural entropy. **Why?**

a) EXTREMES ARE EASY

Extreme views are always simpler and easier to defend than moderate views. Pictorially, extreme views require very limited definition since they originate from specific and limited angles. Moderate views must visualize all issues from many angles. Oops? Looking at issues from more than one angle creates complications. These complications—even if they encompass much more of the truth—are far harder to understand and enunciate than splinter views from isolated angles.

Thus **extremes** are always popular among people who would avoid thinking greatly about real understandings and consensus. Most important, extreme views come with the great bonus of **extreme** emotions— anger, horror, hatred, and malice. Such *extreme emotions* are great entertainments for humans in need of emotional release. Extremist speakers can allow vent for group anger far more convincingly than those counseling

peace and moderation. And when extremes and intolerance dominate, chaos is soon to follow.
>Why?

b) **MIDDLE DESTRUCTION**
The moderate middle quickly disappears when legislatures are dominated by extremes. ***And without a middle to reach consensus, government cannot function.***

Issues are far different today than in Roman or Greek times, but the results are quite similar: Extremes create dysfunction.

Divisive, intolerant, extreme emotions are unavoidable. However, a legislative body with a **strong middle** can still find consensus.

The middle is actually where most humans exist. The extremes are, and always have been, **extreme**. In very few cases do extremes constitute the real majority of the human population.

So why do the extremes apparently wield such an unusual degree of power? Why is polarization so easy? And why do those in the middle apparently disappear?

In the biological world, the answers are straightforward. When toxicities grow between extremes, the middle becomes a **no man's land**. Nothing can live in a toxic no man's land without rules. The only safety lies in protected extremities.

Bacteria, as opposed to humans, have no brains. They can't weigh the irony of their situations. Bacteria are unfeeling to the inhumane carnage rash actions often create. Bacteria cannot analyze results to improve outcomes. Bacteria are governed totally by **numbers. Numbers,** like bacteria, have no brains.

On the flip side, bacteria have no emotions. Thus they can actually remain tolerant of each other far longer than emotional humans. They don't react in anger or petulance. Bacteria don't carry grudges. Bacteria have no secret motives; they don't lie and deceive.

Human **emotions** predictively lie on the **extremes** of rational consensus. Humans apparently *enjoy* extreme emotions. Movies, sports, the arts, and roller coasters constantly supply humans the emotional extremes they crave. In like manner, political pundits on both sides of all political questions draw their crowds by supplying emotional stimulation, not verifiable truth.

Thus ministers of angst and derision—religious or political-- lead their disciples in daily quests for simplistic emotional fulfillment and not toward **alternatives** intended *to improve any* **real** situation. **Actual progress is not the desire.** The desire is to foment feelings of anger and derision that many humans apparently find cathartic and unifying.

Unfortunately, emotional stimulations, anger, and hatred, usually lead away from truth; in fact, most rational alternatives require rational thought, compromise, calm, and understanding. Verifiable truths and reasonable alternatives are of little use to pundits leading their adherents on spinning Ferris wheels of angst.

Among rational, unemotional humans, rational agreements are easily found, particularly when the alternatives are chaos or tyranny. If humans agree to share a **common self-identity** [Ch. 8, 9], they realize they can all benefit together from common goals. And apparently, ignoring all the smoke and madness, humans actually do share common desires and even enjoy the happiness of others. ***Most humans are actually wonderful, caring people—really! We don't really need to hate each other.***

Highly emotional humans, however, who feel they are divided by highly emotional issues, can never come to consensus. ***Violent emotions lead only to violence***—that is why we *have* violent emotions.

Over human history, fear and anger have allowed humans to act in *inhuman* ways to survive, summoning extra degrees of strength and ferocity, battling savage carnivores and crossing wide oceans, impossible without extreme degrees of emotional power.

But when we wish to live in harmony, such madness causes problems. Modern humans have invented wonderful games to dissipate their terrible needs for conflict—football, hockey, basketball, video games, hunting, drag racing, marriage, and checkers—to name a few. We love games and movies precisely because they provide the drug of action-and-conflict many of us crave, without the accompanying death and destruction of actual warfare.

Unfortunately, legislatures and those seeking election, often seek the same action-drug as sportsmen. When **violent emotions** enter the room, rational alternatives exit.

When the middle disappears, rational consensus is impossible, conflict is eternal, and the opportunity for a tyrant to appear to end the chaos grows exponentially.

IN CONCLUSION:
The forces of cultural entropy act destructively on all capital sharing cultures and divide capital sharing concepts. Democratic institutions are most strongly impacted, since such institutions depend on common understandings and moderate sensibilities easily overwhelmed by tyrants and divisive emotions; random forces of cultural entropy negatively affect these symbols of cultural unity over time.

Strong-man, tyrannical governments replace democratic institutions whenever cultural entropy has corrupted the legislative process into toxic extremes and paralysis.

Only work in opposition can keep entropy from increasing.

If a strong middle exists, then irrational extremes and tyrants can (perhaps) be minimized. The problem is—how to create a strong middle? The middle is often derided and overlooked.

Perhaps a first step is to recognize a democracy desperately **needs** a strong middle? The moderate middle—those willing to work with each other—need to recognize they are being victimized by the **extremes**. The way to progress forward—rather than backward--is through moderation and compromise, rather than extremism and violence. The middle must recognize the critical situation and work to continue to purposefully exist against the forces of extremism.

Steven King's, **"IT!"**
"We will never be free, unless we stop denying! We must face the invisible monster, or **IT** will destroy us!"
[See Ch. 10 –The literature.]

Important for human progress to avoid the intoxicating allures of irrational, emotional extremes. *"Romantic extremes are almost always dead ends."* If you disbelieve, read the original, *Hunchback of Notre Dame*. Or, read almost any book of human history. Great authors have recognized the truth since the beginning of humanity [Ch. 10 -- The Literature].

Extreme views consistently lead to violence and despair and away from harmony and love and God. Those who recently heeded the puritanical call of *Isis,* to free Islam from heretics, will inevitably find: Violence only creates violence and not purity—the lesson repeats through history.

Simultaneously, central governments—for all the power they wield to create helpful **infrastructure**—can also be stifling and restrictive of change, whether those governments take orders from religious leaders, legislatures, or dictators.

The most important aspect of successful democracies is to maintain the free circulation of all capital, particularly information capital. Capital information—also known as the **truth**—can be very helpful when a society must make difficult decisions. **Without the truth, wrong decisions are rather inevitable.** *Verifiable truth is the most important human capital to circulate.*

G. TO WIT, THE SOCIALIST/COMMUNIST FOOD CRISIS

We don't need to look very far to find examples of how misinformation and ignorance lead to catastrophic unforeseen consequences. The Soviet system under Joseph Stalin organized several social programs on principals contrary to healthy capital circulation. These programs restarted in earnest after World War II. Well-meaning bureaucrats were taught capital circulation, or capitalism, was uniformly evil.

Social planners forcefully assigned peasant populations profitless farm work without understanding these humans, and their living regions, required revolving profits to prosper. These peasants were affectively *enslaved* in profitless occupations.

Slavery, we have seen throughout history, over and over again, does not create profits or circulate capital, and so large areas of once-profitable farmland turned into capital wastelands with no diversity or return capital flow. The food-capital produced in these areas simply entered government coffers elsewhere and disappeared. When capital profits did **not** cycle back to the area, entire farm districts suffered capital blight. Farming towns *disappeared* along with the trade and progress that normally accompany capital circulation.

Social programmers, who had hoped to move forward, actually adopted ignorant policies that moved their society backwards to an era of slavery, and stagnant feudal hierarchies. These theorists did not understand how human slavery strangles capital production.

As part of production control, social theorists also strictly controlled the **capital information flow** over these enslaved areas. Information is capital. Capital is life. When the wheat harvest began to diminish, those in control were able to affectively deny the truth for many years. Later, when the shortage of bread could no longer be hidden and food shortages ravaged the entire economy, those who controlled the information flow blamed irrelevant factors—not the failed program—as the culprits. In particular, they claimed enslaved peasants were hoarding food for their own capital benefit.

The peasants had no powers to deny the assertions—capital information did not flow from peasants--and those at the top had no knowledge the assertions were untrue. Peasants were severely punished for activities that had no factual basis. The **truth** might have beneficially and easily solved the problem, but the **truth** had been erased from existence by numerous levels of bureaucracy and power control.

Ignorance, on the contrary, or the *lack of information circulation*, replaced the truth; and based on ignorance, wrong decisions—idiotic decisions—were repeatedly affirmed.

The soviet system further communicated with the Chinese system; in doing so, the soviets claimed their farm principals were functioning perfectly—they circulated an **untruth**. With this misinformation, the Chinese embarked on a farm program similar to the soviets.

Over a few years, the Chinese bureaucrats reached the same impasse as the soviets, farm production by enslaved peasants diminished severely. Food shortages rocked the entire economy. Bureaucrats—out of ignorance—found the same culprit to blame; the peasants must be hoarding the harvest. Without the circulation of **truth**—or other capital from the affected areas—peasants suffered unfair repercussions. The peasants were denied food—on the assumption the hoarding accusations had to be correct.

The resulting crisis of wrong decisions circulating again and again might well have led to hilarious soap-opera comedic relief—only the truly tragic affects of these wrong decisions overwhelmed any hilarity. An estimated thirty six million peasants starved in China in the years 1958-62 due to policies based on repeated lies and misinformation.

The bureaucrats involved were not evil. Sorry, these people were simply misinformed. By rigidly seeking to control capital flow, ignorance replaced truth; the results of making decisions based on ignorance were predictably catastrophic.

The conclusions now are rather clear and obvious: Without the open flow of capital, economies die. Without the open flow of capital knowledge, humans reach idiotic decisions.

Again we cannot claim **truth** always allows people easy access to progressive movement forward. But the opposite of truth, **ignorance**, inevitably leads to ignorant decisions; and ignorant decisions are more often than not, well, ignorant.

Ineffective soviet farm policies continued until the seventies; then, new Russian leadership introduced glasnost or the policy of truth. The glasnost policy simply allowed the free circulation of known facts, or the truth. New farm policies returned capital to farmers and farm regions and immediately returned Russia to dominance as a farm producer.

China followed closely with similar policies. No system, socialist or capitalist, can be successful without circulating capital, or profit. Profit enables cooperative capitalism. Capital is life. Capital is the blood that feeds the entire organism. If one part of the organism dies, the entire being is threatened. If one part of the capital stream is stifled, the entire stream diminishes.

CONTROLLING THE TRUTH

Throughout history, tyrants often seek to control the truth in an effort to conceal their own missteps and inadequacies. By controlling the information flow, tyrants can hide atrocities and genocides; they can also hide catastrophes caused by government corruption and misinformation. However, as pointed out repeatedly, the **truth, or information capital**, tends to circulate in line with all other forms of capital, economic, technological, food capital, and so forth. **Stifling the flow of one capital segment generally stifles the flow of <u>all</u> capital.**

So--governments that stifle or strictly control the truth also limit the flow of other circulating capital, including enlightenment, learning, food products, innovation, and social progress. Restated: **Stifling information flow tends to stifle all economic development.**

Recent government initiatives to place more control over information flow in both Russia and China, do not necessarily bode well for economic progress and future innovations.

Vast flows of Internet **misinformation in the USA**, a new device by some to control the information flow, may stifle human progress in a fashion similar to old-fashioned authoritarianism. The result of both methodologies is to create relative **ignorance** and paralyze the democratic process.

In the absence of verifiable truth, only tyrants who control their own views of success can govern. We would assume such governments would enjoy only short-term success, because at some time, actual reality might surface. Or maybe not? Who know how long authorities can extend untruths?

In general, however, all capital flow is intertwined and interdependent. Slaves may be well fed, for example. However, long term, a slave system cannot be expected to produce innovative returns (growth) without the presence of information capital, the truth, and actual capital returns (profits) to fuel the wider system--capital profit circulation feeds and grows the entire system. Only the circulation of verifiable truth can limit catastrophic decisions based on ignorance. Human culture is a single, connected organism. Truth is a type of human *profit* that needs to be circulated.

Untruths oppose human survival. Half-truths can be equally deadly.

CH. 7
POPULATION WARS

Cultural entropy divides biological and human families. Divided families engage in competitive capitalism and eternal population wars. These destructive wars continue indefinitely.

**POPULATION WARS AND COMPETITIVE CAPITALISM STRESS RESOURCES
CREATE TOXICITIES
LEAD HUMANITY TO DESTRUCTION
AND DEVALUE LIFE**

A. TRIBALISM/CULTURAL WARS
B. THE WARRING TRIBAL SYSTEM (MALE/FEMALE ROLES)
C. RESOURCE STRESS CAUSED BY CULTURAL WARS
D. WAR CULTURES DESIGNED FOR WAR AND NOT PEACE
E. CULTURAL WARS BETWEEN RELIGIONS
F. RACISM AND INTOLERANCE ARE HARD WIRED
G. CULTURAL ENTROPY ASSISTS EXTREME LEADERSHIP

A. CULTURAL WARS

Human cultures follow the same rules as all biological cultures. The forces of **cultural entropy** divide human cultures and force these divided cultures into eternal wars (competitions) with each other to claim the future. Cultural wars diminish the ***value*** of individual human life.

Biological cultures must ***compete*** with all other biological cultures if they wish to control resources and survive into the future. Whether we are referring to bacteria or humans, the rules are the same: The future is crowded. Resources are limited. To survive and claim limited **resources**, cultures must push their **numbers** into the crowded future—and as they compete (growing like cancers), they will incidentally push against the numbers of competing cultures. If cultures don't compete back, they disappear.

Cultural wars (family wars) create **competitive capitalism**, a zero-sum game. Competitive capitalism is violent. A culture that loses the game of **competitive capitalism** is pushed away from resources it needs to continue living; it is outnumbered, overwhelmed, eaten, starved, strangled, and crowded out. A culture, that loses the **numbers** game, disappears. So to continue surviving, cultures have no choice in the matter. Only by continuing to aggressively produce **numbers,** playing violent, **competitive capitalism,** can any culture (family) live into the future. Cultures, good or bad, that have not won the game, have disappeared. When we look, we only see the winners—nice or not so nice.

The forces of **cultural entropy**—not human reason--create the rules and the games and the outcomes. Competitive capitalism stresses resources. Numbers have no impulse control.

Individuals have limited lifetimes. But cultures and social cultures—we're talking families, religions, ethnicities, governments, corporations, clans, human tribes, and such things—these can be nearly immortal. These cultural associations can continue without limit, but only so long as they continue to play **competitive capitalism** and out compete the competition—plus incidental forces of death--and only so long as they can simultaneously withstand the *divisive* forces of cultural entropy internally.

THE HAMLET TRILOGY BY WILLIAM FAULKNER

Say a tiny hamlet (a tiny town) is filled with a number of happy, hard-working families. Then one day, a new family arrives—call them the Snopes family. (That is the name William Faulkner gave them.) The Snopeses are not happy or successful. They steal, they lie, they are con artists, they are stupid, they are losers, and they are barnburners. A barnburner will burn your barn if they don't like you, close to a death sentence in a farming community. Hard working, successful people fear, hate, and are disgusted by the Snopes family. Good, moral people look down their noses at the Snopeses and their uncared-for children. The Snopeses are gullible, ignorant, laughable, vengeful, silly, and stubborn. They are untrustworthy, lazy, and stupid. The only thing the Snopeses are apparently good at is having lots and lots of children.

Good, moral people try to ignore the contemptible Snopeses as much as possible. But after a few generations, the Snopses can't be ignored. In fact, they have taken over the Hamlet with their numbers. The Snopses run the bank and the hardware store and have married the town's richest and most beautiful woman. The Hamlet, now a town, should be called Snopesville.

The point is, numbers eventually overwhelm any adversity. Faulkner's Snopes culture did not need to be educated, or reasonable, or moral, or smart, or honest, or hard working to conquer—it simply needed to be large and insistent.

Most authors, and human beings, are trapped in a limited time period. We are blind both to the history and future of most human activities. Faulkner took his characters through generations in several novels to reveal the strange changes **time** reveals.

Cultures, or religions, or families can win the future, not with the strength of their beliefs, or work, but with their persistent **numbers**.

On the contrary, good families or cultures that fail to reproduce, eventually disappear. Their assets (resources) fall to those who survive—in this case, the irrepressible Snopeses.

C. POPULATIONS COMPETE FOR RESOURCES

When animal populations outstrip their resources, their numbers are punished with diseases and starvation. Human populations, in many cases, are smart enough to continually access and create *additional* resources to match their population increases. When new lands are available to create more and more foods, human population wars can continue and continue without an end in sight.

Napoleon Bonaparte is credited with saying, "An army moves on its stomach." Armies of early humans moved across the earth everywhere in every direction—these armies moved on their stomachs. Human populations now cover most of the world, all in an effort to access newer and newer resources.

But population/cultural wars can't go on forever. New, untouched farmlands have already begun to diminish and grow increasingly expensive. Eventually, the resources feeding our human population wars will become deleted and humans will face the same consequences—disease and starvation—facing **all other** life forms. Fossil fuels, new energy sources, and arable lands are (probably) limited.

Specific human sects can grow at cancerous levels, advancing themselves while suffocating less aggressive cultures around them. The result to the entire society resembles cancerous growths in any animal organism, lack of diversity and a failure to survive.

Even assuming extraordinary technological innovations continue, the end is in sight. If we allow random forces of cultural entropy to guide us, we stumble blindly into darkness.

C. WHY ARE RESOURCES STRESSED TODAY?

We know cultural wars, tribal wars, numbers wars, place stresses on resources. Resources are the actual ***goal*** of cultural wars. Thus, since resources are what cultural wars are all about, the ***stresses on resources are unavoidable***. The crowded world today is a direct result of cultural wars. Global warming, ocean acidification, water conflicts, and all the other resource stresses today are not problems that can be eliminated by methodologies, or economics, or technologies--they are problems of population/cultural wars. Facing population wars directly is the *only* method to solve such problems.

Stresses on resources will continue as long as cultural wars create larger and larger human **numbers**. These wars will not halt naturally—other than through momentary ceasefires caused by diseases, starvation, or other catastrophes. Thus the future scenario is not optimistic, unless catastrophes are preferred.

Cultures or religions, rapidly increasing their numbers, place stresses on all other cultures and religions to compete for common resources. No one can play the game differently, unless they wish to disappear. Recall: The future is crowded. There is not enough room for everyone, particularly when big **numbers** are pushing everyone around. If one culture starts a war, all other cultures must respond in kind, or they will be destroyed. The wars began millions of years ago, long before humans.

If the value of all existence diminishes, cancerous cultures don't care. Cancer has no brain. Numbers have no values.

Something or someone will eventually lose. Will it be your culture? Will it be my culture? Will it be our united family? Place your bets. But if you want your culture to win, you'd better start reproducing. If you don't keep reproducing, when you take a look in the future, your grandchildren won't be there. Never mind that your grandchildren may be forced to live in a toxic, violent world—better that, than to have your entire culture smothered by competitors. (?)

We may pause a moment here to recognize most cultures and religions have much the same goals; real differences are actually marginal. Like ants of the same species that kill each other due to differing scent markers, the wars have no real *meaning*. Human population competitions are likewise conflicts between roughly similar colonies.

The forces of **puritanity** enlarge small differences, so we think we are different, and these differences create wars and human torment. At the same time, by not recognizing the cultural wars going on, we may find the future dominated by ignorance and memes of division we could easily avoid.

For many of us, the problem will be time. Humans don't notice population conflicts because they happen slowly and human lives are limited. Cultural changes, that take several generations to occur, can take place beneath our human radar. By the time the results are in, it is too late to go back; the uncultured Snopses (**numbers**) have taken over the town; and the value of human life is not what anyone wants.

Cultural wars stress resources and lead us in directions we have not chosen.

A BETTER WAY

Globalism (seeking common paths) leads to fewer conflicts than tribalism or patriotism (seeking separate paths).

Cultural entropy leads to unnecessary division and conflict over and over and over again. Ignorance keeps humans from understanding the dilemma. Given shared understanding of the problem, (unwinnable cultural wars), humans have the intelligence to find a peaceful solution, (don't play the no-sum game).

We need to understand the no-sum games we are playing and play **cooperative capitalism** (wherein all players can win) instead of **competitive capitalism** (wherein everyone generally loses).

Winning wars can provide wonderful drama. Roman armies were victorious in over 1200 separate wars. The parades were impressive. But the dramatic results did little to improve the diminishing value of Roman society. Rome still eventually **lost** everything. If the goal is to improve the *quality* of human life, population wars are not the answer—in fact, such wars are the problem.

Tribalism (false patriotism) is a product of the forces of cultural entropy; tribal goals lead directly to resource stress and conflict. Globalism, in which humans (from all tribes) seek common goals, is a *humane* concept that may lead in a more cooperative direction.

But nothing is easy—**work** is necessary to oppose increasing entropy; and always will be necessary.

THE BIOLOGICAL IMPERATIVE TO REPRODUCE
"...*The Inviolable Right of Motherhood.*"

In *some* human societies, the right of reproduction is inviolable. Poverty, however, creates poverty. When children are born to poor parents, those children are also poor. When children are born to single women without means, those children are also without means. Encouraging fewer children in poverty situations is a simple way to limit the increase of poverty. However, the right of motherhood is inviolable in some societies, particularly if those societies are engaged in aggressive population wars.

All successful, living organisms possess biological imperatives to reproduce. If they don't possess this biological imperative, and if they don't successfully reproduce, they disappear from existence. Everything living today is here because it has learned to successfully reproduce into the future. If our forefathers hadn't successfully reproduced over the past million or so years, we would not be here.

Recall: Mortality in the past was much higher than today. So having as many children as possible was an absolute necessity simply to *maintain* **numbers**. In the past, humans also needed family to accompany them through the years, since no other assistance was provided by society.

Memes and social activities that **do not win** the numbers wars disappear from existence. So when we look at modern cultures we view the winners—not the losers--in the numbers game, memes and social activities that have aggressively survived past numbers wars.

Thus cultures—religions, ethnicities, beliefs, and economic customs--successful today are those that most successfully play the population game and reproduce their populations. **These cultures are *not necessarily* the best, or the nicest, or the most joyful, or the ones most filled with human love and understanding—they are simply the ones surviving with the biggest numbers.**

THE CHILDREN'S ARMY OF POVERTY

Cultural Wars: In human hierarchies, **wealthy** statuses grow by extending their control of *capital resou*rces. **Poor** statuses can conduct population wars by extending their own *capital population numbers*.

The soldiers of poor statuses worldwide consist of armies of poor children. Like male soldiers, poor children are expendable. Poor children can push in all directions to widen the area of their birth culture. Cultures do not require great **capital outlays** in weaponry to conduct population wars if they have an army of children.

Human cultures, life bacteria, use their populations (children) to push against other cultures. Rapidly reproducing populations in limited areas make cultural conflicts **unavoidable**. [Israel, Malaysia, Venezuela, East Asia, Africa, Central America, Eastern Europe, everywhere—to name a few places.] Population wars devalue the lives of children and turn children into expendable population soldiers.

Since public opinion widely supports children, opposing an army of children can be problematic for any government that respects its media image.

Israel is an excellent example: Israeli forces have established control over capital resources. Palestinian forces fight back with their population. Since 1948 the Palestinian population has grown at roughly twice that of Israel, from 1.4 million to over 11 million in 2018. Half of the Palestinians have migrated to other countries, leaving only 5.5 million still in territories controlled by Israel—still a substantial rise. Though the Jewish population is also rising, the Palestinians staying in the area are expected to outnumber them by 2024. By 2030, Palestinians in the total territory should outnumber Jewish citizens by several million people, if the population continues to rise.

The numbers confound any concept of a shared **Jewish** state, since the Jews will apparently have fewer numbers going into the future—the **shared** state will be dominated by non-Jewish ethnicities and will no longer be a Jewish state.

Numbers confound democratic concepts, peace, and minority interests throughout the world, particularly if we also seek human equality, in which number rule. The concepts directly contradict. [Read Ch. 10 –The Literature: Theatre of the Absurd]

With no stable *population* in sight, stable economies and stable governments in the Mideast territories are ***not possible*** in the foreseeable future.

Population wars create military conflicts and stress resources. As the Palestinian population grows, poverty grows as well. Poverty begets poverty.

The forces of cultural entropy push populations into conflict.

Religious differences are merely decoys that blind us to the truth—human civilizations are actually controlled by primitive forces of cultural entropy and chaos.

C. CULTURAL /POPULATION WARS STRESS RESOURCES

Aggressively populating cultures, war-cultures, by cancerously maximizing their population **numbers**, place stresses on resources, political systems, and other cultures. Cultures waging population wars add to the biological imperative of their members to reproduce; to do so they create **social structures that require their young people (women) must maximize their reproduction** at the cost of all other priorities.

To be utilized as reproductive machines, young women must be kept from all activities that might interfere with reproduction—such as attending school, working at a job, or making free choices. The fewer choices young men and women have, the better they can serve as expendable soldiers and reproductive machines—the primary needs of a culture conducting an aggressive cultural war using an army of children.

We can see today the effects of population pressures on resources throughout much of the world in cultures that use their population numbers as weapons of conquest. Cancers are self-destructive; they have no brains.

When biological and social imperatives combine, reproduction can always outstrip resources. [With humans in population wars, a catastrophe may take time, but the end is certain.] Increasing numbers lead to increasing conflicts both **within** a culture and in wars against other cultures.

CULTURAL WARS DEVALUE HUMAN LIFE
To repeat the obvious: Cultural wars devalue human life. Men give their valueless lives in violent causes; women are reduced to breeding units. Children are population soldiers created to push against other cultures. Religious values are twisted to assist cultural wars and lead away from God and understanding.

All human priorities, not assisting cultural wars, are devalued. Stresses on resources limit capital (life) circulation throughout the culture. Limited capital circulation limits the **economic health** of the entire society. (Military manufacturers may be an exception.)

Limits placed on capital (information) circulation by warfare increase superstition, circulation of untruths, and the ignorance meme. Decisions made in ignorance are often counter-productive.

Cancerous sub-cultures—predatory gangs, parasitic religious organizations, for example—reproducing out of control, can overwhelm and destroy an entire economy and society. **No man's lands**, a creation of cultural conflict, can eliminate laws and social infrastructures over wide areas.

Numbers make the rules; not human reason. **Numbers** do not lead to understanding or God. **Increasing numbers inevitably lead to conflict, and not progress**; this is true both **within** a culture and in opposition to other cultures.

D. SUCCESSFUL WAR CULTURES MUST CONTINUE TO MAKE WARS EVEN DURING PEACE -- "They are built that way."
Human cultures, *like all biological cultures*, are *naturally* at war with each other to extend into the crowded future. Expendable males make human wars possible and bloody. Early tribes paid only a small population price to conduct wars, particularly when rewarded with resources or fertile women. The deaths of significant young males are of little concern to the final **numbers**.
Numbers don't care about the lives of young men.

Numbers only suffer if not enough men are available to fertilize the young females—and this is difficult, since one male is generally capable of fertilizing several women. [The numbers change when males are *absolutely* necessary for childcare, as in most bird species.]

Some human social systems have evolved over thousands of years into military hierarchies designed specifically for constant warfare. War societies must maximize female fertility. Maximum female fertility maximizes population numbers and ensures a renewable supply of expendable, male soldiers. Such societies stress the importance of military involvement for their young men. Women in such societies must be limited to the single task of reproduction. **Numbers don't care about the lives of young women.**

Military societies, however, have particular difficulties dealing with peace. A surplus of young men, often unemployed, and also a surplus of children, makes extreme demands on resources and creates an unsteady political situation.

War and conflict is the **only alternative** for such social organizations. These cultures **were designed** for war, division, and conflict. These cultures were not designed to increase the value of human life. These cultures use human lives and human **numbers** as weapons of war against other cultures.

War cultures evolve in long-contested areas, most often *those ancient places the forces of* ***cultural entropy*** *have been working longest in human populations*--The Mideast, Eastern Europe, Africa, for example. Afghanistan is a poster child of warring states. Regions have been at war in Afghanistan, one way or another, for several thousand years, without much change. These states, designed for war, date from long before Islam. Modern weapons make recent conflicts ever more deadly. Religious ***puritanity*** allows conflicts over increasingly smaller issues.

We may argue, the Trojan Wars, which began 2500 years ago in the region, never actually settled; these ancient animosities continue in renewed cycles of vengeance, through changing religions and governments, across the world, even today. (?) [Read Ch. 9, the Literature]

E. CULTURAL WARS WAGED BY RELIGIOUS SECTS

The world's largest religions today are Christianity, Islam, Hinduism, and Buddhism. These religions dominate today, some say, because they have taken the hearts and souls of humanity.

Even more important, however, these religions are successful because they have continued to conduct **cultural wars** over many years, using population pressures and military force. If their populations hadn't continued to push against other cultures—using military might, technology, capital, proselyting, and numbers--these religions would have been overwhelmed by other religions that do these same things (pushing) better.

The Buddhists were once the largest religion on earth. They once dominated from Africa through Asia. Many humans chose Buddhism for its stance on non-violence, and its respect for learning and understanding. Today, the Buddhists have been pushed from many areas of their ancient domain by religions waging more aggressive cultural wars—increasing their numbers and proselytizing more aggressively than the Buddhists. You play the game hard or you lose.

The fastest growing religion today is Islam. The Muslims, begun in the 7th century, are presently the second largest religion in number, but they should overtake the Christian religion, begun in the 1st century, within two decades if their numbers continue to grow. (Both religions are growing.)

The Muslim religion today pushes in all directions, mostly against older religions, such as the Hindus in India, the Jewish state in Israel, the Buddhist in Myanmar, the government in China, and against Christianity and native religions in Africa and the Philippines. Muslim religions *particularly* push against *other Muslims* where splits have occurred between Shia and Sunni. Cultural wars have become bloody in all these regions. And resources in these regions are also under growing stress from these cultural wars.

The Christian religion overwhelmed ancient Europe and later pushed native religions from nearly every part of the Americas. The Christian and Muslim religions have been engaged in cultural wars throughout the world for hundreds of years. The result is a highly conflicted, highly populated world with quickly diminishing resources and no end of conflict in sight.

The works of Jesus and Mohammed counsel peace and harmony; but followers of these religions have taken roads of terrible violence and intolerance.

But religions are not the primary culprits. Religions are only *pawns,* dupes in a more ancient struggle: **Cultural entropy** places **all** cultures, ethnicities, language groups, beliefs, skin colors, and species in conflict, and has since the beginning of life. Humans and their imagined human concepts (good and evil) are not in control.

The point is: When religious cultures make population wars against other religions or cultures, these **wars *devalue human life*** generally, and debase the basic ideals of their own beliefs. The culture may win momentarily; but humanity—all humanity--will surely lose value in the conflicted future.

And further, on the day any religion or culture dominates completely, ***the wars will not end***. The forces of cultural entropy, and ***religious puritanity*** will continue to divide surviving belief systems into competing parts, and new wars will continue—this is human history. The future, without understanding, should continue as the past.

As an example, if the Muslim population succeeds in taking over Israel or the entire world, the victorious dogmas will split (these splits already appear worldwide), and conflicts—between divisions of the same religion—will continue. Muslim cultures splitting into new factions will continue to battle each other forever for future dominance.

Such a scenario has already repeated historically over and over both in the Christian and Muslim religions. Population wars end only when populating cultures—whatever they may be—stop aggressively populating. Only worldwide catastrophes, no man's lands, or total resource exhaustion can end such wars ***naturally***. Using human reason is a much *kinder* solution.

A similar cultural scenario will occur no matter what culture—religious or atheist--eventually claims victory in the future of the world, as long as the forces of cultural entropy continue to divide and create conflict without opposition. **Recall: To oppose entropy requires focused work.** Without **work** opposing it, entropy naturally and always proceeds to division and chaos. In addition, stresses on resources will continue to occur until resources are exhausted totally, or humanity decides population wars are not worth fighting.

THE CULTURE OF THE NON-RELIGIOUS

Religious publications often fear a future world taken over by the irreligious—atheists and agnostics. These fears are probably not warranted. Something like 40 percent of the world's urban populations considers themselves non-religious in the US and Europe. But this population is not united or particularly focused.

Worldwide, the movement for atheism is small. More important, the irreligious as a culture do not aggressively reproduce. On the contrary—though we have no hard facts—people of non-religious minds probably under reproduce those of religious minds. The **future** thus belongs to the cultures—religions—that today are most aggressively reproducing. These cultures have little to fear from non-aligned non-believers *who do not necessarily share a common culture.*

Numbers will eventually dominate, not morality or hopes.

F. INTOLERANCE AND RACISM ARE HARD-WIRED

The forces of cultural entropy created racism (billions of years ago) and make certain it continues in animal and human societies today.

Ch. 7 CULTURAL ENTROPY CREATES ETERNAL POPULATION WARS

Every human being is racist by nature. Intolerance is part of all biological systems [Ch. 1, 3, 4]. Your loving teacher, your neighbor, your parents, the people on TV, your minister, your friends, your enemies, your dog, people with different skin colors or religions, yourself. Yes, all humans and animals are hard wired to be suspicious and fearful of things that are in any way different. Racism, fear, and intolerance are parts of **all** animal biology.

Racism helps animal populations survive—staying protected with their own kind, avoiding contact with anything unknown, fearing the darkness and parasites.

If something is different than us, it may be a threat to our survival. It is not part of our *self*. Differences arouse our suspicions. Suspicions arouse our fears and hatreds.

We males know that women are *naturally* intolerant. If our colorful feathers are not perfectly arranged and beautiful, if our songs are not perfectly on key, if our nests are not exquisitely arranged—any imperfection and we will be denied our chance to reproduce. If we fail to reproduce, our songs will disappear forever from the immortal future.

To be accepted by society and gain the right to the future, both men and women must reach a high bar of cultural perfection. We can all judge each other severely. We notice small differences. We have learned for millions of years that small differences are important. We fear small differences. **Parasites still kill far, far more people today than wars.**

We seek protection by herding with others that appear to be of our own kind, our own family. Frightened white people seek out other white people when they feel threatened by blacks and immigrants, or people that talk and act a little differently than they do. Fear causes intolerance and avoidance.

Rwandan people, Hutu and Tutsis who lived side by side for hundreds of years speaking the same language, began to massacre each other in 1994, why? They were from different tribes. (Check online) The Rwandan Genocides) **Extreme** leaders took control by massacring moderates from both tribes. Without a moderate middle, consensus was impossible. Divisive propaganda circulated by **extreme** leaders, accentuated divisions. **Extreme emotions** overwhelmed all morality and reason. Millions of innocent people were massacred and millions more starved when the war continued in Zaire.

Racism causes racism; violence causes violence; hatred causes hatred. Extreme emotions destroy moderation, understanding, and reason; extreme divisions generate ignorance. Extreme actions cause absurd reactions. Violence creates **no man's lands** that destroy capital circulation and bring famine. Decisions made in ignorance are inevitably wrong decisions.

Humans are all racists. Wars of cultural intolerance have occurred or are occurring everywhere in the world; these tribal, cultural wars began at the beginning of humanity. The only real change is the advantage of modern technology to make these wars even deadlier.

Racism is stoked by our ***fears*** of others. **Extreme** politicians use these **fears** to control us. Few can be so courageous as to resist racial fears and stand selfless in the vulnerable, moderate, toxic middle. Without a common middle, consensus becomes impossible. Fears, and **extreme** emotions, can cause us to commit extreme inhumane acts. Extreme emotions **overwhelm** morality and reason and twist normal human life to ***absurdity***. Artists and writers have been bringing this absurdity to our attention for generations.

Racism is *natural* to all humans. Children learn to be intolerant when they learn to fear and evaluate others. Racism and intolerance have been part of the animal **self** since the beginning: What is me? What is us? What is not us? What must we avoid? What do I fear? What will hurt my family? Who are my people? Who are not my people? This is racist thinking.

To ***not*** be a racist is unnatural. The disease is in all of us. To survive, perhaps, we all *need* a tiny touch of it, along with some suspicion, and angst, and paranoia. But the edge is very close; and we can all, easily fail, choosing sides and destroying our human family.

We must be vigilant to fight this disease, intolerance, for it can be deadly and totally controlling in **extremes**. *To oppose* extreme emotions, such as racism, requires **work**, continuous work, unending work. Success is not easy.

All the forces of **cultural entropy** push against us. These forces never sleep or tire.

Extreme leaders, to further their search for power, utilize *small* differences and fears to create racist conflicts. Once established, the tools of racism and fear raise **extreme** leaders to greater power. The forces of cultural entropy assist such tyrants. A human ethnicity guided by extreme emotions can wield extreme power even if it is small. Leadership over extremist groups allows a political party or a politician, extreme control.

Moderate groups, on the contrary, even if they represent a large populace, are often unwieldy and lacking in focus. Moderate emotions are less productive of actions than extreme emotions. And reason, as Hamlet well knows, is a time-consuming, often difficult process.

Extreme human emotions always urge violent alternatives over rational consensus. Violent alternatives are quick and easy. Unity and cultural understandings are hard work. Cultural entropy assists extremes.

Forces of division and cultural entropy, always set emotional humans on collision courses. Racism is present in all humans—blacks, whites, browns, yellows, and chartreuses. We are all racists in our own ways. Racism cannot be conquered. Racism is part of our self-identity, our biology.

Racism can *only* be opposed in one manner—by continued hard **work** in the opposite direction towards understanding.

Capital is life. Capital circulation is capitalism. The forces of cultural entropy oppose stability and capital systems. To oppose the continual forces of entropy, requires continual work.

Cultural entropy will not diminish naturally. Human work is *continually* necessary to oppose entropy—cultural chaos, extreme emotions, ignorance, lies, and racism.

G. CULTURAL ENTROPY (Human Biology) ASSISTS INTOLERANT, EXTREME LEADERS.

Humans with large, extreme *egos* often seek positions of leadership and authority. Historically, however, good common sense, morality, intelligence, or human understandings do not necessarily *accompany* **extreme** human **egos**. Egos stand alone.

So--you don't need to be honest, or smart, or sane, or talented to egotistically *want* to be a leader. But to succeed, you need to find something to propel you into a leadership position. Racism, tribalism, patriotism, extreme emotions, chaos, ignorance, and fear are often *convenient tools*. The forces of **cultural entropy** (chaos) manufacture these emotional and divisive tools constantly, and make them widely available to all who wish to use them.

Adolf Hitler could not get into university, because he flunked the mathematics exam. He was **not** a brilliant person, far from his propaganda image. But he had some artistic talents, and, by all accounts he had a creative, artistic temperament--he invented his own truths, like his paintings, out of thin air. When the opportunity arose, he was able to follow his extreme emotional fantasies and his extreme racism to lead his extreme political party to absolute control.

With extreme emotions in control, rational alternatives and moderate opinions soon disappear. When the capital profits of verifiable-truth and human understanding stop circulating, catastrophes due to ignorance are inevitable. Truth becomes whatever fantasy the leaders say it is.

Millions paid the price when they allowed destructive, extremist leadership to take control in Germany. Hitler, of course, was not the first such tyrant to ride the forces of **cultural entropy** and fake patriotism to power. ***Certainly, he will not be the last.***

The world is filled with Hitlers—small, egotistical, fearful, delusional men who wish to be important. **Moderate leaders can only oppose extremism with hard work in the direction of unity.**

All capital sharing systems proceed to maximum **entropy** unless opposed by **work**.

COMING EVENTS

Have you seen the next new extreme leader? He or she will appear soon. We may not yet know what he or she looks like. But we are rather certain what these persons will do. Using divisiveness, intolerance, untruths, fake patriotism, and the assistance of the forces of **cultural entropy**, they will seek to destroy our human family.

CH 8 --
HOW FORCES OF CULTURAL ENTROPY DESTROY CIVILIZATIONS AND CAPITAL ECONOMIES OVER TIME

Rome and Greece
The Anasazi
Stonehenge
The Maya
The Ottoman Empire
The Chinese
The Khmer
The African Continent
The Norse in Greenland
Northern Tier Countries

    Authors commonly conclude civilizations disappear due to calamities, such as invasions, plagues, famines, soil erosion, or climactic changes. These are very good reasons for terrible things to happen—and no way should they be ignored. These reason explain why many small populations disappear from existence. But terrible calamities are only a partial explanation for the demise of larger cultures.
    When large civilizations share unifying resources they can often survive, pull together, and rise again and again. Cultures form initially as survival mechanisms. Final declines, like incurable diseases, only begin when resource sharing ends--in other words, when the culture has already lost the sharing traits and unifying identities that once made it a true culture or united family.

<u>EXAMPLES OF CIVILIZATIONS SHATTERED BY CULTURAL ENTROPY</u>

THE RISE AND FALL OF THE ROMAN AND GREEK EMPIRES

We discussed the great civilizations of Greece and Rome previously (Ch. 5). Why did they rise? Why did they fade? The reasons, beyond understanding at the time, are quite clear today. Humans failed to understand the invisible forces of **cultural entropy** that would eventually disassemble their economies and infrastructures.

Healthy farming and trading *economies* brought both civilizations to power. Human labor created **profits**; these profits enabled sharing cooperative capitalism. *Cooperative capitalism builds empires; competitive capitalism destroys empires.*

Circulating capital profit provided the economic energy to fund armies and massive infrastructure.

Over time, however, the presence of slavery, and strict status levels destroyed the value of human labor (or the middle class) and limited the circulation of profit capital. **Due to slavery, free human labor could no longer generate profits.** When profit capital stops circulating, other capital stops circulating in tandem.

Cultural entropy (chaos) consistently increased populations. Population pressures stress resources, create erosion, and foment constant warfare.

The divisive forces of **cultural entropy**, over time, **polarize political institutions** and magnify regional differences. Polarized political institutions can no longer affectively govern. Strong individuals and tyrants dominate with force and conflict. Ensuing **Population wars** cause deforestation, stress resources, **and form no man's lands.**

Without circulating capital profit, the empire could no longer support infrastructures, including the military, aqueducts, roads, schools, and protected trade. Status levels and language dissolution further hindered common understandings and capital profit circulation between divided states. Without capital (blood) circulating to its various parts, the empire could not function as a single organism.

As central government weakened, extreme elements, and criminal gangs took over and created **no man's lands,** toxic, lawless areas in which human commerce could not succeed, and profits could not be created. Pirates terrorized trade in the Mediterranean, often protected by local powers. Local gangs attacked overland trade.

Without **profits**, trade disappears and human families cannot feed themselves or education their children. Wheat rotted in Egypt, while children starved in Italy. Stagnant, divided, slave states dominated the empire. Without circulation, the organism dies. When the economy fails, the empire falls.

Cooperative capitalism was overwhelmed by **competitive capitalism. No man's lands** grew between entrenched climax populations. The profits of enslaved humanity diminished and ceased to circulate. With fewer and fewer profits to circulate, the economy slowly stagnated.

Reasons for failure commonly blamed in these times--religious controversies, immorality, population movements, pagan invasions, immigrants, leadership changes, political decisions, and military campaigns—actually had little or no *long-term* contribution to the final economic resolutions.

The destructive economic events that shatter civilizations take place beneath human radar: Over time, the random and divisive forces of **cultural entropy** combine with ignorant, competing cultural hierarchies, slavery, and status levels to ever-so-slowly strangle capital flow and devalue all human life. The written *histories*—including battlefield heroics and the colorful rise and fall of powerful individuals—these human stories are dramatic but rather meaningless decoration, ornamentations that changed the dire situation little over time.

The misunderstood forces of random chaos that guided The Roman Empire to destruction were not human. Since they were invisible, they were beyond human control.

THE ANASAZI

The Anasazi were a successful people established in what is now the southwestern United Sates and Mexico. They colonized a wide area and successfully farmed corn and other crops beginning in 1250 BC. But after several thousand years of prosperous growth, suffering through droughts and good years, the entire culture erupted into warfare, economic devastation, and tribal isolation.

Anasazi peoples abandoned central cities from Colorado to New Mexico. Eventually, after 1250 AD, only isolated pueblos remained, many on high mesas or even hidden away in stone caverns. What happened?

Cultural entropy eventually divided the Anasazi family into separate, antagonistic **extremes**. Drought caused famine, and famine turned Anasazi tribes into warring bands. Because of war, populations fled major *indefensible* areas. Large swaths of once-productive territory became **no man's lands**; these could no longer support human populations. Atrocities included cannibalism and genocide. **Extreme** leaders took control.

The total population diminished due to lack of food, but when the drought ended, populations did not return. **Cooperative capitalism** was replaced by **competitive capitalism**. The Anasazi had suffered through a dozen droughts of equal intensity. But now, the family could not come together or **share**. The **no man's lands** remained abandoned, dangerous, and uninhabitable. **Extreme emotions** remained in control. Small defensible villages remained, but the **polarized** Anasazi family never returned to their former glory. A polarized family that refuses to share capital is no longer a family. An organism without capital circulation dies.

When a culture's economy fails, the culture divides and decays. As opposed to river systems that **helped re-unite** other cultures, the Colorado River system disappears for much of its length in deep desert canyons, and is not easily navigable.

What drove the Anasazi to retreat to the cliffs and fortified villages? And, later, what precipitated the exodus? For a long time, experts focused on environmental explanations. Using data from tree rings, researchers know that a terrible drought seized the Southwest from 1276 to 1299; it is possible that in certain areas there was virtually no rain at all during those 23 years. In addition, the Anasazi people may have nearly deforested the region, chopping down trees for roof beams and firewood. **But environmental problems can't explain everything.** Throughout the centuries, the Anasazi weathered comparable crises—a longer and more severe drought, for example, from 1130 to 1180—without heading for the cliffs or abandoning their lands.

Another theory, put forward by early explorers, speculated that nomadic raiders may have driven the Anasazi out of their homeland. But, says Lipe, "There's simply no evidence [of nomadic tribes in this area] in the 13th century. This is one of the most thoroughly investigated regions in the world. If there were enough nomads to drive out tens of thousands of people, surely the invaders would have left plenty of archaeological evidence."

So researchers have begun to look for the answer within the Anasazi themselves. According to Lekson, two critical factors that arose after 1150—the documented unpredictability of the climate and what he calls "socialization for fear"—combined to produce long-lasting violence that tore apart the Anasazi culture. In the 11th and early 12th centuries there is little archaeological evidence of true warfare, Lekson says, but there were executions. As he puts it, "There seem to have been goon squads. Things were not going well for the leaders, and the governing structure wanted to perpetuate itself by making an example of social outcasts; the leaders executed and even cannibalized them." This practice, perpetrated by Chaco Canyon rulers, created a society-wide paranoia, according to Lekson's theory, thus "socializing" the Anasazi people to live in constant fear. Lekson goes on to describe a grim scenario that he believes emerged during the next few hundred years. "Entire villages go after one another," he says, "alliance against alliance. And it persists well into the Spanish period." As late as 1700, for instance, several Hopi villages attacked the Hopi pueblo of Awatovi, setting fire to the community, killing all the adult males, capturing and possibly slaying women and children, and cannibalizing the victims. Vivid and grisly accounts of this massacre were recently gathered from elders by Northern Arizona University professor and Hopi expert Ekkehart Malotki.

By David Roberts
SMITHSONIAN MAGAZINE | SUBSCRIBE JULY 2003

Cultural Entropy invisibly decays economies and divides civilizations over long time periods. Cultural entropy favors extremes, and **destroys** *the moderate middle*. **Extreme** leadership creates polarization and **unresolvable** conflicts. Population wars create **no man's lands**, place competitive stresses on resources, force land erosion, destroy shared infrastructures, and turn cooperative capitalism into predatory capitalism.

STONEHENGE

In 3500 BC, Paleolithic people began creating one of the world's most enigmatic arrangements of huge stones. Early settlers put thousands of man-hours and massive planning into placing these stones. They returned again and again to the same region at regular intervals for hundreds of years.

Visitors to the monolith traveled from such distant places as the Shetland Islands and Europe; some took journeys that must have taken weeks to complete.

After a thousand or so years, around 1600BC, construction at Stonehenge ended. The area was abandoned except for sparse local populations; these people eventually looked at the massive structures without comprehension. What happened and why?

There are other hypotheses and theories. According to a team of British researchers led by Mike Parker Pearson of the University of Sheffield, Stonehenge may have been built as a symbol of "peace and unity", indicated in part by the fact that at the time of its construction, Britain's Neolithic people were experiencing a period of cultural unification.[35][45]

Simply put: The Neolithic family that built Stonehenge, and worshipped there as a family for over a thousand years, stopped being a family. Their languages became garbled to each other. They failed to recognize their real family connection. They engaged in constant, vicious, non-family warfare. The original *family* of people split into antagonistic pieces. The new tribes refused to share resources. "You aren't us anymore! We don't need a common place of worship."

Stonehenge, a place for *family* burials and common solstice rituals, no longer had a common family to tend it--that family was destroyed by time and **cultural entropy.**

Large areas of common land became too dangerous to inhabit or travel, **no man's lands.** Competition replaced cooperation. The concept of *ownership* split the land into defensible parses with trespass forbidden. Common trade routes had to be abandoned because of lawlessness and lack of common regulations.

Cycles of unification and chaos continued for generations, and these cycles continue in Britain today. The forces of unity and division are always in conflict, **cultural entropy** battles central control—and tomorrow will be no exception.

Extreme random elements have been struggling for hundreds of years to divide the British islands into small antagonistic pieces. One day, perhaps, they will succeed completely.

THE MAYA

Beginning in 1200 BC, the Maya inhabited (and continue to inhabit) the Yucatan peninsula of Mexico. They created the largest and best designed stone structures constructed by early American peoples.

The early settlers found the peninsula an excellent place for small farms. Slash and burn agriculture worked well over an extremely large area. Burning the trees and then farming the cleared areas returned excellent crops including corn, beans, and peppers. The resources depleted were able to return to productivity in cycles as low as six to ten years.

The extended population increased to an estimated six million people.

The Yucatan area was unique in possessing ***few waterways***. In lieu of water transport, the people spent time creating roadways to facilitate trade and travel. Water management was also problematic since the area was dependent on underground aquifers and seasonal rains. Early populations, however, were apparently equal to the infrastructure challenges.

In their growth period, the Maya enjoyed immense prosperity; they created stone pyramids for common rituals and made strides in mathematics and astronomy. They were ahead of their time in construction, levies, and water maintenance. They built sophisticated wooden boats; and trade, overland and sea, extended for hundreds of miles. They constructed dikes to stop soil erosion on hillsides and increased production up to three times with fertilizers and irrigation.

Topographical hurtles and cultural entropy, however, divided the once-cohesive population into small divergent language groups. Over 70 divergent dialects were spoken. Soil erosion consistently made growing crops more difficult. When the area was plagued by drought and the crops failed, these separate cultures plunged into vicious warfare.

Large areas turned into **no man's lands. Extreme** leaders took control. Fertile terraced areas were abandoned. Populations plummeted in these areas and never returned, not even when the drought passed and the lands recovered from resource depletion. Competitive capitalism (warfare) replaced cooperative capitalism.

A sophisticated Maya calendar, carefully kept over a thousand years, abruptly halted in the year 906. At the same time, infrastructures, such as roads and aquifers, stopped being maintained, so both trade and small farming suffered. Human labor could no longer yield tradable profits. The population dropped over 60% or more over wide areas, and many population centers created for common use were abandoned.

The common family, the common economy, the common population of the area, no longer existed. **Violent no man's lands** continued to be uninhabitable and impossible to farm over many years even when fertile.

No man's lands over wide areas starve women and children and destroy human populations.

The forces of **cultural entropy** were particularly strong in the Yucatan area. Forest growth and topography acted quickly in these regions to separate the Maya language into multiple idioms. **Seventy separate languages** **eventually developed from the same root.** No river system provided easy access from tribe to tribe across the region, either to facilitate trade or cultural continuity.

Water storage systems and roads required constant maintenance, without which they were quickly overgrown; and during wartime, infrastructures quickly suffered extreme neglect.

Dikes and levies, which decreased erosion and increased soil fertility up to three times in certain areas, had to be abandoned.

Food and trade generally moved on foot, and in times of war, difficult overland trade must have diminished, leaving many regions isolated. **No man's lands** spread across the interior, hindering the movement of capital, cultural understanding, and the production of farm capital long after drought conditions ameliorated.

The irony is, during times of **unity**, drought conditions caused little apparent long-term unrest. The Maya civilization and populations recovered through dozens of difficult historic cycles while sharing the pain. Only when the region divided irrevocably because of language changes, **cultural intolerance**, and **warfare**, did the cyclic problems of famine, erosion, and resource depletion become insoluble.

Intolerance **polarized** the Maya and lingered for generations, and no single tyrant grew powerful enough to unite the warring states. The final entrance of European powers interrupted whatever cycle might have reoccurred.

Cultural entropy destroys capital flow. Capital is life. Focused work is necessary to oppose cultural entropy. Extreme leadership destroys moderation and creates eternal conflict. No man's lands diminish populations by destroying infrastructures, and starving women and children.

THE OTTOMAN EMPIRE

The Ottoman Empire grew in much the same way as the Roman Empire. Conquests over several hundred years extended Ottoman rule throughout all of North Africa and Eastern Europe. The conquests were primarily funded by the control of trade routes.

For several hundred years Ottoman rule brought **economic success** and relative peace and prosperity to its domains. Ottoman rule integrated numerous ethnicities and religions into a successful commonwealth close to the size of ancient Rome.

The loss of trade routes in the fifteenth century led to weakness in central authority and growing polarization. Status levels led to economic stagnation and increasingly limited profit circulation.

Over time, religious divisions, and ethnic divisions that had existed without conflict for hundreds of years, **polarized** against central government and each other. **Extreme** and divisive elements grabbed control both in government, religious, and ethnic arenas.

The last century of the empire erupted into intolerant ethnic and religious wars. Genocides of Greek, Assyrian, and Armenian peoples were last gasp efforts of an **extreme** leadership with limited resources trying to keep together a topographically and linguistically divided empire.

No man's lands reduced trade and economic development. Status levels and military hierarchies denied profits to human labor and devalued human workers who struggled to merely survive. **Extreme** religious *puritanity* validated states of slavery and encouraged constant religious conflicts.

Capital from the new world plus revitalized world trade empowered European economies in the sixteenth century. But this profit capital did not reach the Ottoman state and its many isolated parts.

CULTURAL WARS placed increasing demands on scarce resources. Population pressures continued a pattern of soil erosion and depletion over many centuries (and exists in many areas to this day) that diminished farm production.

Like Rome, The Ottoman Empire died due to the lack of capital circulation, erosions of soil and infrastructure, enslaved poverty, and the polarization of its intolerant parts. **Climax populations** stifled industry and opposed change. Elsewhere, in Europe, increasing capital circulation funded a revitalized middle class. Middle class efforts created technological advances in trade, manufacturing, social change, and warfare—these advances left the Ottoman Empire economically and technologically behind and unable to defend its empire militarily against European incursions.

Today, ancient Ottoman territory is ravaged still by some of the world's most oppressive **extremes**. **Extreme** religious, political, and ethnic divisions still dominate the once-united area. The region is an excellent example of the erosive effects of long-term **cultural entropy**.

Recall: This same area was once united by Alexander, the Great, and later again by Roman forces. The forces of **cultural entropy** have had many years to fester and create human divisions and animosities in this region.

THE CHINESE

The Chinese state is a bit of an anomaly compared to other regions. The difference is that China—though it has suffered great divisions and violence over its history—has managed somehow to regroup on several occasions into long-term dynasties, sometimes lasting for extended periods, hundred of years.

Over long time periods, China is a poster-child for the effects of cultural entropy. Chinese have described their own region as a place that continually divides into warring states and then reunites over and over and over. But compared to other regions—Europe, the Mideast, Africa—continuity is apparently far greater, and divisiveness far less. Why is this?

Is the Chinese temperament simply better suited to civilization than other races? Are Chinese more submissive, less emotional, more reasonable than other humans? Probably not. Scientists have so far found little difference in human populations when brought up under similar conditions. European children brought up by Chinese, and Chinese children brought up by Europeans tend to adopt the same manners as their parents. And ancient Chinese history rivals all other areas for social division and constant, bloody warfare.

Topography, however, probably *has* assisted to stabilize the Chinese population and language. The two major river systems both drain to the same eastern plain. These rivers were united by the Grand Canal [See below]. Though, in the ancient past, the river systems divided the country, major population areas developed down the eastern coast with little to segregate them. The ethnic Han comprise nearly ninety percent of the Chinese population. The Cantonese are nearly seven percent. In this situation, minority ethnicities are truly minorities.

Europe is a combination of numerous peninsulas and divided valleys. Each peninsula and valley—Greek, Italian, Iberian, Ionian, French, or German—have separate drainage areas; these areas remain segregated from each other in greater linguistic isolation than mainland China.

The notable divisions on the Asiatic continent—the Korea Peninsula, Mongolia, Japan, Viet Nam, and Cambodia—occur, as in Europe, when mountains or oceans manage to divide populations over long time periods.

Monotheistic, puritanical religions that divide the European continent—though they appeared in China—never achieved divisive power as they did in other areas.

And not to be ignored: The Chinese developed early in their history a common **symbolic language**. Even when languages changed in divergent regions, the written language and meanings stayed the same. Literacy among the elites continued in China when it dimmed in Europe. This *understanding of a common history* then, and now, still unites the large Chinese population over a large area less apparent in other regions.

Thus cycles of division and unification caused by **cultural entropy** have occurred more slowly in China than in other regions; but they should continue to occur in the future as elsewhere—unless work towards unity continues in a healthy fashion.

THE GRAND CANAL UNITED CHINA'S DRAINAGE SYSTEMS

The Ancient Chinese built early canals to help with transportation and commerce. One early section was the Han Gou Canal built by Kin Fuchai of Wu around 480 BC. This canal stretched from the Yangtze River to the Huai River.

Another ancient canal was the Hong Gou Canal which went from the Yellow River to the Bian River. These ancient canals became the basis for the Grand Canal over 1000 years later.

Building the Grand Canal

It was during the Sui Dynasty that the Grand Canal was built. Emperor Yang of the Sui wanted a quicker and more efficient way of transporting grain to his capital city at Beijing. He also needed to supply his army that guarded northern China from the Mongols. He decided to connect the existing canals and expand them to go all the way from Beijing to Hangzhou.

Building the canal was a huge project. It took over six years of hard work by millions of laborers. Emperor Yang was a tyrant. He forced millions of farmers to work on the canal. Many of them died during the construction. However, when the canal was finally completed in 609 AD, China had a new waterway that would enrich the country for hundreds of years to come.

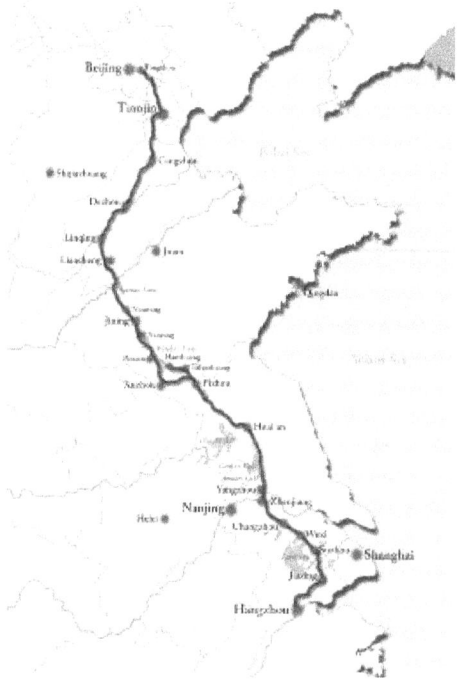

Modern Course of Grand Canal of China
by Ian Kiu

Later Improvements

The Ming Dynasty rebuilt much of the canal in the early 1400s. They made the canal deeper, built new canal locks, and constructed reservoirs to regulate the water in the canal. The main purpose of the canal continued to be the transport of grain. This continued throughout the Ming Dynasty and most of the history of Ancient China.

Interesting Facts about the Grand Canal
- Historians estimate that the oldest section of the canal was built around the 6th century BC.

- Emperors would sometimes travel along the Grand Canal to inspect the locks.
- It is estimated that it took over 45,000 full-time laborers to maintain the canal during the Ming Dynasty.
- The canal was also used as a courier route for carrying important government messages.
- In the 1400s, the Chinese government operated over 11,000 grain barges on the canal to transport food to the north.
- The Grand Canal also proved to be an excellent source of taxes for the Chinese government.
- Portions of the canal fell into disrepair after the Yellow River flooded in 1855.
- The pound lock was invented during the Song Dynasty in 984 AD to help raise and lower the water level of the canal.

DUCKSTERS EDUCATIONAL SITE
Cite this Page

THE KHMER

The Khmer of what is now Cambodia occupied one of the most fertile areas of the ancient or modern world.

The **Khmer Empire** Khmer" to the Khmer people), was a Hindu-Buddhist empire in Southeast Asia. The empire, which grew out of the former kingdoms of Funan and Chenla, at times ruled over and/or vassalised most of mainland Southeast Asia[3] and parts of Southern China, stretching from the tip of the Indochinese Peninsula northward to modern Yunnan province, China, and from Vietnam westward to Myanmar.[4][5]

Its greatest legacy is Angkor, in present-day Cambodia, which was the site of the capital city during the empire's zenith. The majestic monuments of Angkor, such as Angkor Wat and Bayon, bear testimony to the Khmer Empire's immense power and wealth, impressive art and culture, architectural technique, aesthetics achievements, and the variety of belief systems that it patronised over time. Satellite imaging has revealed that Angkor, during its peak in the 11th to 13th centuries, was the largest pre-industrial urban centre in the world.[6]

The beginning of the era of the Khmer Empire is conventionally dated to 802 CE when King Jayavarman II declared himself chakravartin ("king of the world", or "king of kings") on Phnom Kulen. The empire ended with the fall of Angkor in the 15th century.

Wikipedia

The Angkor region, during its peak in the 11th through the 13th centuries, was the largest pre-industrial urban center in the world. The region was more populous and productive than London, Paris, Tokyo, or Beijing.

The Tonle Sap, a large freshwater lake, floods regularly. The early Khmer converted the Tonle Sap floods into fertile rice fields. By controlling water, up to *three* rice harvests occurred yearly. The lake was, and still is, home to abundant harvests of fish.

The Khmer created irrigation and building projects unequaled in the pre-industrialized world. The extreme harvests freed massive numbers of workers for use as year-around builders and soldiers. Khmer traders ventured as far as India and Northern China.

The administrative and design capacities of the Khmer were quite advanced. But less is know of the society than might be hoped. Though the Khmer were quite literate, the damp conditions of the region destroyed most of the bamboo manuscripts once held in the Khmer's preeminent library system.

Damp and rainy conditions over eons also severely impacted major constructions such as Angkor Wat, perhaps the world's largest and most impressive religious monument. Brick suffers from molds and paint decays in such situations without constant infrastructure maintenance. *Entropy never sleeps.*

Central government historically commanded an immense work force to maintain the hydraulic flow of the area. Slaves were common and cheap according to Chinese documents. But large numbers of rice farmers and fisherman constituted the primary population. The king had the power to conscript all layers of the populace for common work.

Over time, however, the gap between slaves and free workers diminished. Free work no longer created a profit and workers had little to trade. Profits supported an ever-richer elite with massive, extraordinary pageantry. Profit circulation diminished otherwise. Workers had little time to spare for massive projects or infrastructure repair. Hunger dominated the wealthiest region in the world.

In the same way that water and wind decay brick, **cultural entropy** slowly decayed the Khmer civilization.

Later Khmer administrations were plagued by foreign invasions and abandoned by their vassals. The central government divided into feuding states.

When forces of **cultural entropy** divided the central government, infrastructures declined. With the decline of infrastructures, the huge population supported by huge rice crops, also declined sharply. Irrigation projects and common constructions had to be abandoned.

Like the Romans, without powerful central government, invading armies stole resources. Lawless areas created **no man's lands** that made farming and trade difficult or impossible. Without cooperation and *infrastructures*, the total population suffered famine and diminished by more than half. The economy collapsed.

In the fifteen century, the jungle overwhelmed abandoned, once-great monuments such as Angkor Wat. The center of government moved from the indefensible central plateau to the defensible coast.

While resource depletion, deforestation, and overpopulation were problems in the final years, these same problems had been encountered in earlier times and overcome. **Cultural entropy** slowly destroyed the integrity of the culture and its ability to react as a *single organism* over many years. Capital did not circulate fairly, and as a result, parts that kept the society together, died.

Cultural inequities lasted for hundreds of years. During modern times, the region suffered a terrible genocide, primarily of the upper classes, perpetrated by the Cambodian Khmer Rouge. Famines and purges affected all classes. The Khmer Rouge slaughtered and starved approximately ¼ of the total population. The policies devastated hated status levels, but poverty, inequity, and other problems remained and even increased severely. The government was attacking the wrong problem.

Mind control, mass murders, economic slavery, stifling farm programs—these activities inhibit needed capital circulation and place an economy in constant famine and poverty. Such programs create conditions completely contrary to economic fertility and healthy profit circulation. Unfortunately, the Khmer Rouge leadership was clueless and uneducated. They recognized status differences were part of the problem, but did not understand, mass murders were not the solution.

Capital is life. When capital profit stops flowing, the organism dies. The Khmer Rouge took no steps to facilitate capital circulation among their peoples. In fact, every decision, made in ignorance, had the exact opposite effect.

Recovery is slow, but the region is now making excellent progress and tourism is welcome.

Following their victory, the Khmer Rouge led by Pol Pot, Nuon Chea, Ieng Sary, Son Sen and Khieu Samphan renamed the country as Democratic Kampuchea and immediately set about forcibly evacuating the country's major cities. The regime murdered hundreds of thousands of their perceived political opponents. Ultimately, the Cambodian genocide led to the deaths of 1.5 to 3 million people, around 25% of Cambodia's population.

ISLAND NATIONS

Island regions, like England and Japan, have some advantages in central control. They also have disadvantages. The advantages are isolation and natural borders. An island nation does not need to worry about where its territory ends, since the sea creates a natural territory. Isolation can create a naturally united population, or not.

Sea borders also offer natural defenses. Both England and Japan have benefited from storms that wiped out invading fleets.

Do natural borders also create a sense of natural unity? Obviously, not always. Sri Lanka, an island country south of India, is recovering from a civil war of terrible proportions. The British islands have suffered great polarization and disunity throughout history, and are still prone to divisive elements. Given the opportunity, separatists in Scotland, Wales, and Ireland would happily divide the once-united confederacy into warring tribes.

Pie shaped island valleys on separate river systems can easily degrade into portions that feel they have nothing in common. Island divisions also increase, as island cultures grow less dependent on sea trade.

Easter Island is a perfect example:

EASTER ISLAND

Easter island is one of the world's most remote islands, and one of the last islands to be inhabited by Paleolithic humans, perhaps as late as 1200 AD. The early colonists enjoyed success and the population soared to five or six thousand individuals.

Large palms originally grew on much of the island. Whether Polynesian rats or human hands destroyed these palms—the points are still debated--the trees disappeared after several hundred years of human occupation. Without trees, the islanders had limited ability to build suitable fishing craft. Together with the disappearance of the palms, much of the accessible wildlife disappeared also, including several species of flightless and nesting birds.

The human family divided the island into pie-like divisions. Capital exchanges diminished between these divisions.

With limited fishing, large human and rat populations overwhelmed the island's ability to provide food. Soil depletions diminished crop yields. The sea no longer provided a common exchange of culture. [Recall how the Grand Canal in China united a large population.] The original settlers divided into warring clans, and cannibalism and other atrocities apparently became common. Large areas of the island became **no man's lands** too dangerous to farm.

The population diminished badly. When the Europeans arrived in the sixteenth century, only a few thousand islanders inhabited the entire island. The enslavement of a large part of the population and European diseases at one point reduced the survivors to approximately 200 individuals.

The irony of Easter Island is the presence of large numbers of huge stone carvings, called Moai. These carvings required the work of thousands of individuals over many days and months and years. The carvings describe a healthy, vibrant, well-fed society, with island-wide participation, and social cooperation on a wide scale over a long, peaceful time span. What happened?

Well, of course, the record is not totally clear: But the forces of cultural entropy certainly played a part. The single family that colonized the island; the cooperating families that later built huge monuments and moved them long distances to look out at the sea—these extended families ceased to exist. The island-wide economy of **cooperative** (sharing) **capitalism** collapsed; it was replaced with **competitive** (predatory) **capitalism.**

Famine conditions created **intolerant** warring clans and **no man's zones.** Lack of material for boats, limited the island's ability to unite as a single sea-going culture. No man's zones and lack of infrastructure further limited the islander's abilities to feed themselves. Farmers could not farm unprotected areas. Resource depletion and deforestation were both causes and effects of human social chaos. Topography can unite large populations (China) or create many divisions on a tiny, tiny island.

Why didn't humans think to replant their vanishing palm trees? They once used these trees to build boats. The palm trees may have disappeared so slowly, short-lived humans never realized what was happening. Each generation of islanders merely accepted the diminished palms as the status quo. ***Time dissolves understandings.***

Or perhaps—as they do today--vicious wars forced intelligent people to be so shortsighted and stressed, they had no ability to share intellectual capital or plan for the future.

David R. Montgomery and Patrick Kirch compared two islands, not terribly unlike Easter Island, Tikopia and Mangaia. Mangia met a fate quite similar to Easter Island. Tikopia, strangely, enjoyed reasonable peace and prosperity until the arrival of Europeans.

Tikopia, uniquely, adopted strict population controls early in its history. Tikopia's population, kept within the limits of its resources, maintained a united single-family identity. The populace carefully attended common gardens without conflict. The society enjoyed family unity and continued to share. So they avoided the vicious wars of Easter Island and Mangia.

Larger populations, such as those in Mangaia and Easter Island, without population controls, engaged in population competitions that divided the island into non-sharing, vicious, apocalyptic violence.

A society that does not *share* capital resources does not function as a family. Intolerance creates extreme leadership. **Extreme leaders** are not reasonable leaders and do not make decisions based on the common good. Warfare, polarization, and **no man's zones** cause famines and **destroy infrastructures**--including, apparently, the palm trees that once made life on Easter Island much more comfortable.

THE AFRICAN CONTINENT

Across the earth, the forces of **cultural entropy** work similarly on all human populations. Language and cultural differences, customs of dress and religion, topographical variances, hairstyles and skin colors—these simple, random divisions **over long time periods** tear human families apart and ravage capital circulation among the human social organism.

The European, the Asian continents, and the Americas—these areas were populated at later dates than the parent continent of Africa. We might expect the forces of **cultural entropy** had longer to work in Africa than elsewhere. The results are exactly what we would predict: The chaos and divisions created in Africa are quite extraordinary and **exactly as expected** after eons of cultural entropy.

Language entropy: The large and topologically diverse African continent is home to a nearly incomprehensible number of languages and tribal divisions. One quarter of the world's languages are spoken in Africa. The power of central governments and democratic institutions are feeble. **Infrastructures** are poor. **Intolerance and polarization** are high.

Parasites and diseases had millions of years to develop alongside the hominid populations in Africa, far longer than on any other continent. Animal species in Africa are thus less naïve and parasites more virulent than on other continents. *Invasions* of foreign religions and military technology have further destabilized the regions.

We should also repeat: **Parasites benefit from proximity.** Whenever a single species exists in close proximity, parasites can quickly establish resistant and successful strains. This is particularly true in the corn belt of the U.S. Vast plantings of one crop allow parasites to quickly develop immunities to all pesticides. [See Ch. 5]

But back in Africa, **large** hominid populations—verses small, divided populations--are particularly susceptible to parasitic infections. This situation, working out over hundreds of thousands of years, put **parasites** on a parallel track with **cultural entropy**. In other words, parasites discourage the creation of large human societies in Africa. Parasites act as a *divisive force* against central governments and human unity. Parasites assist cultural entropy.

If the results of **cultural entropy** and **extreme emotions** over time lead invariably to the creation of **no man's lands**, then much of Africa is a prime example of such effects. To repeat: Africa may **not** be an example of humanity's past, its primitive origination—**Africa may actually be an example of humanity's possible *future*, the place numbers are guiding *all* human activities *forward.***

If so, then we clearly need to understand the situation, and avoid the pitfalls of the **future** we are pursuing. Rational understanding aside—**cultural entropy** is leading our entire human family into a vast **no man's land,** a place of conflict, division, and chaos.

To increase the *value* of future human existence, we should consider pursuing a different course.

THE NORSE IN GREENLAND

The Norse settled in Greenland in (985). They disappeared around 1400. They practiced similar techniques in Greenland as in their home countries, farming, and herding. However, for unexplained reasons they may have refused to eat fish. Experts assume some superstition led the settlers to be intolerant to fish consumption. For unknown reasons, they did not harvest salmon. (?)

Farming practices and overgrazing led to wide scale land erosion and soil depletion both in Greenland and Iceland.

During warm years, the settlers managed to get by, but when the area became too cold to farm, after several hundred years, settlers suffered famine and eventually disappeared from Greenland. Diminishing trade in walrus tusks also may have played a part. (Reports that weather did *not* change are difficult to accept.)

Inuit in the same area who traded with these European settlers continued to prosper. The question is, why did the Norse fail to adapt Inuit practices when their own survival was at risk. The Inuit had learned to create watercraft out of skins—rather than only wood—and to fish for seals and fish, which were abundant.

The evidence apparently reveals the Norse were too proud or superstitious to change their survival customs. The settlers were guided by superstitions and untruths rather than verifiable truths. **When decisions are made on untruths and superstitions, those decisions are often**

catastrophic. Memes of ignorance can be deadly to prosperity. The settlers, rather than change their self-concepts—choosing Inuit methods--chose to starve or leave their homes.

As discussed in previous chapters, in the dark ages, memes of ignorance contradicted the circulation of truth. Similarly, Soviet planners created farm programs utilizing memes of untruth, while at the same time abridging the circulation of verifiable truth. The consequences were economic disasters. Truth is a real, capital item; and when verifiable truths stop circulating, circulation of other capital items simultaneously stop circulating.

When human societies make decisions based on untruths, those decisions tend to be bad decisions. Untruths oppose survival and consensus.

THE AMERICAS

Cultures throughout the new world suffered simultaneous, critical insults to their structures from European invasions. European military technologies overwhelmed defenses. Foreign diseases diminished entire populations. And European religious orders overwhelmed indigenous beliefs.

European political systems replaced indigenous systems often without great effort. The Inca and Aztec societies were based on military power, and at their heights were uneasy, unstable alliances of conquered peoples. The Europeans simply used rebellious forces already smoldering to topple those in power and place themselves in control.

New powers in control, however, did little to alter continuing cultural and economic divisions. Europeans increased the economic enslavement of the indigenous populations. Forces of cultural entropy continue to sow polarization, cement status levels, diminish capital circulation, and place continued stress on resources.

THE LATIN AMERICAN COUNTRIES TODAY

Mexico, central, and South America are often seen as places of poverty and divisiveness. Europeans overwhelmed these areas with massive **enslavements** of indigenous peoples, an enslavement that continues to this day. Enslaved peoples are unable to create profits they can trade to improve their lives. Human labor, without skills and resources, is of diminished value.

Like Africa, economically enslaved Latin American areas are topographically divided, weakening the role of central governments, hindering trade and opposing the creation and circulation of profit capital.

Water systems—that often act to bring humans together to trade—are notably absent or (as yet) uncontrollable in many areas of Latin America

The effects of **cultural entropy**—tyrants, weak central governments, anemic economies (lacking circulation), ineffective infrastructure, cultural polarizations, language divisions, status divisions, extremism, no man's lands (slums), gangs, overpopulation, population wars, resource stresses—are all evident in the Latin American countries. The people and food are wonderful, however.

The result is what would be predicted in an area in which the forces of **cultural entropy** and *human enslavement* are very active and central governments are limited.

THE TROPICAL COUNTRIES TODAY

If a person traces a line around a globe between the equator and the 30th parallels, most of the world's poverty would be included. The concept is initially counter-intuitive, because the areas around the tropics contain much of the world's most lush areas.

If we consider the forces of cultural entropy, however, the reasons for poverty are quite obvious. The tropical areas are some of humanities' earliest areas of habitation. These areas today hold a large percentage of the human population, often in crowded conditions.

Cultural entropy has worked long in the tropics to create crowded populations that stress resources. Topographical divisions have created cultural divisions and language entropy and religious differences have created conflicts.

Again, the great abundance of the tropics explains its contradicting poverties, when divisive, chaotic forces have long been empowered.

THE NORTHER TIER OF COUNTRIES

The northern tier of countries—Europe, Russia, China, Japan, The United States, Britain, and Canada—are all considered first world civilizations; in other words, nations in this tier generally have strong central governments, and growing first-world economies, with profit circulation, adequate wages for human labor, and strong infrastructures for capital movement.

The divisive voices of cultural entropy, however, are still active in the northern tier. Entropy (chaos) can only be opposed by work. Polarizing forces in Great Britain hope to divide the country back into small antagonistic divisions. Many states rights groups exist in the United States with the intent to divide one country into many. Many countries throughout the world are on the verge of anarchy or tyranny, and cultural conflicts between puritanical religious factions seek to end the world in an Armageddon.

Well, no world is perfect.

We may look at northern tier countries as areas not yet overwhelmed over long time periods by chaotic forces of division and cultural warfare. Harsh winters may also serve to limit population growth compared to the tropics, thus sparing resources.

Future development will surely be interesting.

Entropy can only be opposed by work. Ignorance can only be opposed by verifiable truth.

Ch. 9 -- THE HUMAN CULTURE OF SELF

CHAPTER 9.
THE HUMAN SENSE OF SELF

A. Cultural Wars
B. The Human Sense of Self
C. The Intolerant (selfish) Self
D. The Manipulated Self and Culture
E. Self manipulated for the purpose of wars
F. Male expendability
G. No Man's Lands
H. Causes of Human Wars (Not Good or Evil)
I. Male dominance
J. Recreational Sex (Not Tolerated by War Cultures)
K. Human Poverty

A. WARS CAN BE HELL -- CULTURAL WARS ARE VIOLENT, UNENDING COMPETIVE CAPITALISM:
No doubt about it--almost every living organism competes with almost every other living organism for the same resources. Nature **is** fundamentally **competitive capitalism**. Some say the entire struggle is a no-sum game--life battles other life; and a win for one life form is *always* a loss for something else. Only so many poker chips are in life's mix; so we can only win by being con artists, ripping off someone else's gains. Cooperation is an illusion. Kill or be killed.

But the no-sum game strategy is not quite correct either. Capital must circulate; and circulation requires, well, some teamwork, agreed upon or not by the combatants. It may appear when a gazelle eats grass, the gazelle wins completely and the grass loses totally. But eventually the gazelle will spread grass seeds in its dung, so the grass wins too. Capital circulates.

Competitive capitalism is violent and mean—nothing like the Disney version of nature most people enjoy--but it allows the circulation of capital that is necessary to all life. In fact, without circulating capital, violent or not, life could not exist.

In the circle of life, capital, or life is what is circling; and the struggle that brings life also brings a nearly equal amount of death.

To repeat: The struggle in nature is not very harmonious. The gazelle eats the grass without asking permission; eventually a leopard may eat the gazelle, also without permission. Overtly, the leopard wins, the gazelle loses in a violent exchange of capital. But from high school biology, we recognize the leopard keeps the gazelle's population under control, so all the grass is not eaten, so ultimately everything—grass, gazelle, and leopard—can continue the competitive capital cycle (violently trading capital) in the future (assuming, of course, the sun keeps providing new energy to **work** against entropy).

In nature, numbers battle numbers, often to a relative standstill. People talk about nature being in balance. Being in balance basically means everything fights everything else to a *momentary* standoff.

Over short time periods, the balance seems inviolable, but over larger time periods, the balance is always changing--fighters win and lose. Nature is always slightly *out of balance*. The losers disappear. The winners readapt and continue to fight in new arenas. **In nature, permanence is an illusion.**

The leopard needs the gazelle, and the gazelle needs the grass. What does the grass need? Would grass be better off never being eaten? The grass won't come to a conclusion.

The point is: Both grass, gazelle, and leopard, and all living things, are momentary players on a very, very violent stage. One day, they may all disappear, but the dramatic show, life, (capital trading), competitive **capitalism** will continue as long as it can.

Human society changes the game plan slightly. A moose, eating grass and sticks, can grow to several hundred pounds its first year and become independent. A human child, fed milk and cookies, only grows a tenth as large in its first year and will remain dependent for decades. It seems impossible a slow-growing human child could ever compete with a moose.

But humans, we have discussed, put their milk and cookies, not into physical growth, teeth, horns, and claws, but into language, verifiable truths, and social development—other capital investments. Language and social development allow humans to extend their **senses-of-self** to large family units and tribes. Thus human colonies can function as single, large, extended, specialized organisms. Against these *large organisms*, solitary animals are outgunned and outflanked.

Societies, and human families, only work, however, when capital is shared (like a common blood flow). By **sharing** capital—including information capital and social understanding--humans can practice **cooperative capitalism**. *Cooperative capitalism does not require we kill each other at each capital exchange.* We can share profits. But when humans cease sharing, they immediately place themselves back on the level of solitary animals wherein capitalism grows harsh.

To repeat: As solitary creatures, the human strategy fails miserably. Individual humans, without knowledge and tools, who refuse to share capital, are reasonably helpless. Individual humans must compete in a competitive capitalistic economy with animals that grow bigger, run faster, and have much sharper teeth. As a cooperating family, however, the human strategy is far more adaptable than any other animal strategy. And when humans exchange capital—food, tools, information, or comfort—we are not required to **kill** each other. (This is rather nice.) Competing animals are outgunned.

In cooperative capitalism, we can exchange profits, not life. In cooperating capitalism, humans can act as a single organism.

B. THE SENSE OF SELF AND CULTURE

A moose lives most of its life alone, and while alone, it defends its **self** over all other things. A moose is ***intolerant*** of close associations with almost all other creatures. A mother moose momentarily extends her **sense of self** to include her calf. But after a year or so, the mother changes that sense of self, and no longer includes her calf as part of her own self. She chases the calf away to fend for **its self**. "You aren't me anymore!" she decides. "I don't need to defend you. I don't even like you anymore. Go visit your dad!"

The **sense of self** originated billions of years ago in simple organisms. *Self* simply differentiates between what an organism must defend, compared to what that organism must avoid or destroy as a competitor or predator. The question is: "What is me, and what is not me? What is my *self?*"

When organisms cooperate in large cultures, the question extends to: "What is us, and what is not us? Where does capital sharing begin and end?"

In hierarchical social colonies, like wolves, the question grows even more complicated: "How does my particular **self** fit into *our* particular **us**?"

Human societies are more complicated than those of wolves, and humans must constantly ask changing questions of self-identification throughout their lives.

"Who am I?" "Where do I fit?" "How do I get along with others?" "What has changed as I get older?"

Good questions. No wonder most humans are confused.

A CHILD'S TEARS

Children possess no language. Tears are a simple language with one message: "I desire the attention of a parent." Young children look widely for stimulation and play, but they remain children as long as they are dependent on their parents. Gradually children acquire language other than tears and social connections other than their parents. Some authorities feel children start becoming and independent the day they stop crying. They learn, or are taught, tears can no longer summon a parent; other language is more affective.

Real words replace tears. Children learn other behaviors must protect them or allow them to gain what they wish.

That child's growing self, and nothing else encompasses the consciousness of a child. As children mature, a wider definition of self includes family and friends. Maturing children seek places in their peer groups. Gangs are natural formations of young people seeking peer-sharing identification. Gangs may be peaceful or violent. Social connections can provide the means to integrate gangs into social activities or antisocial activities. The hormones of young people are historically rather indifferent to being violent or non violent.

C. THE (INTOLERANT) SELFISH SELF

We probably all realize the *unextended* self can be quite selfish. The self is intolerant. **Intolerance is a primary force of cultural entropy.** The self evolved to defend **only** itself and nothing else. Self-defense is the **job** of self. The animal self has no concern for anything **but** its self.

The human self, however, is quite flexible. Humans have the choice to extend their selves to include others or not.

ARTIFICIALLY INTELLIGENCE SELVES

If robots ever develop a separate sense of self—that **excludes** humanity—the human race is probably in the junk pile. The only hope humanity has, is to make certain the **sense-of-self** developed by artificial intelligence **includes** humanity. That way the robots may include us in **their** future.

Are we alone in the world with nothing but ourselves to worry about? Or are we part of a greater family? Humans can make rational decisions and increase their self-awareness, or not. Animals have little choice. Computers must be programmed.

Sociopaths apparently have no feelings for anyone but themselves. Some sociopaths may have no sense of self whatsoever.

Conversely, some holy people claim identity with the entire universe. The happiest humans claim wide associations, even love, with family, friends, nature, and all society.

Hopefully, future robots will make equally humane connections. Robots need to think of humans, and nature, as part of their extended selves. If not, humanity, and the natural world, may be in deep, deep trouble.

SLEEP AND ENTROPY

We require random, chaotic thoughts to think creatively, but too much randomness can cause us to harm others or ourselves. Sleep-immobility allows our brain to experience random sensations without consequence, since we are physically immobile. Immobility is a wonderful solution created by nature to allow randomness without undue consequences.

Those with mental instabilities often have difficulties differentiating dreams from reality, sorting out reality from creative chaos. Many creative types live their lives close to darkness and chaos. All creative thinkers have a touch of madness—booga, booga, booga.

But too much madness leads to Apocalypse and conflict—and demons like Adolf Hitler. So: Moderation in all things, particularly our use of chaos.

Question: If we wish to create robots that can think creatively, we will need to provide them a chaotic side. If so, to keep these robots from harming themselves or others, they may need to sleep like us humans. Interesting. Snore. (Recall: Thinking Robots must include us humans in their self-awareness, plus nature, or we are all quite dead. Rather important.) "I wonder what robots will dream."

Intolerant artificial intelligence could be deadly to humanity.

The self is absolutely necessary. However, society can be manipulative:

D. SENSE-OF-SELF MANIPULATED

The **sense of self** can be badly manipulated to its own detriment in some social arrangements. Worker ants spend their lives serving a queen, serving DNA, that is in the family, but not directly their own.

Worker ants are being manipulated, and this manipulation can extend further:

Polyergus, Po-ly-er-gus, Ants, social parasites, steal the eggs of *other* ant species. Once these stolen, infertile, female slaves integrate into the *Polyergus* nest, they perform all the necessary functions *Polyergus* cannot, such as feeding the colony or cleaning the nest. Ant species, like the enslaved *Formica*, use scent to differentiate colony members from non-colony members. These *Formica* slave ants, via scent trickery, have their **senses-of-self** relocated to the *Polyergus* colony. They maintain the unrelated *Polyergus* colony as if it were their own **self,** their own scent, their own family, even though they are not related. Their **sense of self** has been fooled.

Humans—using social understanding, rather than scent--enlarge family self-identifications beyond any other mammal. Recall, humans place extreme amounts of their life capital into their brains and their abilities for social organization. With social powers—rather than scent--humans extend their senses-of-self through extended society.

Humans can include, in their senses of self, stuff they own—personal items, cars, and houses. Hoarders include all types of accumulations in their intimate sense of self. Hoarders find getting rid of any of their accumulations, even trash, nearly impossible, like losing an arm or a child.

Human mothers include their children in their self-sense, often throughout their entire lives. Young human males often seek a larger **self** by forming alliances with friends, teams, or a gang of other males. Adult humans may extend their senses of self to include their extended families and even their community and country.

Humans are not simply taking care of children; they are taking care of an extended part of themselves. By extending our senses of self to our children, and grandchildren, and extended society, we are including ourselves in a type of immortality enjoyed otherwise only by the gods.

But human growth is not completely progressive or always open. Young children, like young puppies, can be widely open to play and sharing with contemporaries. Later, as adults, humans may be closed to new relationships and **intolerant**.

Other social animals, such as wolves and lions, suffer from the same self-strategy. As young animals they may accept other animals into their pack concepts, but as adults they lose the ability to make new relationships. Adult selves become exclusive, rather than inclusive. The reasons are obvious: Adult, reproducing animals must protect their own future DNA from foreign or family competition. Young animals don't as yet have this need.

Young human adults may selfishly resist extending their **selves** to include others. However, once they bond with a child or lover, they experience a new self-identification.

Human families, in general, can function as single organisms because they **share** accumulated capital and a **sense of self**. Indeed, most humans include their entire tribe within their capital sharing system and their senses of self. They will defend their tribal self as much or more than they will defend their own selves, even taking extreme personal risks and sacrifice to protect the larger tribal society from perceived harm.

The dividing factor arises between what is self (what must be defended) and what is not self (what must be attacked as foreign). Humans perceive their own tribe as a single organism, an extended self they need to defend.

In the military, young soldiers learn to identify with their unit, placing their own self-needs, even their own lives as secondary to the self-requirements of their unit, a society that acts as a single organism.

On the contrary, humans attack foreigners from other tribes without feeling, because, "Those tribes are not part of us. They have a different *scent*." Humans perceive foreign tribes as outsiders, intruders, competitors, and exclude other tribes from their capital sharing process.

The excluding, ***intolerant*** situation is the same as in other life forms. Ant colonies will fight other ant colonies of the exact same species, because their scents are not exactly the same. Each culture competes to secure the same resources. *Every life form is in population war with all other life forms, even those in their own species.* Every human tribe that generates a **social-self** is in natural war forever and always with every other tribe over resources. The prize is the future.

Describing something as *foreign* is the same as defining something as not *us*, not our tribe, not our scent, not our family—in other words, *foreigners* are tribes that can be attacked as **competitors** and not embraced as *family or part of us.*

These distinctions may seem petty and small—and they are—but such petty distinctions have caused human warfare, death, and destruction for countless years.

Political pundits, who make their pay by circulating angst, utilize cultural distinctions to stir up misunderstandings. They choose a culture, any culture, and gain power and money by pretending to represent and defend particular values against those of competitors. By misrepresentations and exaggerations, they create constant drama and conflict which many find entertaining.

Those *not us,* or in-the-family, are *them,* parasites or predators, taking bread from whoever is identified as *us,* our hard-working family. These foreigners—be they democrats or republicans or immigrants or whatever—have values that are abhorrent to our particular us, or family. We (us) must rally together to protect ourselves and our family values from (them), these foreign invaders. We are mutually enraged by the ordacity of them, or those-who-are-not-us. We celebrate the wonderful rightness of *us* over the ridiculous wrongness of *them,* these others who-are-not-us. To protect our (us), we must be intolerant of (them).

Within our family we practice cooperative sharing capitalism; but with competing families we practice **competitive non-sharing capitalism** wherein trade can turn violent.

Lost in the discussion is the Christian/Muslim/Buddhist concept that all people belong in the same human family; we are *not* separate; we are not different. God sees **us** as one sharing family.

Simultaneously, the pundits are absolutely correct!!!: All populations *are* at war; all human values *are* in conflict. *The forces of cultural entropy place all human cultures in population wars with each other to claim the future.*

Any culture, no matter how progressive and loving, that ignores the population war principal—and forgets to aggressively reproduce and separate itself intolerantly from other cultures--will one day simply disappear.

On the contrary, cultures--including despotic-religions and parasitic ethnicities--that conduct intolerant population wars adamantly, will one day overwhelm and grab the future from us all. **Real numbers** always win over abstract **qualitative** factors--unless of course, human reason recognizes the situation and intervenes in some rational direction.

Alternatives are quite simple: Every culture must recognize (or be bound to) a population boundary. But extremists and chaotic emotions (products of cultural entropy) tend to make rational alternatives impossible. The concept of free and unlimited procreation by whoever intentionally or accidentally procreates is inviolable in many cultures. **Intolerance** is natural in all life.

And those who would foment tribal warfare (and overextend boundaries) are everywhere; the divisive forces of **cultural entropy** work invisibly over long time periods to divide human unity. Extremists and violent human emotions always seem to have a political *advantage* over moderation. Extreme positions—we have discussed previously--are simple to enunciate and popular among those who prefer emotional stimulation rather than complicated truths.

The forces of cultural entropy foment divisions (natural intolerance). Extremist leaders ride these divisions to power.

The methods used by Hitler—utilizing cultural divisions (intolerance) to gain power--are not unique; they can easily be repeated in the future from all sides of the spectrum. Surely, they *will* be repeated.

E. WARS are HELL: HUMAN SELF--MANIPULATION BY OTHERS

Humans, like ants, can have their **senses-of-self** horribly manipulated by the forces of *cultural entropy*; and when this occurs, humans will sacrifice themselves blindly for interests that are not their own.

In particular, the results of most modern human wars tend to give little or no benefit to the warriors or their extended families. These benefits, on the contrary, usually fall exclusively to elites who take little part in actual bloody conflict. And the argument continues: Even elites historically gain little from modern wars.

In general, wars, particularly **modern** wars, make little difference to boundary lines or social structures. Then why do humans make wars so frequently? Because they can—human males are expendable. And further, because of the forces of cultural entropy, humans are always divided (intolerant). **Intolerance** allows violent **extremes** to rise to power.

Almost any war is an excellent example: The U.S. civil war stands out in particular, since those fighting on both sides originated from similar European stock, separated by only a few generations of cultural entropy. Why would two populations of nearly identical genealogies fight to the death?

The dividing concept was slavery and regional power; however, fewer than 35% of those fighting in the southern army came from slave-owning families (Only 5% actually owned slaves), and even fewer had the resources to participate in regional politics. A slight majority of whites in slave owning states worked in activities that benefitted directly from slave activity or acted to manage slaves they did not own. But approximately half of whites in slave states did not work directly with slave activities or lived in areas in which slavery was impractical.

Though poor whites may have yearned for slave ownership, and felt entitled, since they were told they were superior to blacks, most did not realize how slavery sorely affected the value of all work and the total economy in slave states. Memes of ignorance dominated the understandings of poor whites and prevented them from considering their actual predicament.

Many poor whites worked at subsistence wages, barely above those of slaves. Profits, stolen from black labor, accumulated in slave estates, not unlike the feudal hierarchies of the dark ages. These profits certainly did not circulate back to black labor, and gave little advantage to white labor not connected to slave management.

The majority of southern soldiers fought to preserve an aristocratic culture that gave them little or token benefit. The argument grows even more ironic since the presence of virtual slavery, even after the war, robbed most poor whites—as well as **all** blacks--of their ability to profit from their own labors. Even today, after modern migrations, the poverty of the south, a residue of slavery, perseveres in many rural areas. Slavery steals the profit from free labor and presents that profit to those who possess land and slave capital. By pinching the capital flow, the entire society—except those at the very top—grows impoverished.

Recall: Capital circulation includes the circulation of skills and human understanding. A culture without circulated skills and human understanding is impoverished—as was the southern US. Ignorance and *intolerance* flourishes in such situations.

Before the civil war, the forces of cultural entropy succeeded in convincing the southern population they were culturally different from those from the north, even though most shared the same recent European origins. Southern newspapers convinced southern whites, northern interests were victimizing them and that northerners, Yankees, were a separate, foreign tribe from those in the south. The northerners were foreigners, and vice versa. Foreigners were the enemy.

The forces of **cultural entropy** enlarged linguistic and cultural differences (intolerance) and set the northern and southern regions on a collision course. Men who felt they were being patriotic chose to support trivial tribal differences over reconciliation. Extreme emotions on both sides destroyed those in the middle and any hope for compromise. Only a powerful president and extreme force kept the union together.

Ironically, many of the elites who benefited specifically from slavery, continued to benefit after the civil war for the next hundred years (from the low cost of labor). Also ironically, after reconstruction, the civil war changed the south very little economically, particularly for blacks and poor whites. The status hierarchy remained stable. Elites still benefit today, while others, poor whites and blacks, suffer hardship.

Approximately 500,000 young men died on both sides of the civil war. But long-term economic changes in the south after the war were quite minimal. Despite the loss of an entire generation of young men, the total US population continued to grow rapidly.

A new form of slavery based on custom and **status levels** immediately replaced legal slavery; and this cruel situation lasted for a hundred years and still exists in some areas. A situation of suspicion and angst remained in many regions until recently. The point is: Modern cultural, or status **wars** often accomplish next to nothing of positive value in the long run. But they create a tremendous amount of human agony and emotional turmoil over short periods.

We can pound our chests proudly over wars, won or lost, and we can worship our dead war heroes. But changes from wars are usually minimal or the exact opposite of what was intended. Everyone is better off with diplomacy. War is hell. And the results of wars are usually counter-productive.

Martin Luther King accomplished more with persistence and pacifism than hundreds of years of conflict. The same should be said of Gandhi.

Cultural economics dictate morality to religions

We might think religions dictate moralities to human cultures. However, the opposite is historically correct. Religions historically grow morally malleable when cultural/economic factors are in conflict. Economic factors are controlled by cultural entropy, capital flow, and population wars. **Thus religious moralities follow, rather than lead human behavior.**

The Baptist church, for example, was originally established with abolitionist, anti-slavery directives. But, over time, Baptist churches in the south changed in sentiment to become pro-slavery, creating a Southern Baptist split from north to south that continues to this day.

Other northern denominations, abolitionist in the north, turned blind eyes to slavery in the south. Churches that maintained anti-slavery sentiments in the south gradually lost their parishioners and disappeared. Cultural morality won; religious morality lost.

The meme of ignorance, a product of slavery, still survives today in particular southern regions. Why? When capital circulation is stymied by slavery, ignorance and intolerance grows according to the laws of cultural entropy. Capital is not available for common education.

And strangely, for all the contrary evidence supporting the many benefits of unity, many areas of the rural south still support regional differences and separation today. Extreme emotions can almost always overwhelm rational thinking.

The point is: The human **sense-of-self** is easy to manipulate. Humans seek a tribal identity and are commanded by that perceived tribal identity over more thoughtful, global alternatives. Extreme violent emotions usually overwhelm calm thoughtful emotions. Forces of division are much easier to create than forces of unity and oneness.

Tyrants, like Adolf Hitler, are quick to use perceived cultural differences and the forces of cultural entropy to rise to power. And thus, warfare without benefit has plagued human history from the past to the present.

Recall, in addition, *in human societies*, warfare has a specific advantage: Male **Expendability**. We have mentioned expendability before, but it is worth mentioning again, in the context of self. Male humans don't count for much in **numbers** wars over time.

F. EXPENDABILITY, HUMAN WARFARE MADE EASY: Historically, warfare in human populations is made particularly common due to the expendability of human males.

Human males, like the infertile females in insect societies, are extremely expendable. Losses of human males in population wars make little difference to the total future **numbers**, as long as surviving males stay available to maintain female fertility—most males are happy to do this--and as long as male losses simultaneously increase or defend tribal resources.

As in insect societies, new births can more than offset losses in battle. At times, new births or recruits are more energy-efficient than caring for injured veterans. Such cruel expendability strategies were actually practiced in some armies. Roman veterans were a social liability. Dead soldiers presented no problem.

Expendability, as previously mentioned, can make tribal wars extend over thousands of years.

Extreme events can appear to skew the numbers but actually have little affect on the future. For example, if the men in a small tribe are totally wiped out by a larger tribe, the existence of the losing tribe is in doubt. However, all the tribal *women* may still be victorious in fertility. If the victorious tribe takes the women from the losing tribe as conquests, these women's DNA may continue to reproduce without interruption. Total **numbers** produced by these *women* can suffer little or nothing from the loss of their entire tribe of men. Numbers win; men lose. Sorry boys. Men are not important to the **numbers**.

In modern wars, however, the equation changes somewhat. Victorious warriors seldom find rewards in resources and mating privileges. Women, both from victorious and losing societies, seldom receive resource prizes. Thus modern wars bring dubious benefits to any status of society.

In addition, as opposed to early tribal wars, modern wars—using modern weapons--can bring massive casualties. Such massive casualties, however, seldom affect population growth.

Both world wars ended, after massive casualties—nearly a hundred million combined dead--with the total population actually rising soon after. Births apparently increased in the most affected countries, assisted occasionally by government initiatives. The point is: War, by itself, is not an effective population deterrent. Wars murder primarily young men. Young men don't count.

G. NO MAN'S LANDS DESTROY POPULATIONS

However, throughout history, when economic decay occurs to create **no man's lands**, populations tend to diminish rapidly. No man's lands starve women and children. **No man's lands** have entered the discussion on several occasions and are generally a product of warfare and famine, often worsened by environmental stresses.

No man's lands originally came into common definition as areas of devastation between opposing armies in a stalemate situation. Due to constant bombardment and hostility, nothing living can long endure in such areas—vegetation, animals, all life eventually succumbs to the toxicity of such an environment.

Throughout human history, **no man's lands** can occupy large swaths of once-fertile territory over long time spans, even when standing armies are not overtly fighting.

In the Greek enclave of Olympus, a marble wall, several thousand year old, describes Apollo slaying the Centaurs. The centaurs were originally invited to the home of Pirithous for the marriage of his daughter, Hippodamia. Once in the house of Pirithous, however, the wild centaurs drank too much, and, overcome by lust, decided to rape the bride and her retinue, killing a number of guests and Pirithous in the process. Enraged, the Greek God, Apollo took out his bow and slew the offending centaurs.

However, the rapes and murders were not what actually enraged Apollo or the other heroes. Apollo, like others of his time, was enraged because the violence occurred after the centaurs were *invited* into Pirithous's house. The centaurs had violated the rules of **hospitality**.

Apollo was not opposed to violence. He used violence whenever he desired. And if Apollo met a woman he wanted, he took advantage however he desired also. Apollo's morals were impeccable for his time. Might is morally right, unless it breaks an important rule of hospitality.

We can do whatever violence we want to other people in the *wild—the wild has no rules.* Had the centaurs raped and murdered in the wild, Apollo would not have cared. In the wild, force rules. But we should not be rude at home. Home is sacred. *Home* has rules, particularly when we are invited there.

When Greeks from opposing states met in the wild, far from their homelands, they recognized no rules applied to their behavior. Rapes and murder, and all types of violent behaviors, had no moral barriers in the wild. The wild was a **no man's land** beyond the scope of laws or morality.

Any Greek state with power (such as the Spartans) could overwhelm the states around it, and murder and enslave other populations, without any moral stigma. Why not?

However, when the Greeks from many states met at Olympus for sport, they realized they needed hospitality **laws,** laws of accepted behavior, to keep the games from degenerating into chaos.

Those who broke the rules of hospitality in a protected venue could expect severe punishments from *every* state, and from *every* individual, even including the **gods**. For this reason, the wall at Olympus was created.

Cultures can turn into large civilizations by creating homelands in which laws of property and hospitality are widely understood and obeyed. Infrastructures, such as canals, and roads, and farms, and trading areas, can thrive in areas in which the rules of hospitality dominate. Hospitality rules can enable **cooperative capitalism** and all its benefits.

However, when a culture divides into warring parts due to cultural entropy, many productive areas can no longer be occupied—these areas return to wild **no man's lands** unfit for human occupations. **When infrastructures disappear, so do the toilets.** And without toilets, trade, farming, and other amenities--human life becomes very difficult.

Human populations diminish in a very few years when **no man's lands** dominate. The reason for population decline is simple: Famines occur over unstable, violent, lawless areas that cannot be farmed. Famine, as opposed to warfare, impacts **females and children** as much or more than males. And when the number of reproducing females diminishes, the entire population plunges. Male deaths mean very little. Female deaths mean the end of a population or an entire civilization.

Fertile women are the force necessary for population wars. Men are decoration. Civilizations disappear when women can no longer raise healthy children.

TOXIC NO MAN'S LANDS

Toxic **no man's lands** answer the question of why civilizations fail, and further, why failed civilizations sometimes fail to ever recover past population numbers. When a culture splits into vicious warring divisions, mistrust and unproductive **no man's lands** may continue for years.

Cultural entropy, extreme emotions, animosity, famine, disease, parasites, and warfare can turn a single culture into competing cultures that no longer work together, that no longer share resources, and that disallow proper government and infrastructures which might diminish future problems. Cooperating capitalism becomes competitive capitalism.

Excellent examples (we have discussed) include Easter Island, Rome, the Maya peninsula, China, the Khmer, and the Anasazi [Ch. 7]. Each civilization, from conception to demise, progressed through the same phases:

> Early colonization
> Population expansion
> Topographic, linguistic, and status divisions
> Population warfare
> Famine and resource stress
> Infrastructure abandonment
> Growth of no man's lands
> Population and cultural decline.
> Chaos to Tyranny

Sometimes, societies never return to their former glories. At other times, tyrants can re-unite the divided areas under a single rule. Once united, the forces of cultural entropy, intolerance, and division begin anew, and often the entire process repeats again and again over many years.

H. WHAT CAUSES HUMAN WARS??? THE IGNORANCE MEME

The actual causes of human warfare are often illusive:

Some people like to believe horrific forces of human greed and ambition stand behind all wars. Others believe economic forces eternally pit the workers against the elites. Wars, they feel, must all be part of some great class struggle.

Many religions believe wars eternally pit **evil** against **good**. In the end, we will all be involved in a final battle, an Armageddon. We must all take sides. But which side is evil, and which side is good? The distinctions between good and evil usually depend on the view. And the view changes frequently--depending on where people happen to be standing *at the moment*. Is evil only a form of ignorance? Yes, it apparently is. Most of evil is simply *"failure to communicate."*

Ah ha! We must finally wonder—

Are wars simply a product of random forces? The invisible, random forces of cultural entropy that divide humanity and evolve ignorance?? For many, this explanation is not at all acceptable (humans prefer more *romantic ideas), but this view may actually be the most accurate:* Random forces enslave human civilizations to conflicts over and over and over again.

What causes world wars? The forces of good and evil have nothing to do with it. **The blind and mindless forces of cultural entropy** lead us to mindless family divisions. A single family that once survived by sharing resources now engages in deadly combat over those same resources. Growing numbers and intolerance force conflict, create starvation, and stress resources further. Long time-periods blind human understanding to the changing situation. Religions and cultures are pawns in the struggle, not controllers.

Humans are hard-wired to defend their perceived cultural selves, no matter how manipulated those selves become. Ignorance and extreme thinking (products of cultural entropy) guide humans to perform unspeakable acts in imagined self-defense of cultural self-unity.

The forces of cultural entropy lead us to cultural wars again and again and again. Religion, good, evil, loss or gain, human reason, love— these romantic concepts have little to do with it.

Human maturity has not yet developed to understand and control the entropic forces that inhumanely **determine** human conflicts.

I. MALE DOMINANCE

Some women's publications still blame wars and violence largely on male dominance. They may have a point. Male hormones have evolved over millions of years to push young males to violent competitions. Humans are far from unique in this situation.

Male animals in all species seek dominance in order to reproduce. Males that are not dominant fail to reproduce, and those that fail to reproduce disappear from the gene pool. For this reason, most animal populations do not contain a preponderance of meek, less dominant, or feminine males.

And women are not guiltless in this situation. In fact, it is fair to argue, women are the ones in charge. Females have been rewarding dominant males for millions and millions of years. And it is incorrect to argue; women have had no choice in the matter. Women in heterosexual species must have choices: **Female choice and male expendability are the reasons for heterosexuality.** Without female choice, heterosexuality would not be successful or meaningful. The sole purpose of heterosexuality is to eliminate undesirable (mostly male) genes. Romance and pleasure are minor attributes that mask heterosexuality's true purpose.

[Note: When males share child-rearing duties—like most bird species--the choice situation is more equal. But male mammals do not lactate, so child rearing in mammals is almost exclusively in the hands of females.]

In most cases, large animal life we see today is a product of female survival choices made over millions and millions of years. Heterosexual male behaviors of today are efforts to win female approval.

Some **human** cultures, however, control the reproductive choices of their women and men. Parents, or society, may make reproductive decisions, not young women.

Male and female behaviors evolved over millions and millions of years. We are probably not terribly different from our forefathers and foremothers in our chemical dispositions due to these recent social innovations—a tiny blip on our evolutionary calendar.

Females are hard-wired to choose their mates. For this reason, females who feel their mating choices have been compromised can be totally unforgiving. Males, who do not share women's choosiness, can be terribly *confused* by female behaviors. Why, they wonder, should anyone balk at a behavior that should be fun? Female hard-wired choosiness is the answer.

The *Me-Too* movement catches traditional, aggressive heterosexual males unprepared—particularly if they have had too much to drink. (Young, aroused males think this is very unfair.)

Males act today as females (and survival) have trained them to act over vast time scales. Men can't be choosy; they need to grab whatever is available. Those who hesitate, lose. Men beat their chests and battle to the death for breeding rights. Men grow beautiful feathers and sing lovely songs in order to attract women. Women *decorate* themselves specifically to attract and control men. Both males and females act as they do today because of behaviors that have facilitated **survival** over millions of years. The point is: No one is at fault. No one is the greater victim.

Random forces place humans in positions in which conflict is inevitable. We repeat: No one is the greater victim.

J. RECREATIONAL SEX AND HOMOSEXUALITY

Children are the **soldiers** of cultural wars. To maximize the number of children, warring cultures must encourage maximum reproduction by their followers. But when cultures allow sexual expression for purposes other than procreation, fewer children result.

So recreational sex and homosexuality cannot be tolerated by cultures engaged in aggressive population wars. Any tribal culture that allows such practices will be overwhelmed (**outnumbered**) by competing cultures that reproduce more quickly.

Thus the bans against homosexuality and recreational sex in today's successful religions are understandable; maximum numbers continue to make such cultures successful competitors.

The competition, however, has effects that devalue human life. Human **numbers** place increasing stresses on resources and the conflicts (wars) caused by **population competitions** can be hell.

J. HOMOSEXUALITY AND RECREATIONAL SEX

Male animals of all species seek dominance in order to reproduce. Males that are not dominant fail to reproduce, and those that fail to reproduce disappear from the gene pool. For this reason, most animal populations do not contain a preponderance of meek, less dominant, weak, non-heterosexual, or feminine males.

Female animals in heterosexual species must choose male animals in order to reproduce. Females, that do **not** choose male animals for reproduction, disappear from the gene pool. For this reason, most animal populations do not contain a predominant number of non-heterosexual females.

When conducting cultural wars, homosexuality if difficult to explain—since homosexual relations do not aggressively increase numbers. *Homosexuality, inscrutably, does <u>not directly support</u> the forces of cultural entropy.* (?)

Has God or nature decided humans no longer will be dominated by numbers? Hm?? The prevalence of homosexuality in human cultures may spring from recent *priority changes* in human societies—assuming homosexuality is either genetic or behavioral. (The jury is still apparently out.)

SOME SPECULATIONS:

Females exclusively control lactation in mammals. So, very few mammal males participate in child rearing. In fact, many mammal males with high testosterone levels are dangerous to young and so are avoided by females with children.

Human women may complain about men as fathers, but among mammals, human males are at the very top. Why?

Well, of course, humans, as opposed to most mammals, are a social species. Males with more feminine (nurturing) characteristic make sense in tribal groups, groups in which male proximity to children is unavoidable.

Many hominid males in social groups exhibit nurturing skills—including baboons, gorillas, and bonobos. Beavers and wolves, among non-hominid mammals, also assist with child rearing.

If less dominant males (with more feminine characteristic) can help bring more human young to maturity, then the **numbers** would certainly favor less aggressive (or mixed) characteristics in human males.

In addition, if less dominant men fit better in social hierarchies, the numbers would again favor less dominant, more flexible males, males capable of assuming multiple roles.

More **masculine females** may also result from needs in tribal cultures for humans to assume multiple roles. Females must assume masculine (aggressive) roles when males are absent, hunting or engaged in warfare for extended periods.

Social requirements for human flexibility may largely explain the commonality of homosexual behaviors in human societies.

Or, human homosexuality may simply be a characteristic of human genetic divisions. A quirk of human development—either in DNA or in early development--may make homosexuality more prevalent in human societies than in animal societies.

Homosexual humans may not be inclined to heterosexual activities, but they can reproduce successfully when required by family needs, so homosexuality is not an absolute bar to family continuity.

Flexible homosexual activities may also serve to lessen sexual tensions at times when the sexes are severely segregated or heterosexual activities are severely restricted. For example, human wars can separate the sexes over long time spans. In ancient Greek times, heterosexual soldiers, long separated from women, adapted homosexual solutions without social difficulties.

Sexual relation without progeny, between extended members of a culture, such as Bonobos, also apparently serves to lessen tension and increase cultural stability.

Diseases and parasites, however, oppose all close contact between animals. Most animals are thus **intolerant** of contact beyond the minimum requirements for reproduction. Extended sexual relations in social animals usually exist only in isolated communities—Bonobos and Tahitian Islanders, for example--wherein the spread of diseases may be limited.

The advantages of contact must equal or outweigh the disadvantages. The **primate grooming instinct** is a prime example: Touching between grooming primates is made positive, since the groomers are relieving each other of parasites.

For whatever reason, the increase of less masculine males and less feminine females into the breeding pot allows sexual styles in human populations to differentiate in greater degrees than in other animal populations.

Acceptance of sexual styles may facilitate greater sharing and value in future human societies.

And importantly: *Rigid heterosexuality has evolved over millions of years primarily to facilitate cultural wars and create large, healthy,* **warring populations**.

Recreational sex (without progeny) may have the opposite effect, **limiting population stresses on resources**.

However, the wars continue:

In conclusion: Non-progeny or **recreational sexual practices** together with on-line porn (all practices without progeny) are apparently the wave of the future.

Cultures, however, that allow recreational sex to be practiced by their members, will lose out to cultures that allow only procreation sex. So population wars, otherwise, will continue.

On that topic, no society engaged in aggressive cultural wars can allow their children to practice recreational sex or homosexuality widely (not in any manner that keeps them from maximum procreation).

Women's role must be restricted to maximum reproduction without other alternatives. Otherwise not enough young will be born for child soldiers or male expendability in wars. A society that condones homosexuality or recreational sex would not maximize its **numbers**, and would lose a population war against a competing culture.

Remember: **Numbers** create the future, not moral values, or right, or wrong. Cultures that fail to reproduce will disappear—no matter how much *fun* they have. Cultures that *force* their members to reproduce—*"It's the only allowable way to have sex!"*—will claim the future, no matter how much fun they **don't** have.

The future belongs to the **numbers**, not humanity, not to pleasant relations, not to peace, not to the pursuit of God, unless human beings decide upon a different direction.

Early tribal wars may have made some sense to the combatants. On the contrary, most modern wars have no meaning or purpose. Modern wars diminish the value of all human life in all parts of the hierarchy, particularly when atomic bombs add to the mix.

Unfortunately, human ignorance, extremism, violent emotions, and the invisible forces of cultural entropy encourage cultural wars to re-occur again and again.

K. WHAT CAUSES HUMAN AND ORGANIC POVERTY???

Poverty is partly capital inequity. Poor people today may possess as much or more capital resources than wealthy people a thousand years ago. But these people still feel they are poor, since they possess much less than others around them.

Poverty is partly an absence of profit capital and partly a lack of emotional capital. Monks may possess little or no real capital items, their diets may be sparse, and their workload high. But they may consider themselves emotionally wealthy and tranquil. They feel they possess a great deal of social capital.

Ch. 9 -- THE HUMAN CULTURE OF SELF

Slum residents and orphans may never miss a meal and may even dress in fancy clothes, but they may be harassed by emotional poverty, social instability, and violence. Such individuals suffer from a lack of capital/social infrastructure. Even wealthy individuals can be trapped by emotional stresses that make them feel socially impoverished.

Young boys gravitate to gang memberships mainly to satisfy their needs for social capital. Young girls often seek motherhood for the same reason. The need for real capital (money, possessions) is only secondary to the need for social capital.

Young people who possess adequate capital (social capital, financial capital, social connections) are less drawn to violent gangs or motherhood to assert their needs. We are always shocked when individuals from "good" families commit violent actions. We are also shocked when individuals from "stressed" families grow to be happy, well-adjusted adults.

Generally, individuals that possess circulating profit capital, together with circulating emotional capital, are thought to be doing quite well. We create profit capital from our labors; and we receive social capital from the world around us.

Individuals without profit capital or circulating social, educational capital are denoted as doing badly, in poverty.

The USA is a country in which education and profit from free labor are widely available. The USA is a country presently considered near the top on the wealth standard.

Poor countries are poor primarily because skill education and profit from free labor are often not available (do not circulate) to large percentages of the population. When free labor cannot create for itself a profit, then little profit can circulate. When profit circulation is low, human life is of low value, along with a lack of circulating social enlightenment.

Much poverty arises from human slavery. The enslavement of blacks in the southern US, and the peon system that enslaved Native Americans in Mexico and South America, contributes to a legacy of poverty that continues today. Slavery, warfare, and cultural entropy that divided cultures over many centuries in Africa, Europe, India, and Asia, combine with population wars that stress resources and limit capital distribution. Poverty is the result.

Simply controlling population increases in the poorest of people may benignly eliminate a great deal of poverty in the future. Poverty breeds poverty. Also, improving the profit on free labor increases the circulation of all capital from the bottom. Such bottom-up circulation is the most beneficial both for biological and human cultures.

If we view poor people from all countries as a separate culture, then this culture—like all other natural cultures—is seeking to overwhelm the world with its numbers. On a human level, many poor people have only their children and family as a social network in their old age. Societies that provide stable social networks for their populations generally have less difficulty with overpopulation, since many children are not necessary for elder care.   But, as we have discussed, many cultures have traditions of large families otherwise. Such traditions make population wars inevitable.

        Wars are hell.

CH. 10 –

SUMMARY
CONCLUSIONS AND THE LITERATURE

Cultural Entropy
Cultural Entropy verses Democratic Concepts
What is Capitalism?
Population Wars in Philosophy
In Religion
In Literature
Theatre of the Absurd
Catch-22
Human Monsters from Chaos

SUMMARY –
CONCLUSIONS AND THE LITERATURE

CULTURAL ENTROPY

For most of human history, humans did not recognize bacteria existed. Humans attributed the diseases caused by bacteria to evil spirits; in so doing, humans ignored real cures.

Today, by recognizing the once-invisible effects of bacteria, humans have found actual cures, and can live healthier lives.

The forces of cultural entropy, over long time periods, destroy and divide human cultures and families.
Since these forces are invisible, we attribute the effects and diseases caused by cultural entropy to human evil or imagined monsters; in so doing we ignore real cures.

Ch. 10 -- SUMMARY AND THE LITERATURE

Entire civilizations have perished without knowing why.

By understanding the destructive forces of cultural entropy, humans may live more joyful lives.

Without work in opposition, entropy will always increase.

CULTURAL ENTROPY VERSES DEMOCRATIC CONCEPTS

The forces of cultural entropy particularly and critically impact democratic institutions. Discussed previously [Ch 6, 7, 8, 9, 10].

Chaotic forces continually work to turn democratic assemblies into dysfunctional systems. Forces of cultural entropy favor **extremes** over consensus. These divisive forces increase greatly with ***the passage of time***. General human ignorance of the processes of cultural entropy allows invisibility.

Numbers wars (evolved from entropic processes) thwart the ***basic concepts*** of democracies—individual rights and human value—and turn feuding cultures into ungovernable states. Tyrants are quick to recognize chaotic states and grab power.

The forces of **cultural entropy** push the human future, like the past, into tyranny and a nuclear Armageddon. Loving humans must oppose this movement.

Democratic institutions require human love and human labor to maintain legitimacy and integrity. Extremes are deadly. Only continued **work** toward unity can keep the forces of **entropy** from **increasing** to chaos.

CAPITALISM

Life (God) transfers the energy-capital of the sun into growth and diversity—from molecules, to plants and animals, to humans. We call this energy-transfer, **capitalism.** Capital exchanges or capitalism allows all life to originate and grow.

A healthy economy—biological or human—depends on healthy capital circulation. No circulation; no economy. No economy; no capitalism; no life.

The random forces of **cultural entropy**—sunlight, wind, water, the sporadic movements of all elemental particles, chemical interactions, gravity, endless time, and the *random*, emotional, chemical permutations of humanity--continually stir life's ordered economies in **chaotic** directions. The resulting conflicts, over extended time periods, create the violent history of life and humanity.

Humanity has added a drop of reason to the stew. Humans can utilize ***cooperative capitalism*** (profit trade) over **competitive capitalism** (violent predations) to circulate capital. **Cooperative capitalism** allows profit sharing without violence and death. But the overwhelming flavor of the stew is still dominated by random chaos, extreme emotions, and dark ignorance. Forces of **cultural entropy** invisibly and repeatedly re-establishes **competitive capitalism** in human societies.

All human and biological cultures continue to be at war with each other over an endless timeline. These wars will not halt naturally or nicely. **Numbers** have no impulse control. Chaos has no brain.

Numbers force us to be predators; **population wars** demand human cultures compete violently against other human cultures to claim the future; **population wars** stress resources and create inequity and poverty.

Only the **work** of loving humans can stop these wars.

Population Wars

All human cultures survive today because they **aggressively compete**, and continue to compete, against other cultures in population competitions. If they did not compete in the past, they would not exist today [Ch 6, 7, 8].

The point is, **the rules of society did not evolve to increase the joy and value of human life.** On the contrary, social rules evolve, as competing societies evolve, to preserve the **intolerance and prejudices** necessary to assist competitive capitalism, or ***population wars***. Social rules do not assist human happiness or lead to social tranquility; they assist a **culture** to compete *and overwhelm other* **cultures**.

The concept (cultural war vs life) is not new. Humans have argued the situation for ***thousands*** of years:

In 400 BC, the Greek philosopher, Diogenes, practiced public masturbation to demonstrate he—and not *society*—was responsible for his own wellbeing. Human desires, he claimed, were *easy to satisfy* when not shamed and opposed by society.

To emphasize his philosophy, Diogenes, a noted teacher, ate scraps from the public market and lived in an old wine vat. Social expectations, Diogenes argued, were contrary to the rules of *actual* human nature. Shame was merely a device *societies* use to control human behavior. The gods did not recognize shame. Why should he?

In statues, Diogenes is a middle-aged man who is very fit. (In his chosen state of poverty, he may not have eaten lots of fatty foods.) He carries a staff and a lantern. He carries a lantern because he is seeking (and not finding) an honest man. Dogs accompany Diogenes. Diogenes felt dogs were his moral compasses. Dogs were brave, loyal, and friendly, and they had no idea of shame or esteem. Dogs were comfortable and happy without any need of luxury.

According to Diogenes, rules for societies evolved over many years according to forces of **cultural entropy** and eternal conflict, and **not** from the gods or human needs. Many *so-called* moral values, created by constant population warfare, oppose **reasonable** human desires.

Societies seek to *control* masturbation and human sexuality (or love) for a single purpose: A culture succeeds through time *only* if it **requires** its breeding members to create soldiers (more children) to take part in population wars to combat other societies. Breeders must not waste their energy on leisure sexual activities that might lead to fewer children soldiers to fight society's wars. If they do, their future family will lose the population war and disappear. But population or cultural wars, we know, **eventually** lead directly to human conflict and chaos—the opposite of what humans (including children) need for happiness or progress [Ch. 6, 7, 8, 9 – Cultural Wars].

At the same time, the **socially mandated** drives for extreme esteem and wealth are not choices humans make to find human **happiness**, peace, or God. Such drives do not benefit the poor or the rich; they do not even benefit the tranquility of society. Pride leads humans **away** from oneness with God and oneness with each other.

Socially mandated **capital lusts** simply make a society more hierarchical, more military, more warlike, more tyrannical—perfect for population wars; terrible for loving humans.

This ironic situation is the unavoidable catch-22 of human existence: *The structures of ordered civilizations, evolved to give order and peace to human lives, naturally over time direct us to intolerance, disorder, overpopulation, resource stress, and eternal conflict.*

In other words, the very systems constructed to bring peace and order to humanity ultimately *over time* lead in the opposite direction--to absurdity, conflict, insanity, and chaos. Civilization's extreme expectations push us to intolerance, constant wars, and self-destructive ends, <u>not</u> to unity or peace.

Society's directions contradict; the forces of cultural entropy lead us to apocalypse, not order.

THE SCIENCE AGREES
"**The Population Bomb**" written in 1968 by Paul and Ann Ehrlich, describes a future world filled with toxic disasters and starving people. Since 1968, the world population has **doubled**, from three billion to seven billion people. Most humans are still **not** starving. How disappointing. Were all the scientists wrong?

Recent technological advances, and the green revolution, have pushed the predicted disaster into a distant future most people prefer to ignore. In fact, in the next decades, new technologies may allow humans to increase our population even further. By utilizing all energy reserves and farming the oceans, we may increase the present (seven billion) human population to twenty or thirty billion happy souls, or even more. Perhaps we can stretch the human population even higher before absolute starvation occurs.

However, the price paid for such a huge human population—extraordinary resource stress and a toxic apocalypse--might be pleasant to avoid. A world with twenty billion starving children might not be pleasing to inhabit.

Population wars push all human events to absurd degrees. We are probably better off using future technologies to increase the **value** (rather than the **number**) of human lives. We might use future energies to travel to distant worlds, rather than risk destroying the one world that supports our needs.

We can eliminate much conflict if we stop fighting cultural wars, if we stop using our children as soldiers, and if we oppose the forces of chaos that guide us to madness.

AND THE LITERATURE AGREES
THEATRE OF THE ABSURD -- Artists have defined the conflicts of cultural entropy for many generations.

Words are not perfect constructions of reality. Socrates, born in 470 BC, Diogenes's mentor, taught the idea several **thousand** years ago. Stresses of many types distort human concepts to non-meaning or absurdity. Socrates revealed common social assumptions, when examined minutely, contradict or grow absurd. Patriotism, courage, family values, faith, love, and morality—all these simple concepts can be twisted and **magnified,** by the forces of **entropy,** to act in complete opposition to intended meanings.

Wars, of course, place the most terrible stresses on human concepts. As soon as humans from one culture begin to routinely slaughter humans from another culture, **human *values*** no longer make sense. The world becomes a ***no man's land***. The *value* of human life no longer exists. Genocides may appear rational. Cannibalism may appear tasteful.

Wars, chaos, and other **extreme** actions extend normal human activities to the point of absurdity or madness. In *"Catch 22"*, the famous novel by Joseph Heller, a prolonged war causes soldiers to lose track of their fundamental humanness. Ridiculous, insane activities become normal. The point Heller makes is: Warfare stretches reasonable human actions to absurdity; this enables the ridiculous--*catch 22.* In other words, human existence becomes a contradiction.

The *existential* and *absurd movements,* personified in the writings of Jean-Paul Sartre and Albert Camus, articulate other philosophical and artistic reactions to the absurd (distorted) activities generated by world wars and chaos. Many artists took up the chant, echoing the meaninglessness of normal human concepts under extreme stress—Ionesco, Kafka, Beckett, Stoppard, Heller, Vonnegut, and many others.

But absurd artistic works are not a recent event:
Shakespeare's **Hamlet** and **Othello** are perfect examples.

Indeed, The ***Iliad***, written *three **thousand** years ago*, is an artistic rendition of an insane event that extends human existence to absolute absurdity and non-meaning. Homer knew *exactly* what he was saying: Enflamed, ***extreme*** passions began the Trojan War; later, glorious and dramatic battles solved nothing; they merely created the desire for more glorious and dramatic revenge, greater and greater absurdity.

The distorted chaos of war pushes all participants to lives of absurd, meaningless violence and purposeless death. Homer pointed out repeatedly: **Wars do not glorify human existence**; on the contrary, wars make human life pointless.

Ulysses is the Trojan War's wisest and most reluctant hero. One of the very few to survive the war, Ulysses loses his way going home. After a decade wandering, Ulysses stumbles into Hades; there, he encounters Achilles. Achilles, the greatest Greek hero, dead and depressed in Hades, affirms—his life seeking glory was empty and meaningless; ridiculous wars stretch human concepts to absurdity (to chaos, also know as, Hades).

Ulysses recognizes—family (love) is what is important; war and fame are counter-productive and pointless. Ulysses returns to earth to find his forgotten family and his true meaning.

Two thousand years later, Irish author, James Joyce, brilliantly rewrites "**Ulysses**." The theme is the same.

Artists have known for thousands of years what politicians and generals do not. Unfortunately, artists are not in control—and neither, incidentally, are politicians or generals. Competing **numbers** define human history, not reason, or humanity.

Cultural entropy enflames passions and puts all cultures into endless competitions and **war**. A human is a culture of cooperating cells. A human family is a culture of related humans. A society is a culture of many families. A civilization is a collection of cooperating cultures.

The forces of cultural entropy naturally push all cultures into mortal conflict (chaos), both internally and externally. Within such conflict (or **competitive capitalism**), stressed human values become insane and lose their meaning.

THE LITERATURE CONTINUES: Cultural entropy creates monsters that scare us:

CREATURES FROM THE ID—
The 1956 movie, "Forbidden Planet", featured a monster that appeared from the human subconscious or ID. While asleep, chaotic madness takes over the human mind. Sleep-immobility is necessary so our nightly dream-dance with chaos will not cause us harm.

The movie took place on a planet that destroyed itself, while sleeping, after they invented a powerful machine they were able to control with their minds. The inventors did not realize they would murder each other in their (chaotic) sleep.

The monster re-appears when humans also seek to use the still-powerful mind machine.

The concept (fable or not) is clear: The human subconscious contains out-of-control and chaotic monsters. When humans are controlled by (chaos), they become monsters.

Unless opposed by **work**, *entropy* **(chaos)** *will always* **increase**.

Recall: Chaotic thoughts are necessary for human cognition [Ch 3,4, 8, 9].

LORD OF THE FLIES--

In the classic novel, **Lord of the Flies**, by William Golding, English boys find themselves marooned on a tropical island. They struggle for a kind, unified society, but evil forces doom their efforts. Dark, extreme human emotions turn to violence and madness.

Love, kindness, and human understanding are not easy; they are **not natural**. On the contrary, rage and tribal intolerance are natural in all humans, perhaps more so in young boys. Finding scapegoats for real problems takes little effort. Mutual understanding is very difficult; it takes **work** and **emotional maturity** to oppose chaos. Emotional maturity is something—by definition—young boys do **not** posses. The forces of cultural entropy pull us apart. Ignorance and fear create dark and dangerous monsters. Random, destructive forces act invisibly to oppose human unity.

These same forces divide our city halls and congresses into tribes of frightened children. These forces divide our country and our world. These **(extreme** emotional) forces act invisibly within our families, friendships, and intimate relationships to created **intolerance**, hatred, and conflict. These **monsters** bring out evil, ignorance, wars, and eventual madness in all of us.

When we choose competitive capitalism, we choose to make ourselves predators (monsters); we dine on our own human family.

When we choose to be predators, like Dracula, we suck the blood of our fellow creatures. Like the undead, we allow the bloody <u>past</u> (the dead) to destroy our future.

The solution is not magical. To oppose random chaos (**monsters**) simply requires **work,** clarity, human understanding, and cooperation—within our own souls, and without.

The solution requires we *understand the problems (intolerance, chaos) exists* **in** all of us; intolerance grows when ignored and becomes infectious over time. We cannot turn away from such diseases; they will not cure themselves **naturally**. We cannot stick our heads in the sand or ask spirits or **false gods** to save us. If we do, we enslave ourselves to random forces of chaos, to entropy, to **monsters**—not the God of love.

Extreme emotions and fears summon us to insanity and ignorance. **Extreme** leaders create scapegoats and seek to lead us into darkness. Natural forces of **cultural entropy** (chaos) act invisibly over long time periods to divide us and turn us away from God and joy. Forces of **puritanity** divide our beliefs and push our common understandings to absurdity.

Intolerance is easy. Opposing intolerance is hard. To find love and unity (sanity verses chaos), we must **work together** over **extended time periods** towards common understandings and enlightenment. ***Only work can oppose the forces of entropy. Madness is easy; sanity is hard work.***

MORE MONSTERS IN THE DARK

In Steven King's novel, *"It"*, the monster thrives in the darkness of **denial**. It can only be destroyed by being **recognized and confronted**. Work in opposition is constantly necessary to confront chaotic monsters of fear, madness, and ignorance. **Entropy will always increase unless opposed by work.** Work towards unity (sanity) must continue as long as humanity desires joy in existence.

We must <u>recognize</u> the chaotic forces (of cultural entropy) actively exist. Otherwise we risk being overwhelmed by invisible monsters.

All systems proceed to larger entropy/chaos unless opposed by work. Perpetual love is <u>not</u> natural; it will dissolve without continuous work.

THE NORSE GODS

The Norse god, Loki, was the god of chaos and mischief, and also of **change**. Does a god exist currently that represents change? Thor appreciated Loki, at times, but recognized Loki could sometimes go too far and become dangerously destructive, crazed, and demonic. Loki was responsible for the death of Balder, the god of unanimity. Loki also helped usher in Ragnarok, the final battle with the giants of Chaos, and the death of the gods.

The most important concept controlling Loki was **moderation**.

EASTERN UNDERSTANDINGS

Understandings in myth and religion from eastern civilizations, Hindu and Buddhist, are quite advanced in confronting the forces of chaos and division—far more advanced than the west, in my opinion.

In particular, the concepts of Ying and Yang and Harmony explicitly dramatize the struggle between opposing forces in the universe.

Philosophers could write volumes more about the subject from an Eastern perspective; however, balance between **extremes** is the prime objective. **In other words: Moderation**.

MODERATION, BALANCE AND REACHING CONSENSUS

In final summary—from science, art, and religion--we must bow to the absolutely obvious: **Cultural entropy destroys economies; cultural entropy** creates divisions, violent wars, *change*, and terrible extremes. **Changes** *may* **sometimes** make us better, but **extremes** destroy us. Balance is the secret to harmony; but balance takes work.

Human reason is a much better road to progressive change than chaos. Recall: **Chaotic evolution** has taken **billions** of years and terrible conflict to bring us to the present. Progressive change due to *reason* should not only be faster, but more pleasant.

Extremes replace the truth with lies. Extremes and warfare push human existence into absurdity and madness. Extremes destroy the middle and any hope of consensus.

Human existence and progressive change depend exclusively on the circulation of actual **truth.** Lies and ignorance lead to disasters.

But the truth exists most strongly, ***not*** at the **extremes**, but balanced somewhere in the **middle**, *within* us all. Finding common truth is not easy. If it were easy, we would have reached this epiphany long ago.

On the contrary, finding the truth (our common family) is obviously extremely, extremely difficult—the effort will probably take love, togetherness, sacrifice, and continuous **work** over a great deal of time. **Extremes** are easy; understanding and moderation are hard, endless **work.**

Indeed, loving humans have worked to achieve unity and love for thousands of years. Their loving efforts have met with some success, but opposition from extreme hatreds and corrosive entropy is unending.

Extremes lead to madness and chaos. Seeking God, finding our common Truth, seeking a balanced existence, depending on reason and not chaos to achieve change, and accepting sanity and joy--these are the very difficult struggles we, humans, must undertake going forward if we wish to go a different direction.

Or, we can continue as always, forever guided away from God and life, not by visible reason and verifiable truth, but by invisible forces of entropy and denial.

However, wars can be hell.

Why Civilizations Fall and Cannot Rise Again
GLOSSARY 11

GLOSSARY OF TERMS:

Why Civilizations Fall
The Destructive Forces of Cultural Entropy

AVOIDANCE AND INTOLERANCE:
[Ch. 1, 2, 4] To avoid **parasites, diseases, and predators**, wise organisms commonly **avoid** close contacts, even with members of their own species.

Intolerance, for the same reason, is often accompanied by chemical or behavioral toxicities between organisms. ***Intolerance and avoidance*** are survival behaviors hard-wired in all animal organisms.

("It's nothing personal. I just don't want to be close to you.")

Avoidance and intolerance **oppose sharing** activities within animal and human cultures.

CANCEROUS CULTURES:
Cancerous cultures, within an organism or larger culture, breed out of control. These cultures can overwhelm or destroy their parent organism or culture (and themselves in the process).

In human cultures, warlike societies impose restrictions on their members to insure maximum reproduction. Rapidly reproducing human cultures (like cancers) force other cultures to compete for resources or be overwhelmed.

CAPITAL: [Ch. 1, 2, 3, 4]
In human cultures capital is tradable **value.** Food items have particular *intrinsic capital value.* All life is food, and thus life has elemental capital value.

Food (life) is valuable **work-energy** necessary to enable life's processes. Tools, mating privileges, resources, human **work**, and domestic animals can also translate into capital (food) value.

Profits are extra capital, capital available to exchange or distribute without the loss of life.

Humans created **token capital** devices to facilitate non-violent capital **exchanges (of profits)**—coins, money, stocks, bonds, for example. **Token** capital **represents** actual capital (profit) value in trade exchanges. Without **profits**, however, non-violent exchanges would be impossible.

Capital Creation: Plants create capital-food-energy by capturing the energy (work) of the sun. Life utilizes sun-energy (work) to organize **resources** for life's priorities, growth and reproduction.

Besides sunlight, some organisms can use (work) energy from chemical reactions or volcanic vents to create original capital (life). Work (energy from some source) is necessary to oppose the contrary actions (work) of entropy.

Organism unable to process original energy sources must grab capital (food) items from plants or other animals. This exchange is **capitalism**. In nature, almost all exchanges of food-energy-capital between unrelated organisms are **violent**. This type of violent exchange is called **competitive capitalism.**

The cycle of life: When people refer to the cycle of life, capital is what is cycling. The circulation (cycling) of capital, or capitalism, allows living organisms to diversify and grow. In nature, exchanges of capital occur violently.

Humans create profit capital over time when they plant crops or create products utilizing human labor (**work**). Shared human understandings are a unique type of human capital profit.

CAPITALISM:
CAPITALISM: Plant organisms use sun-energy and elemental resources to create living capital-energy. **Capitalism is the process** by which Capital energy **circulates** from plant organisms through animal organisms to energize growth and diversity in life, eventually returning to the environment as (unenergized) elemental resources. [Ch. 1,2, 4]

TWO KINDS OF CAPITALISM:
COMPETITIVE CAPITALISM occurs when capital (food) is exchanged violently. In capital

exchanges between unrelated animals, one animal benefits (finds food), the other animal loses (becomes food). Most of nature is **competitive capitalism**.

Competitive capitalism may also be dubbed a zero-sum game—gains can only equal losses.

COOPERATIVE CAPITALISM:

Cooperative capitalism exists in nature in the *fruit-flower exchange*. In **cooperative capitalism**, organisms create and exchange **profits**, rather than **life**.

Flowering plants began using **cooperative capitalism** when plant **work** created **profits,** nectars and fruits, plants could **trade** with insects and animals for desired ends--the dissemination of their pollen and seeds.

In **cooperative capitalism**, exchanges of work and profit between separate organisms can benefit **both** organisms. A violent death is not required.

An even earlier form of **cooperative capitalism** occurs within a single organism or culture of organisms that **share** resources or food. Plants, of course, create capital energies and share this energy with their specialized cells. They pass some of the profit energy along with their pA single organism **shares** food between its different specialized cells. Sharing benefits all the cclls involved.

Humans are unique among large mammals in producing common **profits**. These profits can be **shared**, allowing human cultures to practice cooperative capitalism; **cooperative capitalism** widely benefits human development.

Humans do not need to **kill** each other at every capital exchange. (Although some humans may feel violence is more fun.)

Humans revert back to **competitive capitalism**, in particular, during cultural **wars,** in which violence and force again define capital exchanges, and population competitions between cultures stress resources.

Cooperative capitalism or **sharing profits** allows specialization and diversity and increases human value.

CAPITAL CONGESTION

When climax populations or natural cycles keep capital from cycling, capitalism cannot function.

In nature, when tides, that normally bring nutrients to the ocean's surface, change direction, the ocean economy may die off.

When rains fail to fall, famines may occur.

In human terms, stock market crashes, or burst housing bubbles can severely diminish capital circulation.

Climax populations can dominate capital-resources over long periods. When governments or climax populations hoard resources or limit the profits from human labor, economic circulation can stagnate.

Without circulation, an economy may die.

CLIMAX POPULATIONS [CH. 1, 2, 3]

In nature, climax populations are the final chain in transitional changes in an environment. The tallest trees will eventually dominate a stable forest, and can continue to dominate until displaced—by disease, fire, forestry, or some other violent event. A climax population can diminish diversity.

The death of a large tree or grove of trees allows transitional growth access to resources and sunlight.

Human populations can rise to climax states when a single status dominates capital resources and limits circulation to other statuses.

CULTURAL ENTROPY: [Ch. 2, 8]

The forces of entropy (chaos) affect living cultures in the same way entropy affects physical systems. Cultural entropy randomly exerts divisive, corrosive pressures on *living* cultures.

Forces of entropy in biological systems include avoidance and intolerance. Intolerance generates toxicities.

The forces of **cultural entropy** (chaos) also generate **speciation** (separation of species) and foster natural selection or competitive capitalism in nature.

Human emotions and activities *magnify* the effects of cultural entropy [Ch. 3, 4, 5, 7, 8]. Long time-periods generally make the divisive effects invisible to short sighted humans. Short-term solutions (status levels, slavery, capital sequestration, for example) can often make long-term problems much worse. Human families can be blinded by time, so long-term injuries to the family unit (and social infrastructures) can go untreated.

When things go awry—and they always do—humans historically blame evil forces or each other for the problems. Ignorant understandings end in inappropriate actions—genocides, wars, extreme emotions, polarization, no man's lands; these make the original problems far worse (not better).

The forces of entropy can only be opposed by **work**.

CULTURAL CORROSION (Caused by Forces of Cultural Entropy):

Cultural corrosion occurs in several steps *over long time periods*:
1) **Intolerance** entropy encourages misunderstandings, cultural **extremes (toxicity),** and human status divisions
2) **Extremes destroy** (toxify) the **tolerant middle** and demean common understandings.
3) Without a tolerant middle, a **culture splits into warring parts, fighting over resources, unable to reunite.**
4) Violent population competitions between weak and divided cultures **stress resources** and create **no man's lands.**
5) Violent population wars **devalue human lives**.
6) **No man's lands** can diminish population numbers.
7) **The process repeats**: Divided cultures cannot heal. Newly created cultures, over time, suffer similar splits and cultural wars due to repeating intolerance, misunderstandings, and extremism

The same steps of cultural corrosion divide civilizations, tribes, families, legislatures, churches, and even intimate human relations.

Forces of entropy stir extreme emotions and decay common understandings. A toxified (poisoned) mid-point makes healing impossible.

The **CYCLE OF LIFE** [Ch. 1]

When people refer to the **cycle of life**, capital is what is cycling. Plants create capital-life-energy by combining sun-energy with available **resources**. Plants compete with other plants to grab resources.

Animals violently grab and violently exchange capital energy (food) with each other, utilizing some of the captured (food) energy in each transfer. Eventually, after several exchanges, life processes use up most of the capital-**energy** in the food-capital; the remaining elemental capital resources are returned to the environment.

Using sun-energy for **work**, plants begin the process again by using sun-energy and resources to create new capital-food-energy, also known as life. The cycle repeats.

ENTROPY: [Ch. 2]

The principal derives from the *second Law of Thermodynamics*. **The German physicist, Rudolf Clausius, introduced the entropy concept in 1850.**

The second law of thermodynamics says that when energy changes from one form to another form, or matter moves freely, entropy (disorder) in a closed system **increases**.

Explained physically—entropy is the tendency of free moving particles to randomly (chaotically) bounce/repel away from each other. Entropy causes moving heat (work) energy to disburse, and free gas particles to fill space. Free particles move (**work**) to equalize pressures around themselves. Only work in opposition can oppose the free **flow** of entropy to chaos. Unless opposed by work (**energy**), entropy (chaos) of free particle systems will **always increase**.

INTOLERANCE AND AVOIDANCE:

[Ch. 1,2,4] Avoidance and intolerance are the tendencies of all living organisms to avoid contact with organisms of other species and of their own species. Intolerance generates toxicities. **Intolerance and avoidance are necessary because all organisms must avoid parasitism and disease.**

INTOLERANCE IN HUMAN SOCIETIES:

Intolerance in human societies evolves from the same biological imperative (avoidance of parasites) found in animal cultures.

Humans can **magnify** the effects of intolerance due to contagious and extreme human emotions, puritanity, status levels, religious differences, linguistic differences, ignorance, lack of capital understandings, lack of sharing, and just about any concept that makes humans feel they might be different than others.

All humans are naturally intolerant; we are born with this ingrained trait—it was once necessary for survival.

Over time, small **intolerances** will grow larger, unless humans **work** to reverse the intolerant cycle. This is not easy.

Only **work** can keep entropy from increasing.

LINGUISTIC ENTROPY

Linguistic entropy is one of the more obvious corrosive effects of cultural entropy over time [Ch. 2, 3, 5]. Human languages randomly change over time. People separated by only a few hundred years of change can have difficulties understanding each other. After a thousand years, human languages can become mutually incoherent.

Even small linguistic and cultural changes are enough for tribal people to feel they are different than others, and no longer belong to the same sharing family.

A shared language is necessary for a human culture to share mutual understandings. Language differences favor **intolerance** and extreme emotions.

Most conflicts erupt between humans speaking different languages or dialects; unable to understand (share) they were once the same family.

PERSONAL RELATIONSHIPS:

Even between those raised in similar circumstances, language is an impure medium to describe abstract truths. Nuanced phrases often contradicted by facial and bodily expressions can always be misinterpreted. If we assume men and women speak different languages, we can understand why we often fail to communicate.

The point is the same: Chaotic forces take advantage of human disabilities to persistently divide our senses of self. Only work in opposition (love) can counteract these forces.

GOOD AND EVIL [Ch 6, 7]

In the history of human evens, few concepts are more romantic or divisive than good and evil. The **extremes** of good and evil leave no middle ground for peaceful resolution, no point of common balance.

Dramatic storytellers, from yesterday to today, repeatedly employ these concepts to create fantastic conflicts and satisfying conclusions (assuming good somehow triumphs). In daily life, however, the ideas of good and evil can be divisive. "I mean, I'm good, so if you don't agree totally with me, you must be evil! What? How dare you disagree! You must be even more evil!"

These concepts—good and evil—have not always dominated the human discussion however.

Ancient European religions employed a variety of gods and viewpoints. The tradition continues in India and Asia today. Such religions are often (but not always) more tolerant of diversity in human traditions. They suggest a grey area of human understandings.

Monotheistic, western religions tend to view the situation more narrowly. The concepts of good and evil generate romantic heroes and dramatic battlefields. Given the opportunity, extreme elements can generate extreme intolerance or **puritanity**. Note: Puritanity creates human divisions over increasingly smaller differences.

The more dominant a religious hierarchy becomes in an area, the more that hierarchy will be free to impose its own intolerance. If we, and our religion, are purely good, then we must assume everyone else, not us, is evil. Of course, good must destroy evil or be, itself, destroyed—that's the rule. There is no middle ground.

Without a middle ground, human conflict is inevitable. Areas in which different beliefs prosper side by side for generations may quickly split apart when extreme, puritanical elements (fighting over good and evil) come to power.

Don Quixote, a romantic knight, struggled to find evil he could fight. What he largely found was his own (and the world's) ignorance.

HUMAN VALUE

Human value may be the most important quest in human existence besides survival. Humans like to feel they have intrinsic human value. We wish to be valued for our hearts and souls, no matter what our accomplishments.

In economic terms, however, we are only as valuable as the capital we can produce with our human labor and capital possessions. If I have no capital possessions (to compound future profits), and if in addition, my human labor also has no value (since I possess no marketable skills), then I theoretically have no human (economic) value.

Without the ability to gain capital, then, I am valueless. In this case, if I am an animal, without the ability to accumulate capital, I will starve.

When societies deny their citizens the infrastructures to make their labors productive, then the value of all humanity in that society decreases concurrently. Capital (including understandings) must circulate to create a healthy society.

Economic value increases as an individual's ability to accumulate and create capital increases. Capital technologies, such as spears, fire, tractors, and smart phones, assist in the creation and accumulation of capital. Marketable skills and knowledge (additional acquired technologies) also assist the quest for capital necessary for survival. Children are the most important capital items life can produce. Life *is* ultimately capital.

We know human *economic* value does not necessarily correspond to *human* value, but the two concepts (human value and human economic value) are intricately linked.

Human values move beyond economics to include human understandings, love, joy, spiritual growth, and many other abstract human yearnings. Such quests may not easily translate into economic concepts.

The forces of cultural entropy work randomly against *all* capital sharing systems; thus, cultural entropy works to diminish human value, both physically and spiritually.

Cultural entropy, or competitive capitalism, pushes us to greater and greater numbers and violence. Greater and greater numbers stress resources and create violent competitions that consistently diminish human value.

If we hope for a better future for humanity, then we must design future economic systems to maintain the value of human labor. The future must recognize and work against the destabilizing effects of cultural entropy to maintain the social peace and stability necessary to pursue other (spiritual, artistic, scientific) activities.

POPULATION, CULTURAL, OR NUMBERS WARS

Population, cultural, or numbers wars occur when different populations compete for resources. The primary weapon of population wars is increasing population numbers. Population increases are also the reason population wars are necessary.

Thus population wars naturally stress resources and contribute to resource depletions such as soil erosion, and soil infertility.

Population wars violently create **no man's lands**; these destroy the human ability to create and maintain infrastructures assisting human survival—bridges, safe farming areas, soil fertility, human education, common understandings, etc.

Population wars, generated by increasing populations, contribute to famines, and population crashes. Population wars increase intolerance, ignorance, divisions, and polarization, and thus contribute to future population wars.

Entropy can only be opposed by work and understanding. "The balanced way leads to God."

**STATUS DIVISIONS:
CULTURAL ENTROPY CREATES HUMAN STATUS DIVISIONS, CONFLICT, AND MISUNDERSTANDINGS.**
The forces of cultural entropy (chaos) over time create vertical divisions of a single culture into capital statuses. Statuses claim differing capital or social assets. These statuses can separate further over time and refuse to share resources with equity [Ch 3, 4, 5].

Ultimately, a single culture or family is drawn into status conflicts and misunderstandings between its own peoples. Such conflicts severely divide and weaken the culture's economy and contribute to cultural collapses.

NATURAL SELECTION
Natural selection, also known as *the survival of the fittest*, is the Darwinian description of competitive capitalism. All living systems are in competition (cultural wars) with each other to dominate capital and capital resources.

Over time, random factors favor the lucky over the unlucky, the fit over the less fit. Losing systems disappear from existence. Over time, billions of years, natural selection has improved animal **technologies**—teeth, claws, size, feathers, brains—but technologies do not change the violent premise. More than ninety percent of animal young are killed before maturity. In some species, only one in a thousand may survive to reproduce.

God uniquely favored humans with brains. Human reason, in the future, may allow a process more humane than vicious warfare (between humans) to determine our planet's future. Or maybe not...

NO MAN'S LANDS [Ch. 2, 3, 4]
No man's lands traditionally occur between warring armies. Violence creates a zone in which nothing, plant or animal, can survive.

No man's lands also occur in human zones without government, or when government collapses or is controlled by lawless criminal elements. No man's lands have no barriers to violent human behavior. In such areas farming, trade, and infrastructures otherwise cannot survive. Capital cannot be created or fairly circulated in no man's lands.

When large areas of a country become no man's lands, women and children begin to starve and the population will quickly diminish. Other than plague, no other process is as historically devastating to human populations.

Wars are generally less malignant to populations than no man's lands (often created by wars), since wars generally consume a percentage of the expendable male population. Future wars, with atomic weapons or worse, may prove the exception.

To a degree, all of nature may be viewed as a no man's land, guided strictly by force and circumstance, without human values, and outside the garden of God.

PROFITS [Ch 1,3,4, 5]

Profits enable cooperative capitalism. Without **profits** to trade, the common exchange of capital is life and death.

Human economies work best when **human labor** can broadly create profits. Profits created from human labor can allow specialization and diversity.

PURITANITY [Ch. 4, 5]: An extension of Intolerance

Those practicing puritanity utilize obsessive standards of purity to differentiate belief systems or cultures.

By emphasizing cultural **differences**, rather than cultural *oneness*, **Puritanity** magnifies the divisive forces of cultural entropy. In particular, **Puritanity** magnifies the divisive effects of **intolerance** in human cultures.

Puritanity allows religious institutions and political understandings to be divided over **increasingly smaller** real differences.

Puritanity also works in human relationships to divide families and couples; puritanity creates **extreme** and unresolvable positions.

SLAVERY [Ch. 3, 4, 5]
Conquering cultures often welcomed the short-term benefits of slavery. But long-term, slavery (like a disease) slowly stifles a culture's capital economy.

Slave owners (like parasites) *steal* the labor (**profits**) of their slaves without fair compensation. In so doing, they severely limit profit circulation to anyone but themselves. Slavery, in turn, diminishes the value **profits** available to free workers everywhere.

When slave owners, as a climax population, also dominate land resources, **profits** throughout the culture can no longer circulate in a healthy fashion. Labor (work) of free humans, without access to resources, eventually becomes enslaved also.

When human **work** has little value, working humans have little value. In other words, the value of humanity diminishes.

Without capital circulation generally, the circulation of capital-understandings, education, and skills diminish in synchrony. The value of all human beings--even including the elites—declines over time, often without notice.

Such a weakened slave culture is historically susceptible to tyranny, military rule, and the further chaotic forces of **cultural entropy**.

TECHNOLOGIES
Technologies assist human survival and the creation and accumulation of capital items. Technologies include human languages, fire, spears, farm implements, domesticated animals, use of fossil fuels, and the Internet, to name a few.

Important to realize however—*technologies do not change the violent premise of competitive capitalism.* Used badly, technologies can negatively impact the value of human life. Wars using terrible modern weapons, and technologies that allow tyrants to control and oppose free human understandings are examples of technologies that limit human value.

Technologies can contribute to massive population increases; but again, population numbers do not necessarily coincide with increased human value.

T REX – Why the short arms?
T-REX dinosaurs bit something and then twisted their bodies around until they could rip off a chunk. The maneuver is called a crocodile roll, and crocodiles and sharks use it today. All these animals have massive necks, jaws, and teeth, and none of them use knives and forks.

Most important, the prey of T-Rex included sauropods. These huge herbivores used their *terrible-tails*, as an effective defensive weapon. Whipping a huge tail back and forth like a whip could slash and tumble even a T-Rex. Once knocked head over feet, terrible damage could occur in a large animal, twisted about by its own weight. In particular, large flailing arms might suffer greatly. Evolution might easily favor rounded, heavily-built predators, able to recover from the blow of a *terrible tail* without permanent damage. This evolutionary solution would reward small arms that could be kept out of the way during a roll.

By biting and rolling, a carnivore can use its entire body weight to rip apart its prey, a tremendous advantage, particularly if you weigh a ton or so. Big arms would have gotten in the way of a T-Rex's dinner.

The lethality of a bite and roll technique to badly injure or subdue prey would have diminished the need for arms and lethal claws. But a napkin may have been nice.

Smaller T-Rex's may have benefited most from the maneuver, ripping off a quick bite and then running off before encountering cannibalistic relatives. Twisting off a three-foot swatch of flesh may not have killed a huge, fleeing Sauropod, but the resulting infection from such a gash may have finished the job later.

T-Rex had an amazing sense of smell to track injured prey. So, arms weren't necessary for T-Rex, unless they wanted to scratch their noses.

WHY DO NORTHERN PEOPLE HAVE SHORT ARMS?
Generally, humans from northern, cold climates have shorter arms and legs than those in southern, hot climates—though variables are wide. The reasons are obvious. People in cold climates have difficulty retaining heat. People in hot climates have difficulties expelling heat. Long arms and legs and thinner bodies allow humans to expel more heat. Thick

bodies and shorter arms and legs allow humans to retain more heat.

Variables, however, are profound. Some northerners have unusually long arms and legs. Clothing, fire, and other technologies allow a variety of human body styles to survive. Humans, unlike dinosaurs and other animals, are not *totally* dependent on body structures. Humans can and do use technologies to compensate for physical abilities.

Wearing clothes, and living in areas of constant cloud cover, limit exposure to the sun and the production of vitamin D. Light skins evolved in northern people to assist vitamin D production.

The point is: Human shapes and colors vary from region to region, and human cultures and religions may also vary from place to place, but apparently the various humans are pretty much (99.99%) the same.

Physical, linguistic, and cultural differences are trivial when compared to the humanity we all share.

WHY CIVILIZATIONS COLLAPSE – The Too-Simple Rule:

All economic systems require constant energy input and circulation to achieve stability or growth.

Economic systems that lose energy input and capital *circulation* will collapse.

A civilization divides and falls when it can no longer share (circulate) its common humanity.

Why Civilizations Fall and Cannot Rise Again   227
GLOSSARY 11

www.ingramcontent.com/pod-product-compliance
Ingram Content Group UK Ltd.
Pitfield, Milton Keynes, MK11 3LW, UK
UKHW040806111225
9509UKWII00029B/500